The Relevance of Executive MBA Programs: Student Expectations and Satisfaction

by

Janis Weinstein Dietz

ISBN: 1-58112-039-7

1999

© Copyright 1997
by Janis Dietz
All rights reserved

ISBN: 1-58112-039-7

Dissertation.com
1999

www.dissertation.com/library/1120397a.htm

ABSTRACT OF THE DISSERTATION

THE RELEVANCE OF EXECUTIVE MBA PROGRAMS: STUDENT
EXPECTATIONS AND SATISFACTION.

Janis Weinstein Dietz

The Claremont Graduate School: 1997

Investment in executive education has grown steadily since its inception during the last century. Several studies have attempted to measure the effectiveness of executive programs; prior research has indicated that some programs lack relevance.

This study addressed the topic from the perspective of corporations, whose future executive education decisions are affected by the relevance of current programs, and program alumni.

In a partial replication of a 1959 Harvard study, which queried graduates of 39 residential programs, I surveyed the 1993-1995 executive MBA graduates of four schools: UCLA, University of Colorado, University of Utah, and University of Washington. The main research question was:

Are executive education programs meeting the needs of their mid-career students?

In addition to the above, the changing workplace prompted the following queries:

a) **Is there a difference between the satisfaction of the students with the programs in 1959 and now?**
b) **Are the programs affected by lack of security in the workplace. Are people using the EMBA to change employers?**
c) **Do sponsoring companies use the skills learned?**
d) **Do women have a problem with the 'glass ceiling'?**

In addition to collecting the surveys, I interviewed the four program directors, 10 corporate executives whose responsibilities include executive education, and 24 of the 157 alumni who returned the questionnaire.

Frequency distribution, correlation analysis, and stepwise multiple regression were used to analyze the survey data.

The major findings were: 1) EMBA students today are satisfied with the relevance of their education; 2) Students are dissatisfied with schools that employ professors with outdated or inadequate teaching skills; 3) Instability in today's workplace is prompting some people to change jobs or go into their own business once their EMBA is completed; 4) Corporations will continue to invest in these programs, but there is more specific succession planning in conjunction with the career path expected for the employee; 5) There continues to be little ethnic diversity in the programs.

THE RELEVANCE OF EXECUTIVE MBA PROGRAMS: STUDENT EXPECTATIONS AND SATISFACTION.

By

Janis Weinstein Dietz

A dissertation submitted to the faculty of the Claremont Graduate School in partial fulfillment of the requirements for the degree of Doctor of Philosophy in the Graduate Faculty of the Peter F. Drucker Graduate Management Center

Claremont
1997

Approved by:

David Eli Drew, Ph.D.

We, the undersigned, certify that we have read this dissertation and approve it is adequate in scope and quality for the degree of Doctor of Philosophy.

_____
David E. Drew, Chair

_____
Joseph A. Maciariello, Member

_____
Reed Powell, Member

This dissertation is dedicated to John, without whom this dream would not have been possible, and who really did marry me "for better or for worse."

ACKNOWLEDGEMENTS

No Ph.D. dissertation is ever completed without the help of many people, whose friendship, advice, and aid are critical in the completion of the project. On the chance that one of these many people is inadvertently left off this document, my apologies and my thanks.

David Drew provided me with the support and the belief in my work that enabled me to complete this project. I am forever indebted to his agreement to act as Chair of my committee, even when he was really too busy to take on another student. David Drew embodies the reasons I chose to enter academia. He makes a difference in the lives of his students; he has made a difference in my life that I cannot adequately express in words.

Joe Maciariello and Reed Powell have given counsel and shown interest in my topic, even with their busy schedules. Reed wrote the original work on which my study was based, and his counsel has been very important. Joe has been a very supportive member of the faculty and someone whose ideas have taught me a lot.

Liz Stillman has been my guardian angel. She has laughed with me, cried with me, and told me to push on when I wasn't sure I had the strength. Liz also read the chapters as they were concluded and provided valuable feedback.

The rest of the Drucker Center entering Class of 1991, including Jim Canning, Jim Cook, Gary Gibbons, John Kensey, Dietmar Kluth, Keith McFarland, Emile Pilifidis, and Larry Wangler, have given me constant support throughout the process of finishing this research.

Drs. Larry Meyers and George Ellison, of the UCLA School of Medicine, told me not to give up even when it appeared that the hurdles were too great for me.

Dr. Jill Anne Tronvig, who took my raw data and provided the regression analysis that I needed, was not only an excellent consultant, but became a friend who counseled me in many of the other areas of this process where I needed guidance. Although I appreciated the statistical help, her emotional support was probably the most important.

The Masco Corporation, in particular Delta Faucet, even though they stood to gain nothing from supporting my graduate studies, enabled me to arrange my travel such that I could attend classes at the Drucker Center.

Jesse Overall, my colleague from The University of La Verne, was kind enough to request a copy of my dissertation and to provide his excellent feedback.

No one gets to this point in an education without strong signals and values that can support them when the going gets rough, as it always does. My parents, Al and Joan Weinstein, provided me with love, support, and a desire to achieve that enabled me to pursue any dream I might have. I was luckier than most to have parents who told me that I could do anything I wanted (as long as my grades were good enough to get into college!).

Finally, a dedication is never enough to thank a loved one who provides unwavering support to a wife who, for 5 ½ years, neither cooked nor cleaned nor darned socks. Every wife should be as lucky as I am to have a husband who willingly put up with the tremendous sacrifices that a Ph.D. program requires. Thank you, John.

TABLE OF CONTENTS

LIST OF TABLES xi

LIST OF EXHIBITS xiii

LIST OF FIGURES xiii

CHAPTER 1 INTRODUCTION 16
   Country of residency and gender. 17
   Security in the workplace. 18
   Return to the workplace 18
   Support of industry 18
   Relevance of course work 19
   Importance of the topic 19
   Outline of the dissertation: 20
CHAPTER 2 REVIEW OF THE LITERATURE 22
   1) Diversity 26
   2) Lack of stability in the workforce 27
   3) Relevance of course material 28
   4) Support of industry 30
CHAPTER 3 RESEARCH QUESTION AND METHODOLOGY 32
   Research Question 32
   Methodology 33
   Selection of the sample 34
   Data Collection 41
   Pilot Study 41
   Measurement 50
   Results 52
   Limitations 53
CHAPTER 4 RESULTS 55
   Descriptive statistics 56
   Regression analysis 130
CHAPTER 5 SCHOOL INTERVIEWS 132
   The University of California at Los Angeles. 133
   The University of Colorado 141
   The University of Utah 150
   The University of Washington 156
CHAPTER 6 CORPORATE INTERVIEWS 165
   The current workplace 172
   Are courses relevant to jobs? 176
   Training expenditures 179

TABLE OF CONTENTS, CONTINUED
   Suggestions for improvement 183
CHAPTER 7 ALUMNI INTERVIEWS 188
   Relation to the Research Questions 230
   Conclusion 231
CHAPTER 8 DISCUSSION AND CONCLUSIONS 233

xiii
Discussion of the Andrews/Powell research implications *233*
Implications of the current research *236*
Suggestions for further research *241*
Conclusion *244*
REFERENCES 247

APPENDIX

A.	Pilot survey	N/A
B.	Sample letter to schools requesting their assistance	254
C.	Survey instrument	N/A
D.	Harvard survey	N/A
E.	Cover letter for survey	255
F.	Reminder letter	256
G.	Cover letter for second survey mailing	257
H.	Program director interview	258
I.	Survey response	259
J	Position at time of beginning program vs. position at the end	261

LIST OF TABLES

Table 1 Change in executive development emphasis. 28
Table 2 Major negative comments about executive education 29
Table 3 Support by industry 30
Table 4 Executive MBA Programs used in the research 35
Table 5 Andrews/Powell questions & current research 40
Table 6 Survey Timetable 44
Table 7 Total return 56
Table 8 Year of graduation: 57
Table 9 Gender and Marital Status at Graduation 57
Table 10 Marital Status: All schools 59
Table 11 Ethnic background (Question $#32) 60
Table 12 Industry(Question #1) 61
Table 13 Comparison of Harvard, Current research, and GMAC industry support 61
Table 14 Forbes Industry Classifications: 63
Table 15 Number of years of service 65
Table 16 Age of Participants (Question #30) 68
Table 17 Amount of tuition support (Question #3) 69

List of tables, continued:
Table 18 Have you changed jobs? If so, is there a connection?(Questions 5 and 6) 70
Table 19 , open ended; if there is a connection, what is the connection? 71
Table 20 (Question #9)If you still hold the same position, has the scope of your
responsibility changed? 71
Table 21 Relationship between attendance at the program and an increase in salary,
promotion, or responsibility 72
Table 22 Harvard results compared w/current research 74
Table 23 Position before and after the program 75
Table 24 Positions before and after the program 75
Table 25 Use made of skills acquired (Question #11) 76

Table 26 What did you think the program was trying to accomplish? (Question #12a)... 79
Table 27 What did you think happened to those who attended? (Question #12b) 80
(Andrews Question 22b)... 80
Table 28 Ranking of program benefits... 81
Table 29 What do you think happened to you? (Question #12c)..................................... 82
Table 30 Ranking of program effects.. 83
Table 31 What did you think the program would be like before you enrolled?................ 84
Table 32 Reaction at the end of the program (Question #13b) (Harvard #29) 86
Table 33 What is your reaction now? (Question #13c) (Harvard #30)............................ 87
Table 34 Rating for the program in general on a scale from 1(no current value) to 5(very valuable).. 90
Question #14 How would you rate the faculty's teaching effectiveness at your program?(Harvard #33, open-ended question.)* 1=Poor/2=Fair/3=Average/4=Above Average/5=Excellent.. 90
Table 35 Comments regarding faculty. (Question #14)... 91
Table 36 Which teaching methods did you prefer? 92
Table 37 In which of the following ways would you use the same amount of money? (Question #15)... 94
Table 38 How did you feel about the schedule? (Question #16) 97
Table 39 (Question #17) Other than the effects of the EMBA program mentioned above, were there any others that you received from attending the program? (Not in Andrews)... 98
Table 40 (Question #18) Please check over the following areas of study and indicate for each whether or not it was included in the program and, if so, your reaction to is: 100
Table 41 Mean study score for schools.(Question #17)... 105
Table 42 To what extent is your expression of interest a reflection of the way in which the different areas were taught, and to what extent is it a reflection of your basic interest in these areas (Question #19):.. 108
Table 43: (Question #20) Amount of reading and writing assigned in the program. 108
Table 44 Written 109
Table 45 Overall schedule... 110
Table 46 (Question #21) Please evaluate the personal value to you of the program elements: 111

List of tables, Continued

Table 47 All Schools mean scores of program elements 113
Table 48 All elements ranked in order of mean rating.. 113
Table 49 (Question #22) If you are a woman, have you experienced "the glass ceiling?"116
Table 50 Suggestions 117
Table 51 (Question #24) How applicable to your career was your EMBA experience? 120
Table 52 (Question #25)Would you be interested in on-line education for this program?121
Table 53 Comments about an on-line option 122
Table 54 International Trip 123
Table 55 Use of experienced practitioners as faculty 125
Table 56 Final comments.. 126
Table 57 Program rating as determined by faculty teaching and "use of new skills."..... 125
Table 58 Faculty teaching effectiveness 126
Table 59 UCLA Age profile 134
Table 60 UCLA industry profile 135
Table 61 Industry participation for U. of Washington vs. Harvard 158
Table 62 Corporate interviews.. 165

xv

Table 63 Corporate interviews 187
Table 64 Advanced degrees held by interview participants 189
Table 65 Graduation year of alumni interview participants 190
Table 66 Characteristics of alumni interview participants 191
Table 67 Industry breakdown of interview participants 192
Table 68 Tuition support for those interviewed 193
Table 69 Rating of interview participants 194
Table 70 Mean program rating of interview participants 195
Table 71 Financial support and program rating 195
Table 72 Correlation matrix of questions 3, 13d, and 14 196
Table 73 Personal value of program elements (from surveys) 220

LIST OF FIGURES

| 1 | Credit to the program for an increase in job status | 74 |
| 2 | Ranking of field of study | 96 |

LIST OF EXHIBITS

| 1 | Corporate interview | 45 |
| 2 | Alumni interview | 51 |

CHAPTER 1

INTRODUCTION

Executive education has been growing steadily since its inception. There have been many attempts to evaluate its usefulness, but none have given a clear, quantitative answer to the question about effectiveness that corporations continue to ask in order to justify further funding. Today, there are new questions that should be asked of executive education participants in order to measure the level of quality currently being delivered in this field.

There is little question in the international business economy today that major changes in competitiveness, downsizing, and globalization affect the terms and content of executive education. The goal of this research was to find out how changes in the business world, and the demographics of the student population in general during the past 25 years, have affected the evaluation by students of executive management programs. As there is evidence of the need for a restructuring of many programs (Johnson, et al., 1988; Levitt, 1989; Byrne, 1993; Lord, 1993; Bongiorno and Byrne, 1995; Bryne & Leonhardt, 1996), this study also examined how practitioners in executive education have reacted to the expected changes in student reactions to their programs. This research project used parts of a comprehensive study, conducted from 1959-1965 by Harvard professors Kenneth Andrews and Reed Powell, to evaluate the effectiveness of executive management programs. That survey was entitled "The Effectiveness of University Management Development Programs" and, with a sample of 10,000, was the largest of the studies done to date[1] This study used the 1959 survey as the basis for comparison of

---

[1] P.E. DuJardin, 1981, Residential General Management Programs and Adult Development (351 participants);A. Fresina, 1988, Executive Education in Corporate America (300 corporations); C. Ingolls, 1986, Executive Education Programs: Meeting Strategic Organizational Purposes, (400 corporations); A.

student reactions to the quality and long-term effectiveness of executive MBA programs. I chose to use executive MBA programs, rather than the residence executive programs of the type used in the Harvard research, because of the prevalence of executive MBA programs in existence today which did not exist in 1959 and which are usually the result of self-selection rather than nomination. Only two executive MBA programs existed prior to 1964: The Executive MBA Program at M.I.T. was established in 1931 and the program at the University of Chicago was founded in 1943 (Hilgert, 1992). This relatively new program offered a new target population for me to study by using some of the same questions that Professors Andrews and Powell were asking of individuals who were not getting an advanced degree from their programs, and most of whom were chosen by their employers to attend rather than through self-nomination (Du Jardin, 1981). I wondered if the end result of an earned degree would color responses about the program upon completion. Differences in the population used in the current research from the Harvard study include:

Country of residency and gender.

The 10,000 survey recipients for the first survey were all men, and most of them were Americans. Given the diversity of the corporate and student population today, a study replicating some of the issues might bring a different response on some of the issues. Today's Harvard Professional Management Development Program and Advanced Management Program actively recruit international executives because of their understanding that the US no longer holds a concentration on business leadership (Harvard, 1996). The recruitment brochure for their current programs lists participants from over 30 countries across all continents.

Vicere and V. Freeman, 1990, Executive Education in Major Corporations: An International Survey,(171 corporations); T. Johnson, S. McLaughlin, L. Saari, D. Zimmerle, 1988, GMAC Study of The Demand and Supply of University-Based Executive Education (100 corporations).

Security in the workplace.

The decade of the 1990's is experiencing consistent downsizing of corporations. Men and women whose parents spent their entire careers with one company cannot hope to do the same. Almost 94% of the men who had been sent to the programs that prompted the Andrews survey were still with the same company three years later. The average tenure was seventeen years. The principal significance of this finding to Professor Andrews was that university programs were not used as recruiting grounds for men looking for new opportunities. Today's executive students are facing a decidedly different outlook in terms of job security. I was interested in knowing if my survey participants were using the programs to change employers.

Return to the workplace

Most of the people from the original research were supported in their new knowledge by their companies. How do women fare when they return to the "glass ceiling," which describes the impediments women encounter on their way to corporate executive suites (Groves, 1996)? Is there a difference in the support from companies where there is not as much security for the executive who has spent two years pursuing an Executive MBA? In a 1988 study (Johnson, et al., 1988) commissioned by the Graduate Management Admissions Council, it was found that most companies require little or nothing of substance in terms of proof from executives and managers they have sent to MBA programs.

Support of industry

The earlier work was heavily supported by the petroleum industry. Studying the differences by industry might indicate both expectations and changes. For instance, the

1988 Graduate Management Admissions Council project found EMBA programs heavily concentrated in the banking and finance areas.

Relevance of course work

For the most part, the participants in the Andrews/Powell survey were complimentary about the quality of the education they received. However, these were short-term residence programs. I expected the longer-term executive MBA programs to elicit more diverse responses with regard to course relevancy. Several studies have been critical of the course work relevancy to on-the-job experiences (Johnson, et al, 1988;Morrisey, 1993), even though most studies are complimentary about the "broadening" atmosphere of these programs (Du Jardin, 1981; Hilgert, 1992). However, a recent American Assembly of Collegiate Schools of Business (AACSB) survey found that there was a greater demand by part-time students for classroom information that is relevant to their workplace (Levenson, 1995). In a 1993 report on the question of whether business schools have lost touch with business, Professor Jack Hershey at Wharton noted that "students are beginning to classify schools into two groups; those that have new curricula and those that don't (Lord,1993, p. 55)."

Importance of the topic

The importance of the topic stems from the increasing need by corporations to justify expenditures at all levels. If there are differences in the reaction of students based on some of the differences cited above, a research project might be able to identify how those differences are affecting the impact of today's programs. If practitioners in executive education need to be addressing the needs of their clients/students in a more focused fashion, this research is expected to contribute to the improvement of the programs involved.

There is a substantial body of literature pointing to a dissatisfaction within the sponsoring corporate community with the applicability of coursework to the needs of executive students. This study also investigated whether some of the changes predicted in earlier publications have indeed been made in executive MBA programs. Currently, there are few studies detailing that these changes in relevancy have been made.

The marketing field is increasingly turning to separating customers into targetable groups for the purpose of personalized promotional programs (Grant, 1995). This suggestion has been made by some of the literature, but little response has been uncovered. The importance of treating their students as customers, and as different customers from their younger MBA students, will impact planning for executive programs as we go into the next century. Media reports about the increase of as much as 19% in applications to top business schools, plus the comments that part-time learners are especially interested in course work, raise the question about what the dominant trends are (Bongiorno, 1995). This leaves the interesting paradox of those critics who "deride MBA curricula as outdated and say the degrees no longer guarantee corporate success and wealth (Lancaster, 1995, p. B1)" and the fact that applications, especially to top business schools, are increasing.

Outline of the dissertation:

This dissertation is divided into 11 chapters. The first chapter introduces the topic and discusses the points of research.

Chapter 2 is a review of the literature as it relates to executive training education.

Chapter 3 discusses the research question and the underlying issues that relate to the main goal. It also covers the methodology used in the research. The triangulation method is described as it relates to the way the research was conducted. The survey of four schools, interview of 25 respondents, interview of four program directors, and interview of 10 corporate people responsible for executive training are described in depth.

Chapter 4 describes the results of the survey, using tables to present the descriptive information gained from the surveys. It includes comparative statistics with the 1959 Andrews/Powell work. Chapter 5 also reviews the survey work from the basis of relevant statistical analysis. It supports conclusions regarding the correlation between key variables used in the survey.

Chapter 5 describes the interviews conducted with the four school program directors.

Chapter 6 covers the semi-structured interviews with corporate sponsors and their reaction to levels of skills available in the workplace today, as well as their expectations for future availability of the types of employees they feel they will need.

Chapter 7 describes the semi-structured interviews conducted with the 24 survey respondents who agreed to be interviewed. To protect anonymity and provide for freedom of report, the names of the alumni have not been used.

Chapter 8 discusses implications from the perspective of the alumni survey results and interviews. It also includes recommendations for further research.

CHAPTER 2

REVIEW OF THE LITERATURE

The individual corporation school, which began as early as 1872 (Eurich,1985), offered classes in both basic "culture education" and training for upper level occupations. As industry grew, the importance of ensuring that employees were trained in the proper way grew as well. The origins of the American Management Association come from these roots. In 1913, thirty-five leading corporations sent top officials to provide a forum for idea exchange and training. The participants in the National Association of Corporation Schools, as the organization was named, grew to two hundred (ibid.). The term "executive training" first appeared at the NACS convention in1919. Today the American Management Association, as it is now called, offers over 5,000 training sessions annually (Graham,1993). Research into this subject supports the belief that today's leading companies are also the leaders in sponsored executive education. Names like A. T. & T., IBM, Bell South and General Electric continue to be found in reports of efforts on behalf of corporate business to keep the education of its executives up-to-date.

At about the same time that corporation schools were springing up, the University of Pennsylvania established the Wharton School of Commerce and Finance with a $100,000 grant from Joseph Wharton (Moulton, 1993). Programs were then developed at Berkeley in 1899, and at the Universities of Chicago and California before the turn of the century (Andrews, 1966). Programs developed by corporations, universities and entrepreneurial training companies have continued to grow as the industrialized society has grown. Sometimes men (until relatively recently, there were no women attending these programs) were sent to these programs in order to improve skills, sometimes as a prelude to greater responsibility, and sometimes as a reward for hard work (Humble, 1973; Moulton,1993).

Investment in executive education has continued to grow, to a projected level of $12 billion today (Byrne,1993). This research focused on the Executive MBA programs, which number 139 in the United States and Canada. There are a total of 750 MBA programs, both full and part-time, offered at this time. The investigation addressed some of the many changes that have precipitated a need to update executive education.

Comes and Powers, among others, wrote that "advanced skills will be needed in this volatile atmosphere ," referring to the next century's capitalistic requirements (1994, p.13)." The requirement of a college degree for a lifestyle that twenty years ago would have required only a high school diploma is only one element in the technologically supported knowledge-based organization, "an organization composed largely of specialists who direct and discipline their own performance through organized feedback from colleagues, customers and headquarters (Drucker, 1988, p.45). Knowledge increases in geometric proportions. The ability to understand the shift from products or services to information will be required to take advantage of the next wave of economic growth (David and Botkin,1994). As a matter of fact, on October 5, 1995, The Wall Street Journal noted that Syracuse University is at the forefront of a new program entitling MBA graduates from the '60s,'70s or '80s to upgrade their skills in several locations around the country. This research was designed to ask the following question of business schools: have they updated their skills as well?

The use of extended training gained more purpose with the growth of complexity and the growth of technology. Those purposes include skills upgrading, rescuing the derailed executive, investment into those who are important players in future strategy formulation, and "window dressing" for corporate image. In 1973, Humble described management training as a system that includes corporate and individual needs, evaluation of training options, and planned opportunities. In the 1966 publication of the Andrews study on effectiveness of executive education, over 70% of the respondents mentioned "broaden thinking" in a particular discipline or the total field as the purpose for undertaking the program (Andrews, 1966). Formal training courses as a way to prepare promotable managers for greater authority have always been among the basic reasons for corporate use of executive training (ibid.). In the following paragraphs, I will discuss the reasons behind why managers pursue executive education and then move on to the literature behind the sub-questions asked in the dissertation.

a) Skills:

The first reason that companies embark on executive education is to improve skills or to teach new skills that may be required to master new technology. With each year, new concepts and new methods requires updating and education planning. Many new concepts, such as 'Just in Time'(JIT) delivery schedules, are given a lot of emphasis while they are relatively new ideas.

By mid-life, many managers are missing the broader ranges of thought required to expand their conception of their job requirements (Moulton, 1993). Although that may have often been true of prior aging workers, the current combination of lightning speed technical improvements, global change, and increased competition make this slow-down a critical problem unless continual learning is pursued.

One of the areas being seen is flexibility in education for those whose work and for whom time limitations make attending classes once a week problematic. The American College was the first to experiment with new technologies by developing a course called "Money Manager" that can be used on IBM and Apple computers. Classrooms can be all over the country; the reach and flexibility of this type of education is only beginning to take advantage of pent-up demand. California Polytechnic University, in Pomona, California, was experimenting with modular distance learning (MDL) during the winter quarter of 1995. By using voice-mail and data mail boxes, students and instructors can communicate 24 hours a day, according to Dr. Rhonda Rhodes, College of Business Administration director of graduate studies (Cal. Poly,

1996). A number of Fortune 500 companies have signed up for the Executive Education Network, an interactive satellite network that transmits MBA-level courses from schools that include Wharton, USC, Penn State, and Carnegie Mellon (Anderson, 1995). In addition, distance-learning programs are springing up because business schools see that "the new techniques and technologies of distance learning hold the potential to revolutionize executive education (Byrne, 1995, p.64)." One of the questions in the survey asked respondents whether they would be interested in distance learning if it were available. The reason for this is that a product like distance learning requires training just to use it; the availability of it does not necessarily suggest that potential students will rush to choose distance learning over traditional face-to-face methods of education.

b) Derailed executives:

Moulton (1993) discusses the derailed executive as someone who is demoted, fired or stalled for reasons of their own making. By targeting multiple job assignments and course work designed to motivate more productive behavior, a worthwhile person can be saved. The literature supports the supposition that it is worth the cost to retrain rather than replace a key member. However, the layoff practices of the past several years would tend to open this question to debate for some of the more expensive programs and some of the more expensive managers.

c) Public image/Retention

The Rand Graduate Institute is not only an example of high-level academic work given by a corporation, but of a corporation that has recognized that it is good for the image of the company and is an aid to the recruiting of highly qualified staff (Eurich, 1985). General Electric's corporate schools in Ohio have long been known for their quality education and used as an attraction to hire the best employees.

d) Contribution to Strategy

Many CEO's have turned to executive education to help their strategic agendas, in which case they must oversee the training of the skills necessary to create and manage the strategy (Bolt, 1993). A number of the better known business school professors have consulted with such companies as AT&T, Eastman Kodak and Phillips (Byrne, 1991).

e) Reward

Although less today, there was a time when these programs were taught in resorts and were seen as a reward to executives or as a way to let an impatient young manager know that patience would pay off in the long run.

The reasons of skill development, remedial study, strategic training and reward were all discussed in the literature, but Andrews noted that executive programs were generally designed for the most promotable manager rather than those in need of remedial help (1966).

The following section will review the literature used as the basis for the sub-questions articulated in Chapter 3..

1) Diversity

Today, more than half of all women between the ages of fifteen and sixty-four are in the workforce, comprising 30% of the world's working population (Johnston, 1991) By the year 2000, the percentage of women in the workforce is expected to rise to 47.3% (Greenburg & Baron, 1993). As the Andrews/Powell project did not survey any women, I was interested in the response of today's executive women to the programs available to them. Even Pierre Du Jardin, whose dissertation work followed Andrews' research by some ten years and used the same program as a sample, excluded women and non-Americans from the final sample in order to get a homogeneous sample for his own purposes (Du Jardin, 1981). As late as 1993, the Advanced Management Program at Harvard (one of Andrews' subjects) had only 5% women (Banergee,1993); consequently, I was interested in gender trends and reactions to Executive MBA programs, where women in greater numbers are expected to be going after an MBA that does not require a top spot in management as part of the ticket of admission. My research found that schools list female participation from 18% to 30%.

Because the American workforce is becoming more culturally diverse, issues of culture become important in the planning of management training. In 1980, the workforce was composed of 6% Hispanics and 12% Black; by the year 2000, those percentages will become 10% Hispanic, 12% Black and 4% Asian (Ibid.). America is no longer known as the "melting pot" because of the many ethnic groups who try to hold on to their culture. In <u>Guess Who's Coming to College: Your Students in 1990</u>, Harold Hodgkinson suggested that American colleges and universities were ignoring the rapidly increasing percentage of minorities in the U.S. population, and were not properly planning for future generations of increasingly minority college students (cited in Brown & Rivas, 1993). My interest was to identify levels of satisfaction among members of minority groups who were part of my sample population.

2) Lack of stability in the workforce

Nancy Bern , a Vice President at John Hancock, mirrored the feelings of many when she said that "globalization, change and uncertainty are the three most common themes that I face in my job......these themes are becoming stronger (Ready,1992,p.39)." More than 50,000 managers a month lost their jobs last year and downsizing continues to be among the strategic choices of many firms.

This differs from the era of the Andrews/Powell survey, when most of the participants in the survey stayed with their companies after their programs; in fact, the average seniority was 17 years. In other words, the executive programs in the 1950's were not used as stepping stones by these people. In January of 1996, the 76 million members of the "baby boom" generation began to turn 50 years old at a rate of one every seven seconds for the next ten years. They realize that lack of job security forces them to make sure their skills are up-to-date for either maintaining their jobs or being ready to change careers. The question "do Executive MBA participants look at their education as a ticket to leave their current employer?" is a valid one considering the amount of corporate investment in these programs. If these people do use the MBA to leave their jobs, or even to start their own businesses, will corporations rethink their financial support? Currently, few schools allow part-time students, who usually receive tuition reimbursement, to use the school's placement operations to find new jobs (Levenson, 1995).

In her recent attack on the entitlement habit that she feels is threatening American business, psychologist Judith Bardwick stated that, if members of the labor force are productive and add value, if they keep on learning and their skills are current, they'll be O.K. (Bardwick, 1995). This pronouncement might give solace to people who feel they are on a continuous learning stream, especially by tackling an Executive MBA program. But how do corporations feel about the funds they are investing into this person's portable "security?" Will they still feel that the overall investment advantages outweigh the negative impact of the few who get their education and leave? I researcher predicted that corporations would take the latter view, even though some employers have policies that call for payback of the expense of training should the employee leave within a certain amount of time (Sample, 1995).

3) Relevance of course material

In 1991, Training and Development magazine surveyed directors of executive development in 77 companies in the United States and Canada, with the purpose of understanding their plans to respond to upcoming challenges. Table 1 shows the significant change in the following categories:

Table 1 Change in executive development emphasis.

Topic	Past Emphasis	Future Emphasis
Leadership	38%	89%
Managing Human Performance	22%	73%
Implementation of business strategies	23%	70%
Managing organizational change	15%	64%

Source: Mann and Staudenneier, 1991

Andrews and Powell, in their survey of 10,000 participants in management courses from 1959 to 1966, found that the campus management courses had, "in a short period, won the respect and approval of the men who have attended them

(Andrews,1966,p.184)". But I found a number of examples of conflicts between the most relevant education and that which is currently offered. Conflict between emphasis and needs includes the feeling that the schools encourage a preference for analytical detachment rather than the insight that comes from hands-on experience, and for short-term cost reduction rather than long-term development of technological competition (Hayes and Abernathy,1980; Cheit, 1985). The 1985 GMAC report on "The Demand and Supply of University-Based Executive Education" (Johnson, et. al,1988) noted that the following suggestions were among those made for program effectiveness by the 100 corporations that were studied:

1) Thirty percent said the universities should work harder to identify company needs and then respond to them.
2) Sixteen percent mentioned that the university programs should become less academic.

The report also mentioned dissatisfaction with university professors whose background did not prepare them to effectively teach business executives. A review of the major negative comments about these programs is listed in Table 2:

Table 2 Major negative comments about executive education

Literature source:	Conflict Presented
Hayes & Abernathy, 1980 "Managing Our Way to Economic Decline:"	Schools encourage preference for analytical detachment rather than insight from experience
Cheit, 1985 "Business Schools & Their Critics"	1) Wrong model 2) Ignore important work 3) Fail to meet society's need 4) Foster short-term, undesirable attitude
Johnson, et al, 1988 The Demand and Supply of University-Based Executive Education.	1) Increase responsiveness 2) Less academic, more practical content 3) Appropriate training for instructors
Leavitt,1989 "Educating our MBA's:On teaching what we haven't taught."	Too much analysis in the business school method.
Byrne, 1993. Business Week's Guide to the Best Executive Education Programs	Managers are surprised at the inconsistent teaching quality of prestigious universities.

During my research, I had the opportunity to interview Quinn McKay, whose 1960 Harvard dissertation was based on those who did not respond to the Andrews/Powell survey. Echoing some of the criticisms of executive education, he said that he was "surprised at the limited number of faculty members who could relate to business (McKay, 1996)." This comment was to become important as the comments came in from the EMBA alumni.

Current trends do show that many schools are reacting to the challenge to "reformulate ...executive-education programs in the face of a changing market and increased competition (De Rouffignac,1993, p.R12.)". One of the purposes of my research was to find out, from the student population, if that is true and whether the changes are effective.

4) Support of industry

The 1966 Andrews/Powell report showed heavy concentration in support from the oil industry, with a further representation as follows:

Table 3 Support by industry

Industry	Sending Men to Executive Programs 1949-1958[2]	Sending people to Executive MBA programs in 1986[3]
Agriculture/Forestry Mining/Construction/ Petroleum(17.5%)	21%	5.3%
Manufacturing	46.6%	35.0%
Transportation/Commun	12.4%	10.0%
Services	10.7%(Gov.,Entertainment)	21.3%
Wholesale/Retail Trade	2.7%	14.9%
Finance/Insur/Real Estate	6.5%	13.5%

Service company participation and that of finance and insurance doubled, while manufacturing participation decreased by 25%. This could very likely follow the pattern of industrial employment, such as the increase in service jobs vs. manufacturing jobs, but it was interesting to quantify the mix in 1996 vs. that of ten years ago, when the GMAC survey was done.

No trend in American business is more important than that toward participative "people-oriented management" and more sophisticated decision-making (Johnson et.al, 1986). The Human Relations movement, which evolved from the Scientific Management movement created by Frederick Winslow Taylor, continued to support the need for better kinds of training.

---

[2]Andrews, 1966
[3]Johnson, et. al, 1988

A number of predictions have been made that related to the need to keep executive training current:

1) The growing role of technology will increase the importance of further training.
2) An increased number of firms are regarding employment decisions as long-term commitments to training.
3) The internationalization of the economy will place new priorities on a group of world issues and the needs of the culture.
4) The growth of small companies will require managers who are independent-minded problem solvers.

(Johnson et.al., 1986; Johnston, 1991)

The challenges of the next century will include disappearing natural resources, an aging continual skills upgrading for a very diverse population. Business schools and corporations answer to these needs by pooling their immense resources and brainpower in a focused mar

In the end, Peter Drucker is right. The purpose of a business is to create a customer. The corporation is the customer of the business school. The corporation needs the knowledge infusion that the school provides. The research cited here shows that it is a symbiotic relationship, where the schools must respond to changes needed in the businesses. In the modern society of enterprise and management, knowledge is the primary resource and society's true wealth (Drucker, 1988). This research was expected to support the need for business to continue investing in education at all levels and for schools to continuing listening to the changes that business expects in order to continue to provide financial support.

CHAPTER 3

RESEARCH QUESTION AND METHODOLOGY

Research Question

This is a descriptive study based on answers to surveys and interviews. The research question which served as the basis for the sub-questions follows:

Are the schools which are producing executive training at the MBA level meeting the needs of their mid-career students in ways that address their concerns as working professionals?

Several sub-questions and hypotheses were developed using an inductive approach:

a) Is there a difference in reaction by executive students to the effectiveness of programs in 1993, 1994, and 1995 vs. their reactions in 1959, as measured by the Andrews/Powell study?

b) Are the programs affected by the lack of security in the workplace today and are people using the executive MBA degree to make a career change?

c) Are the courses relevant to the executive's job needs? Do they help him/her do the job better or are they too academic? If the satisfaction level is the same as that covered by the Andrews work, the current results would state that there remains a high satisfaction level with course relevancy.

d) Do sponsoring companies make concerted use of the skills learned? The Andrews/Powell work found some evidence that corporations do not have specific programs to utilize the skills acquired in executive education programs.

e) Do women continue to have a problem with the 'glass ceiling' even after attaining the skills that programs produce? According to Jean Lipman-Blumen, a professor of organizational behavior at the Claremont Graduate School, "it's a widespread problem, not only in the United States but around the world.(Groves, 1996, p.D1)." Recent research points out that women have an easier start on their careers than they did in the past, but "getting women into corporations is not the same as moving them up. (Wentling, 1996, p.255)." A recent study by the non-profit Catalyst stated that, "of the 2,500 top-earning executives, just 50 are women.(Himelstein,L.,1996)"

The research used several methods to build the answers to the above questions:

1) Four case studies, including alumni and program directors of the schools used in the research, combined to answer the research questions.

2) Surveys were conducted of the 1992, 1993, and 1994 alumni from the EMBA programs at the four schools. The survey instrument can be found in Appendix C. Open-ended questions were used to find out how the respondents felt about their experience. Demographic questions were used to describe the population. Likert scales were used to determine level of satisfaction.

3) Interviews of 24 alumni, chosen randomly from the returned surveys, were used to obtain expository comments about the experiences.

4) Interviews of ten corporate representatives who were responsible for executive level training expenditures.

Anonymity was offered both to the schools and the alumni who answered the survey or agreed to be interviewed.

Methodology

This study used the triangulation approach to research (Campbell, et al, 1982) in order to increase the validity of the results(Rudestam&Newton,1992). The triangulation method combines quantitative and qualitative methods to interpret data. By combining a quantitative survey of EMBA alumni with interviews of selected participants, interviews of the four program directors, and interviews of ten corporate managers responsible for executive education reimbursement programs, I expected to be able to cover the entire span of stakeholders in the EMBA programs used for this research. The four case studies, of UCLA, the University of Colorado, the University of Utah, and the University of Washington, provided ample information to work with, as the quantitative surveys and interviews used the same format for each case study.

Selection of the sample

The population was comprised of Executive MBA alumni from the four chosen schools. The Andrews/Powell survey used 39 selected management development programs. For purposes of choosing this sample, the following schools, which were in the Andrews/Powell sample ,currently offer an Executive MBA degree:

Columbia University	Michigan State University
Northwestern University	University of Illinois
Ohio University	University of North Carolina
University of California, Los Angeles	University of Oregon
University of Colorado	University of Pennsylvania
University of Hawaii	University of Southern California
University of Houston	University of Utah
University of Illinois	University of Western Ontario

Four schools were chosen based on, a) their willingness to be involved in the program ; and b) their proximity to the research base. As there was no separate funding for this project, the need to conserve personal funds for travel expenses played a part in the sample chosen. The entire mailing list of the schools was used. Systematic random sampling was used. Every other person on the mailing list was included, to bring the sample to a workable number. Alumni from three specific years, 1993, 1994, and 1995, were used. Details about the programs include the following, listed in Table 4:

Table 4 Executive MBA Programs used in the research

School/Contact	Admitting Class Selected Data	Age of program	Length of program	Cost [4]
The University of Colorado, Denver Scott Guthrie	Mean age:38 Mean years of work experience: 16.	14 Years	22 months 1 day/week Alternating Friday/Saturday Includes international Trip	$24,960 all inc books, lodging
The University of California at Los Angeles Gary Lindblad	70 admitted per yr. 30% 30-34 yrs. Old 42% 35-39 yrs.old 21% 40-45 yrs.old All members follow the same schedule.	40 years	24 months Alternating Friday/Saturday Includes international trip	$26,375/yr Includes notebo computer,book materials,reside weeks,parking,
The University of Utah David Dungan	40 admitted per year/ 30 graduated per year.	20 years	21 months 1 day/week Alt. Friday/Saturday 3 One-week sessions/ Includes international trip	$18,500 entire includes books computer acces
The University of Washington Nina Sanders	35-45 admitted per yr. Mean age: 37 years All members follow the same schedule.	13 years	24 months Alternating Friday/Saturday	$17,000 includ tuition, books,c materials,reside weeks,parking,

There are many similarities in teaching methods, use of international trips, etc., but the cost differential is high and would lead one to believe that there is some major difference in student take-away. This research project hoped to identify some of those differences.

The research design called for the following:

1) Survey graduates of Executive MBA programs for 1993,1994, and 1995. This survey replicated part of the Andrews/Powell document, as well as adding some questions relating to changes that may affect the students' experience. By using the entire

---

[4] Based on 1995 entering year.

alumni mailing list available, it was expected that a representative percentage of women and of various ethnic groups would occur without special effort.

2) Interview program directors at these schools concerning their reactions to the issues raised in the surveys, as well as their prediction for future programs.

3) Interview a sample of the students (total 24) based on their answers to the questionnaire and other feelings on which they are willing to elaborate. Interviews were 60-90 minutes in length.

4) Interview ten executives responsible for executive education funding, concerning their feelings about the future support of their company and the quality of the employees they are getting now and expect to get in the future. This sample was not random, but was based on contacts available through current colleagues.

Survey preparation

The Andrews/Powell survey, written by Reed Powell, contained 48 questions. Some contained more than one part. In choosing what questions to use, I concentrated on my research questions and how the original survey would add to the quantitative and qualitative information I was seeking, without making the instrument so long as to detract from my response rate. The Andrews/Powell questions were separated as follows: The first nine questions were demographic in nature, asking questions about age, which university program they attended, marital status, etc. I used the questions relating to age, program, industry, and marital status, but I did not use the questions relating to prior educational experiences.

The next eight questions, three of which were open-ended in nature, asked who initiated the idea of going to the program, present position, and whether or not there was any relationship between going to the program and a subsequent increase in salary, promotion, or increase in responsibility. I used the one which asked their present position, and added one asking their position at the time they began the MBA program. I also used the original text of Question #17 in the Andrews/Powell questionnaire, which became Question #10 in my survey. It was an objective question which asked the relationship between going to the program and an increase in salary, promotion, or increase in responsibility.

The next four questions, Questions #18-21, asked the respondents feelings about attending another executive development program, what kind of program they would attend, and their candid opinion about having other management personnel from their firm attend a program of the type they attended. Two of the questions were open-ended and two asked the participants to check their opinion (such as choosing the value of the program for all management personnel between very low and very high).

Andrews/Powell Question #22 asked if they noticed any changed in the attitudes of other people in their company when they returned from the program. I used this question in the alumni interviews, but not in the survey.

Question #23, an open-ended question, asked what they felt the program was trying to accomplish, what they thought happened to those who attended, and what happened to them. This became Question #16 in my research instrument.

Questions #24-26 asked the percentage of their class who applied themselves, whether some attended only because their company wanted them to, and whether any of those who had wanted personally to attended had become dissatisfied with the program by the end. I did not use any of these questions because I was focusing on the satisfaction level of those who attended.

Questions #27-30 were open-ended questions which asked what they thought the program was trying to accomplish, what they thought happened to those who attended, and their reaction when they were answering the survey. Parts of these questions became questions #12 and #13 in my research.

Questions #31-33 asked about teaching methods employed in the program, their reaction to those methods, and their thoughts about faculty effectiveness in their program. I did not ask about the teaching methods in the survey, but I did include this question in the alumni interviews. The survey I used included the questions about their reaction to the teaching methods and to faculty effectiveness.

Question #34 in the Andrews/Powell survey was an objective question asking how they would have made use of the same amount of money if given the choice between attending seminars, time off to study individually, attendance at a technical course, visits to other companies, and attending the program they actually attended. In my survey, I added the choice of another program to these questions. It became Question #15 in my questionnaire.

The next four questions, #35-38, asked about the social activities, the amount of recreation engaged in by the group, and to what extent these activities interfered with their studies. In the interest of brevity and because I knew the programs I was researching were not residence programs, I chose to leave these questions out.

Question #39 became one of the most important questions in my survey. It asked the respondents to rate the areas of study in terms of the interest they held for the participants. It became question #18 in my survey, after I added "strategy" to the areas of study because it was not included in the Andrews/Powell work.

Questions #41 and #42 asked about the amount of reading, writing and overall work assigned in the program, and also the personal value of the program elements such as reading, class sessions, small study groups, contacts with faculty outside of class, and informal on-campus discussions with other executives. They became questions #20 and 21 in my research.

Question #43 asked about contacts and their value. I did not use it.

Questions #44 and #45 asked the degree of interest from week to week. Because the programs I was researching were not residence programs of comparable length, I did not use these questions.

The last three questions, #46-48, asked for suggestions and for anything that particularly stood out in their mind, either favorable or unfavorable. These also became my last questions.

I added 11 questions as they related to my research questions. They included questions about:

1. The "glass ceiling" and whether the women had experienced it in their careers. Whether on-line education would have been an interest to them as an alternative to in-class meetings.
2. Using industry practitioners vs. the requirement of a Ph.D. to teach in the executive program.
3. The applicability of the course-work to their career.
4. The importance of the international trip.

I added these questions because they related to elements which were not a concern in the original research, which covered programs in which there were no women and did not include international trips.

Table 5 is a visual representation of the original questions from the Harvard research, and whether or not I included each one.

Table 5 Andrews/Powell questions & current research

Question # in Andrews' Survey	Topic	# in Current Survey
1	Industry ?	1
2	Years with present company?	2
3	Age at last birthday?	Not used
4	Marital status?	33
5	Education?	Not used
6	Title of university program?	35
7	University?	35
8	Length of the program?	4
9	Beginning & Ending date?	Not used
10	Who initiated the program?	Not used
11	Reservations about attending the program	Not used
12	Changed employers?	5
13	Connection between leaving and the program?	10
14	Present position?	8
15	Date of last promotion?	Not used
16 a	Position the same?	Not used
16 b	If same position, has responsibility changed?	9
16 c	Other positions held in the company?	Not used
17	Relationship between attendance in the program and career advancement?	10
18	Feelings about attending another program?	Not used
19	Questions about attending future programs?	Not used
20	Who should sponsor future programs?	Not used
21	Feeling about having co-workers attend the same program?	Not used
22	Change in attitudes of other people at work after attendance at the program?	Not used
23	What was the program trying to accomplish?	12a
24	What % applied themselves?	Not used
25	Were there people there who only attended because of pressure?	Not used
26	How many were dissatisfied by the end of the program?	Not used
Question # in Andrews' Survey	**Topic**	**# in Current Survey**
27	What did you imagine the program would be like?	13a
28	Reaction after a few days?	Not used
29	Reaction at the end of the program?	13b
30	Reaction now?	13c
31	What teaching methods were used?	Not used
32	Reaction to teaching methods at time of program	Not used
33	Faculty teaching effectiveness	Not used
35	Extent to which executives engaged in social activities?	Not used
36	Feeling about recreational time?	Not used
37	Extent that social activities interfered with studies?	Not used
38	What percentage "party boys.?"	Not used
39	Areas included in the program?	18

40	What % reflection of teaching methods and what % reflective of personal interest?	19
41	Amount of reading?	20
42	Rank parts of the program in value?	21
43	Contact with men in class after return ?	Not used
44	Degree of interest from week to week /	Not used
45	What factors influence interest from week to week ?	Not used
46	Would you do this again or take the money?	Not used
47	Suggestions for improvement?	23
48	Anything that stands out in your mind?	28

QUESTIONS ADDED	Topic	# in Current Survey
	Position when began the program	7
	Gender	31
	Ethnic background	32
	Marital status at graduation	34
	Company use of skills	11
	Faculty teaching effectiveness	14
	Rating of the program	13d
	Choice of another MBA program	15e
	Inclusion of strategy in current programs	18j
	If a woman, "glass ceiling?	22
	How applicable to your career was the experience?	27
	Choice of on-line education	25
	Evaluation of international experience	30
	Feeling about practitioner qualifications	27

The final questionnaire used in my research contained 35 questions, seven of which contained more than one part, such as an opportunity to comment on the prior answer. Demographic information was included at the end. The surveys were color coded by school and offered the option of mailing or faxing back the completed survey.

Data Collection

a) Pilot Study

A non-random pilot study was conducted in January of alumni of the Peter F. Drucker Executive Management Center at the Claremont Graduate School and several other colleagues who held executive MBAs.

The pilot surveys were mailed out on Drucker Center stationary. I called each person to ask their help prior to sending out the surveys.

Fifteen surveys were returned.. Data from these questionnaires were entered onto the computer using Absurv software. I then conducted the following analysis:

1) Comparison of pilot responses to responses in the original Andrews/Powell work. For instance, I could tell how many respondents had been with their companies for certain lengths of time for both the pilot and the Andrews/Powell survey.

2) Demographic descriptive statistics to ascertain if there was any diversity in the sample.

3) Comments about the questions in order to clarify or change questions that might be ambiguous.

I noticed the following general information about the original survey vs. the one planned for this research:

1) The men in the Harvard survey had been with their companies longer and more of them were married than the pilot showed.

2) In the Andrews/Powell research, 47% of the respondents came from manufacturing, while the pilot showed only 20%. One of the questions the research was trying to clarify was how the change in corporate support will affect the people who attend these programs.

3) Marketing received a much higher ranking in importance in the pilot than in the original research.

4) Becoming more employable was used as an answer in the pilot, while it was not a factor in the Andrews/Powell survey, where most of the people were sent by their employer because they were on a promotion schedule.

I also added questions relating to the glass ceiling and the use of on-line education. Response to the pilot study indicated the following:

1) Most of the respondents were against using on-line education because they received value from face-to-face interaction.
2) Most women had experienced the glass ceiling.

The following changes were made based on the pilot results:

1) Several questions were taken out because they confused the participants and we were trying to limit the length of the survey to four pages.
2) Several questions were changed from a ranking to a likert scale at the suggestion of Professor Drew because the pilot respondents has a hard time ranking some of the areas.

b) Data collection for the surveys was done in the following manner:

1) During the period April 22nd through May 1st, a survey, cover letter, and stamped return envelope were sent to every other person on the mailing lists supplied by the four schools. The surveys went out on Drucker Center stationary, with permission from Cathy Agne, the Director of Executive Programs at the Drucker Center during the time the proposal was being developed. First class postage, both for the outgoing envelope and the return envelope, was used because it has shown to increase the response rate (Dillman, 1978). Appendix B represents an example of the cover letter used for the University of Utah. The schools will be identified as School Green, School Blue, School Goldenrod, and School Yellow, in order to offer appropriate anonymity to the schools participating in this research. These colors signify the four colors used in the surveys. It was decided to use colored paper because research indicated that steps taken to make a questionnaire look more attractive would have a positive effect on response rates (Fowler, 1984).

I wanted to be able to identify who had sent the surveys back before I did my second and third reminder letters, so I numbered the first page of the survey, at the bottom right corner. In the cover letter to the alumni, I indicated that the surveys were numbered, but that they were numbered for response purposes only, not for follow-through if the respondent chose not to include a name. If the respondent chose not to identify himself or herself, I could still identify them and remove them from the list for further follow-up. I folded the letters and surveys and enclosed the stamped return envelope according to the method suggested by Dillman (1978, p.181), such that the letter opened up to reveal the recipient's name and address immediately. Appendix K identifies the way the surveys were returned. As each survey came in, it was copied and logged against the number assigned to it so that I could keep track of who was not responding.

2) After two weeks, I sent out a reminder letter to those who had not answered within that time. Those surveys returned as non-deliverable (four) were removed from the list. Appendix E shows an example of that letter. Of the 258 surveys mailed out, only 16, or 6.20 %, were returned as undeliverable.

3) Two weeks after the reminder letter had gone out, I sent another cover letter, survey and return envelope by first class mail to the remaining non-respondents. Appendix G is an example of the cover letter used for the last mailing. The process took place using the following timetable, represented in Table 6 :

Table 6 Survey Timetable

	Green	Blue	Goldenrod	Yellow
First surveys sent	April 22	April 24	April 25	May 1
Reminder letter sent	May 10	May 10	May 11	May 16
Second surveys sent	May 24	May 24	May 28	June 5

b. **Interviews**

    Corporate interviews

From January through the middle of July, I conducted the ten interviews of corporate executives responsible for overseeing the funding of executive MBA programs. I used an interview schedule, the text of which follows:

Exhibit 1
EXECUTIVE EDUCATION SURVEY FOR CORPORATE SPONSORS

This survey is designed to measure the current satisfaction, plans and expectations of today's executive with regard to executive education. The questions will involve the impact of job rotation, increased job insecurity, the entrance of minority groups to the workplace and future investment plans.

QUESTIONS FOR DEMOGRAPHIC IDENTIFICATION

1) Into what category does your company fall:
    ____Less than $100 million
    ____$100 million or greater, but less than $200 million
    ____$200 million or greater

2) Is your company multinational?   Yes____   No____

3) What is your position?_____

4) What is your age bracket:
    ____Less than 40 yrs. old.
    ____Between 40 and 50 yrs. old.
    ____Over 50 yrs. old.

QUESTIONS ABOUT THE CURRENT WORKPLACE

5) Do you think the current labor market for managerial jobs is:
Poor___   Fair___ Good___   Very Good___ Excellent___

6) Do you think that, in the future, the market will be:
Poor___   Fair___ Good___   Very Good___ Excellent___

7) Are your plans for hiring managers in the next 5 years:
More than the last 5 years   ___?
The same   ___?
Less than the last 5 years   ___?

8) Do you think the availability of talent in managers is:
Poor___   Fair___ Good___   Very Good___ Excellent___

9) How has increased diversity of workers affected your workplace in terms of productivity (in the past 5 years)?
    It has increased productivity   _____
    It has decreased productivity   _____
    Productivity has stayed the same   _____

10) How has increased availability of workers from other countries or minorities affected turnover in the past 5 years?

    It has increased turnover   _____
    It has decreased turnover   _____
    Turnover has stayed the same   _____

QUESTIONS ABOUT CURRENT TRAINING EXPENDITURES

11) What department is responsible for choosing, managing and funding executive education:(check all that apply)

    Executives choose themselves and are reimbursed 80%   _____
    Executives choose themselves and are reimbursed 100%   _____
    We send out lists of available courses, for which we pay 100%   _____
    We hold off-site sessions   _____
    We hold on-site sessions   _____
    It is handled by the Human Resources Department   _____
    It is handled by the Marketing Department   _____
    Each department handles its own   _____
    Other(_____)   _____

12) How much did your company spend training managers last year in:

    Academic programs like an MBA   _____?
    Off-site programs   _____?
    On-site program run by an internal training department   _____?
    On-site programs run by external consultants or universities   _____?

13) Are you satisfied with the results of the training?

    Yes_____   No_____

If so, in what way? (Please check all that apply)

    Applicable to real business situations   _____
    Contributes to growth   _____
    Reflects action-learning principles   _____
    Is flexible for our needs   _____
    Other(please specify)_____

14) If you are not satisfied with the results of the training, why not?(please check all that apply)

    Not applicable to real business situations   _____
    Does not reflect current global perspective of business?   _____
    Is not a good value for the money   _____
    Do not use the best instructors   _____
    Other (please specify)_____

15) In comparing executive ability to five years ago, in general, do you think the current level of executive ability and skills is:

    Worse than   _____
    As good as   _____
    The same   _____

Better than it was 5 years ago   _____

16) For executive training, which of the following do you prefer:
    Weekend lecture   _____
    Once weekly lecture   _____
    Weekend lecture and case study/group work   _____
    Once weekly lecture and group work/case study   _____

17) There are several locations where this type of training is conducted. Please rate your preference in order from 1-4, 1 being the most preferred.
    Off-site overnight   _____
    Off-site day only   _____
    On-site   _____
    Off-site full week program   _____

18) These programs are administered by different types of institutions. Again, please rate your preference in order from 1-4, 1 being the most preferred.
    University program open to the public, other than an MBA
        program   _____
    University degree program, such as MBA.   _____
    Custom University program planned with the company _____
    Consultants in the area of interest   _____

QUESTIONS ABOUT FUTURE TRAINING EXPENDITURES

19) With regard to investment in executive training in the next 5 years, do you intend to spend:

    The same amount?   _____
    More?   _____
    Less?   _____

20) What programs will you add, if any?
    In-house   _____
    More support for outside academic institutions   _____
    More support for outside professional management training. _____

21) What programs will you subtract, if any?
    In-house   _____
    Outside academic offerings   _____
    Outside professional management training   _____

22) What programs do you wish were available?
    More about managing the global economy   _____
    More about managing diversity   _____
    More flexible programs   _____
    Other (please specify_____)   _____

23) Is there a budget for executive training expenditures?   Yes_____   No___

If so, are the courses taken affected by a downturn in company revenues?
                                                              Yes _____   No___

QUESTIONS ABOUT MANAGEMENT ROLES IN EXECUTIVE DEVELOPMENT

24) Assuming there is a risk that employees will want to change departments or leave the company after they have improved their skills through training, how much of a risk do you feel there is:
    ____Low
    ____Moderate
    ____Average
    ____Above average
    ____High

25) Do you evaluate managers on their role in providing opportunities for further training for their subordinates?
    ____ Yes
    ____ No

26) Is there a system to use the skills that executives obtain in executive training programs?
Yes_____ No_____
If so, what kind?_____

27) How do you reward executives for participating in these training programs (please check all that apply):
    _____We give them financial support to pay for the courses, and nothing more.
    _____We consider their participation in these programs as part of their overall evaluation toward promotion.
    _____Their bonus or salary is positively affected by participation in these programs.

QUESTIONS ABOUT OBJECTIVES IN TRAINING

28) What kind of improvements in skills are you looking for when you sponsor executive training programs? Please be as specific as possible:
_____
_____

If you could be assured of the effects mentioned above, would you be willing to increase the amount of training funding coming from your firm?
                                                           Yes____   No___

29) Which of the following best describes your expectations when your firm supports a manager in executive education?

    ____ Expect quantifiable skill change and increase in affective commitment.
    ____ Expect quantifiable skill change; affective commitment not important
    ____ Expect improvement in affective commitment to the organization--this is the most important benefit.
    ____ Feel it is a benefit to the employee, much like health benefits.

30) As your last question, I am interested in your overall feeling that practitioners of executive education meet the needs of the corporations whose financial support is important to the future of executive programs. Please check the one that most applies to the way you feel.
    _____ On an overall basis, I think the programs are meeting our needs.
    _____ On an overall basis, I think the programs are lacking in real-world applicability to our company's needs.
    _____ On an overall basis, I think that there is some weakness in practical applicability, but the skills the managers are attaining are worthwhile for our purposes.

Alumni interviews

I had set 24 as the number of people I wanted to interview after the return of the surveys. This provided for 6 interviews per school. I accomplished these interviews in the following manner:

School Green:

This school was my first visit, and it occurred before the surveys actually went out. With the permission of Professor Drew, I asked the program director to identify 5 people I could interview on my trip there. These interviews were conducted from March 28th through April 3rd, by phone and in person. I found that the interviews took between 45 minutes and one hour.

School Blue:

From the returned surveys, I chose from those checking the box indicating that they would be willing to be interviewed. I took every other one, as I had the original surveys, and called to set up an appointment for my visit there on July 15th and 16th. During the actual visit, I conducted the interviews at the respondent's office, using a tape recorder to assure accuracy of transcription.

School Goldenrod:

From the returned surveys, I chose from those checking the box indicating that they were willing to be interviewed. Taking every other one, I set up appointments for my visit to that site from July 8th-10th. During my scheduled interviews, which were held in the office of the alumnus, I tape recorded the interviews after receiving appropriate permission to do so.

School Yellow:

From the returned surveys, I used every other person who agreed to be interviewed and set up appointments for a personal interview. After requesting permission to tape-record the interview, I conducted the interview either at their place of business or at their home. Due to problems of scheduling, four of the six interviews I conducted with School Yellow were done over the phone.

Measurement

For the survey, inferential statistics were used to describe the reactions of the alumni because the entire population of Executive MBA graduates from all 139 schools was not used. The surveys included both nominal and ordinal measurements in order to compare the reactions of people in one industry or at one age with other students who fit the same classifications.

The interviews of both the sample of students and the EMBA program directors were semi-structured. Following is the outline for the interviews of the alumni who agreed to be interviewed and of the program directors.

Exhibit 2

Interview of EMBA Alumni

Name_____ Date_____ Time_____

1) From your recollection of the survey, can you think of anything that the survey left out?

2) What was your first reaction to the program?

    Why? What stood out?

3) Apart from what the program intended, what do you really think happened to those who attended?

    What happened to you?

4) Can you tell me a little more about the best parts of the program?

5) What about the less useful parts of the program?

6) Can you expand on your answer about how well the corporation used your skills when you finished the program?

7) What would you most like to see schools do to improve this program?

8) When you returned from the program, did you feel you did your job differently?

9) Can you cite a specific incident as an example of doing your job differently?

10) From the company's point of view do you really feel it was worth the investment in your time and the company's money to send you to this program?

11) Was there anything about the program, favorable or unfavorabled, which particularly stands out in your mind?

12) How do you feel about the length of the program?

    -if you were notified that the length of the program was going to be changed, would you suggest that it be lengthened or shortened?

<u>Alumni Interview, continued</u>

13) What method or methods of instruction were employed at the program you attended?

    What is your reaction to this type of instruction?

Would you have personally preferred more lecture or more discussion type of instruction?

14) How would you evaluate the effectiveness of the faculty?

Thinking specifically of the instructor you felt was the most effective, what attributes or characteristics did he or she demonstrate that made him most effective from your point of view?

15) Can you give me a brief account of your previous experience; that is, prior to entering into the program what types of jobs had you held?

16) What has been your experience since finishing the program by way of promotion, salary increases, and increase of responsibility?

--if there has been a change of attitude of other people toward you, can you describe this change of attitude?

--do you believe that this change is due to your participation in the EMBA program?

17) With regard to the coverage of issues important to you, how do you feel about that?

18) Were there other results of this EMBA program, such as social relationships, networking opportunities, that stand out in your mind?

Comments:

Results

The entire process, which began with sending out the first surveys on April 20th and concluded with the last interviews during the week of July 15th, took approximately three months. My attempt to maintain randomness in choosing alumni to interview was important to the overall validity of the results.

With the data which were produced from the research, I performed the following analysis:

1. Using ABSERV (Anderson Bell), I recorded all of the answers to the surveys for the survey respondents and the interview participants. These data were used to categorize their answers.

2. Using descriptive statistics, I listed the answers to each question in table form, listing the answers of each school as well as including the total. Where appropriate, I included the Harvard statistics.

As a check on my own data accuracy, the data were entered into SPSSX for further analysis. Using these data, I applied regression analysis to determine the correlation of several of the variables with each other.

Limitations

I learned early in my education about research that all research is flawed in one way or another. I was to find out that, no matter how much one could try to follow the dictates of research methodologies, items of availability, logistics, and researcher errors make it impossible to get total randomness or follow the exact methods described in research literature. The following are some of the areas that may limit the results obtained. They are also some of the areas that suggest follow-up research.

Question # 30, "Age", was listed after "year of graduation from the program", Question #29. Some people apparently used their current age, and some people used their age at the end of the program. I discovered this as the surveys came in and some people would add "now" to their age on the survey. I questioned each of the interviewees to confirm that the age I was using was their age when they graduated from the program. Since the surveys covered only three years, 1993-1995, the error is not a significant factor in the results.

As mentioned before, the Utah interviews were non-random because of the timing of my visit to Salt Lake. In reviewing the program and faculty ratings of those interviewed in Utah, I found no difference between the ratings given by the people who were interviewed resulting from a random process vs. those interviewed by suggestion of the program director.

One of my research questions was about the change in response given the expected diversity in the workforce today. Unfortunately, as confirmed by my interviews with the program directors, there is very little representation of African Americans in part-time executive management programs, due in part to the availability of full scholarships for those who choose a full-time program as opposed to a part-time schedule.

I knew that some of the addresses on the mailing lists provided to me would not be current, so I asked the Claremont Graduate School to hold those returned by the post office for me. Of the 258 surveys mailed out, 16 were returned as undeliverable. This cut the original number to 242. However, I received 157 completed surveys, a percentage of 64.88%. In the results shown in Chapter 4, I have used 157 as the total number of responses for data analysis.

CHAPTER 4

RESULTS

I will present the results in two sections: the statistics which describe the answers given to the questions, and the statistical analysis linking certain variables to others, where I will show that there is a relationship between how the alumni felt about certain parts of the program and how they assessed others. The numbers are presented as raw numbers, followed by the percentages. Schools are identified by colors rather than their names.

From the total of 258 surveys which were sent, I received 157 back by fax and mail. This was a total of just over 60% of the original target sample. I attribute the high return to the following factors:

a) In the case of two of the schools, a letter was sent from the program director alerting the alumni to the existence of the survey and supporting its purpose.

b) Several of the alumni shared with me that they wanted to help the school by answering the survey.

c) By following the method suggested in the literature, that of sending the survey, a reminder letter two weeks later, and another survey two weeks after that, I feel that the results were greater than would otherwise have been the case. For instance, after the first reminder letter, the response increased by 13.6% for School Green, by 18% for School Blue, by 10% for School Goldenrod, and by 18% for School Yellow. When I sent the survey again, along with another cover letter and self-addressed stamped envelope, using first class stamps, along with another survey, the response increased by 25% for School Green, by 9.2% for School Blue, by 10% for School Goldenrod, and by 15.5% for School Yellow. It is clear to me that all three methods, including the use of first class stamps on all correspondence, were important elements in maximizing the return of the surveys.

The results will be presented mostly in tables, listing the descriptive statistics for each school, the total of the schools, and the comparison to the appropriate Harvard statistic, where applicable. Comments preceding and following the question will tie the question to the research questions and to the literature. At the end of the chapter, I will comment on how the descriptive statistics added to my research.

Descriptive statistics

Table 7 Total return

	Green	Blue	Goldenrod	Yellow	Total
Total sent	44	65	60	90	259
Returned by postal service	1 2.27%	2 3.08%	4 6.66%	4 4.44%	11 4.26%
Total returned	37 (84.09%)	37 (56.92%)	35 (58.33%)	48 (53.33%)	157 (60.62%)

The return was high for several reasons:

a) Program directors from three of the schools sent letters ahead asking for the help of the alumni.

b) By following a three-pronged follow-up system, with reminder letters and new surveys sent every two weeks, I was able to attain responses for people who might otherwise have thrown away the document.

c) As will be seen from the statistics by year, more responded from 1995 because the survey arrived fairly soon after they graduated; thus, they were able to respond with answers while their memory was still fresh from the experience.

Table 8 is a representation of the year of graduations for each school. Graduation years of 1993, 1994, and 1995 were used. Some people noted a different year than one of the years I was using; this could have been because they actually finished at a different time than was recorded in their respective school's records.

Table 8 Year of graduation:

Year of Graduation	N=	1993 (% of total)	1994 (% of total)	1995 (% of total)	Other/not designated
Green	37 23.57%	12 7.64%	13 8.28%	10 6.37%	2 1.27%
Blue	37 23.57%	9 5.73%	8 5.10%	16 10.19%	4 2.55%
Goldenrod	35 22.29%	11 7.01%	9 5.73%	13 8.28%	2 1.27%
Yellow	48 30.57%	12 7.64%	15 9.55%	21 13.38%	0
Total	157	44	45	60	8
Percent	100%	28.03%	28.67%	38.22%	5.1%

As expected, the largest part of the sample came from the 1995 graduating year. I would have expected this to be because some of the earlier graduates moved, but only 13 of the 258 envelopes were returned to me. The relatively equal distribution of the years for each school adds to the reliability of the data.

Table 9 represents gender and marital status at graduation. The four following tables represent each of the schools. In each table, the representation of the total population is listed. For instance, for School Green, the percentage who were married was 67.57%, while the total for the entire sample who were married was 74.52%.

Table 9 Gender and Marital Status at Graduation
School Green

	Men	Women	Missing	Total	Total Surveys
Total Population Sampled	34 77.27%	10 22.72%	0	44 100%	259
Total Surveys Returned	27 72.97%	9 24.32%	1 2.70%	37 84.09%	157 60.62%
Blank	1 5.88%	1 10%	0	2 5.41%	3 2.0%
Single, Never married	6 22.22%	2 20%	0	8 21.62%	25 15.92%
Married	20 58.82%	5 50%	0	25 67.57%	117 74.52%
Separated	0	0	0	0	0
Divorced	0	1 10%	0	1 2.70%	10 6.37%
Widowed	0	1		1	2

| | | 10% | | 2.70% | 1.27% |

School Blue

	Men	Women	Missing	Total	Total Surveys
Total Population Sampled	46 7.08%	19 2.92%	0	65 100%	259
Total Surveys Returned	26 56.52%	9 47.37%	2 5.41%	37 56.92 %	157 60.62%
Blank			0		32.0%
Single, Never married	3 11.54%	3 22.22%	0	7 18.91%	25 15.92%
Married	22 84.61%	3 44.44%	0	25 80%	117 74.52%
Separated	0	0	0	0	0
Divorced	1 3.84%	1 11.11%	0	2 5.71%	10 6.37%
Widowed	0	1 11.11%	0	1 2.85%	2 1.27%
Not designated		1 11.11%	2 5.41%	2 5.41%	9 5.73%

Table 9 Gender and Marital Status at Graduation, continued.

School Goldenrod

	Men	Women	Total	Total Surveys
Total Population Sampled	41 68%	19 31%	60 100%	259
Total Surveys Returned	26 74.29%	9 47.37%	35 58.33%	157 60.62%
Single, Never married	1 3.85%	3 15.79%	4 11.43%	25 15.92%
Married	25 96.15%	3 3.33%	28 80%	117 74.52%
Separated	0	1 11.11%	1 2.86%	0
Divorced	0	2 2.22%	2 5.71%	10 6.37%
Widowed	0	0	0	2 1.27%
Not designated	0	0	0	9 5.73%

School Yellow

	Men	Women	Total	Total Surveys
Total population sampled	68 75.56%	22 24.44%	90 100%	
Total Surveys Returned	38	10	48	157

	55.88%	45.45%	53.33%	60.62%
Blank				3 2.0%
Single, Never married	5 13.16%	4	9 18.75%	25 15.92%
Married	29	5	34 70.83%	117 74.52%
Separated	0	0		0
Divorced	0	0		10(6.37%)
Widowed	0	0	0	2(1.27%)
Not designated	4	1	5 10.42%	9 5.73%

Table 10 is a representation of all the schools combined, with regard to marital status.

Table 10 Marital Status: All schools

Total Population	Men	Women	Not designated	Total
Total sample	117	37	3	157
Single, never married	14	10		24(15.29%)
Married	96	16		112 (71.34%)
Separated	0	2		2 (1.27%)
Divorced	1	6		7 (4.46%)
Widowed	0	2		2(1.27%)
Blank				14 (3.18%)
Total	107	36	14	157

In the Andrew's survey, 97% of the men were married, 2% were bachelors and "less than 1% reported themselves as widowers or as either separated or divorced (Andrews, 1966, p.51)." This compares with the fact that only 71% of this population were married, more than 15% had never been married, 6.8% were either divorced or separated, and 1.2% were widowed. The 6.8% who were divorced in the current research can be compared to the difference in the divorce rate since the original research. In 1960, the divorce rate was 2.2 per thousand people; in 1987, it was 4.8 per thousand people (U.S. Dept. of Commerce, 1991). The divorce rate more than doubled between 1960 and 1987 (the latest available figures from the Bureau of the Census), but the number of people who were either widowed or divorced in my sample was over eight times the amount noted in the original research. The difference between the small amount who were bachelors in 1959 and the larger percentage in 1996 appears to be consistent with a population that is marrying later or not at all.

In the proposal for this research, I mentioned that, by the year 2,000, the percentage of women in the workforce is expected to rise to 47.3% (Greenberg&Baron, 1993). The total female participation response in this research was 37 of 157 returned surveys, or 23.57%. The total number of women sampled was 70, or 27.13% of the total. However, because the number of women in the original Andrews/Powell study was 0%, substantial progress seems to have been made in women represented in executive management programs.

Question #32 asked about ethnic background. This was because I wanted to know if the ethnic diversity I expected from changes in the US population was represented in the executive MBA programs. Table 11 represents the answers to this optional question.

Table 11 Ethnic background (Question $#32)

Background	Green	Blue	Goldenrod	Yellow	Total
Asian American	0	0	1 2.86%	4 8.33%	5 3.18%
African American	0	1 2.7%	0	2 4.17%	3 1.91%
Latino	0	2 5.41%%	0	0	2 1.27%
Anglo	35 94.59%	31 83.78%	30 85.71%	41 85.42%	137 87.26%
Native American	0	1 2.70%	2 5.71%	0	3 1.91%
Pacific Islander	0	0	0	0	0
Not answered	2 5.41%	2 5.41%	2 5.71%	1	7 4.46%
Total	37	37	35	48	157

In the Greenberg & Baron work referred to above, the percentage of the American workforce in the year 2000 is expected to be 10% Hispanic, 12% African American, and 4% Asian. This means that, if my survey reached a representative population, 26% of the respondents should have been other than Anglo, or White. Only ten people, or 6.37%, fit that criterion. In my conversations with the program directors, they expressed two possibilities for this discrepancy: a) that full scholarships are available for some of those who represent minorities, so that they might choose a full-time program vs. a part-time program and; b) that, although the schools welcomed diversity in their candidates, they could only attract those that corporations were willing to send. Although I expected the ethnic representation in Utah and Colorado to be less diverse than those in Washington and California, I was disappointed to find that the entire set of surveys (N=158) showed nearly 90% Anglo participants. One of my research questions was 'does executive education properly take into consideration differences in cultural background and critical thought.' I took out of the survey the one question that related to the above because it appeared to complicate the job asked of the respondents. That factor, in addition to the low representation of other-than-Anglo participants, makes it impossible for me to answer the question with any amount of validity.

Table 12 represents industry participation.

Table 12 Industry(Question #1)

Industry classifications used in the Harvard study	Goldenrod	Blue	Green	Yellow	Total	Ha S
N=	35	37	37	48	157	6
Agriculture/Forestry/Mining /Construction/Petroleum	1 2.8%	8 22.22%	3 8.82%	2 4.17%	14 8.92%	2
Manufacturing/Aerospace	12 34%	8 22.22%	5 14.71%	19 39.58%	44 28.0%	4(
Transportation/Communication	3 8.5%	6 16.66%	1 2.94%	2 4.16%	12 7.64%	1:
Services	4 11.4%	7 19.44%	10 29.41%	9 18.7%	30 19.1%	1(
Wholesale/Retail	3 8.5%	2 5.55%	1 2.94%	4 8.33%	10 6.37%	2
Finance/Ins/Real Estate	3 8.5%	1 2.77%	6 17.65%	7 14.58%	17 10.8%	6
Health Care	5 14.2%	1 2.77%	6 17.65%	2 4.17%	14 8.92%	
Computer	3 8.5%	4 10.81%	2 5.88%	3 6.25%	12 7.64%	
Not answered	1	0	3	0	4 2.55%	

I wanted to compare the industry support in 1996 against not only the Harvard work, but the GMAC study in 1986 (Johnson, et al, 1988). Table 13 follows:

Table 13 Comparison of Harvard, Current research, and GMAC industry support

	Harvard	GMAC	Current research

Agriculture/forestry/mining/ construction/petroleum	21%	5.3%	8.92%
Manufacturing	46.6%	35.0%	28.03%
Trans./Communication	12.4%	10.0%	7.64%
Services	10.7%	21.3%	19.1%
Wholesale/Retail Trade	2.7%	14.9%	6.37%
Finance/Insurance/R. Estate	6.5%	13.5%	8.92%
Computers	Not used	Not used	7.64%

As expected, manufacturing, even when it includes aerospace, has shrunk significantly both between the time of the Harvard survey and the GMAC research, and between the GMAC research and my survey. As I expected, and the GMAC research confirmed, service businesses have doubled since the Harvard research. I broke out health care because I thought it a significant element for future support of executive MBA programs, but I imagine it was included in "services" for the previous research. If I were to add "health care" to the "services" portion, the total would be 28.02%, or a number as large as manufacturing, the largest category in the Harvard study. In addition, finance/real estate/insurance accounted for 10.8% of my sample and 13.5% of the GMAC results, while it only accounted for 6.5% of the Harvard data. These data confirm the move away from manufacturing toward what Peter Drucker calls the "knowledge workers." Adding together services, finance, etc., health care, and computers, the total representation in these specialized service and technical areas is 46.46%, an area that will continue to grow in importance as the universities look at the industries who are their customers. In my interviews with corporate sponsors, the human resources managers continue to stress the need for employees to have the specialized skills that will be required in the future.

The Table 14 lists the industry classifications according to Forbe's Industry Classifications, which are more detailed than those from the Harvard research.

Table 14 Forbes Industry Classifications:

Industry	Andrews %[5]	Goldenrod	Green	Blue	Yellow	Total N= 157
Aerospace&Defense		11	2	1	8	20 (12.58%)
Bus/Envir/Waste			2			2 (1.26%)
Business Supplies	1%				2	2(1.26%)
Capital Goods/Electrical	3.4%		2			2(1.26%)
Capital Goods/Heavy Eq	2.3%	1		2	2	5 (3.14%)
Capital Goods/Other Indistrial Equipment				1	1	2 (1.26%)
Chemicals-diversified	7.9%	1				1 (.62%)
Chemicals-specialized			1		1	2 (1.26%)
Computers&communications-major systems	0			1	2	3 (1.89%)
Computers&communications-peripherals	2.1%			3	3	6 (3.77%)
Computers&communications software	0	2	4	1	1	8 (5.03%)
Computers, telecommunications	0	3	1	4	1	9 (5.66%)
Construction-builders	1%					0
Construction-building materials	0	1		1		2 (1.26%)
Consulting (added)	1%		1	3	3	7 (4.40%)
Construction			1	1		2 (1.26%)
Consumer durables - appliances				1		1 (.63%)
Consumer durables-automotive & trucks	1.7%[6]	1			1	2 (1.26%)
Consumer durables-home furnishings	.3%					
Education (added)			2	1	2	5 (3.14%)
Electric utilities			3		1	4 (2.51%)
Energy-gas,oil,other	18%			3	2	5 (3.14%)
Entertainment&info advertising,publishing, broadcasting&movies	0	1		1	2	4 (2.51%)
Financial services	6	2	5		4	11 (6.91%)

Industry	Andrews %[7]	Goldenrod	Green	Blue	Yellow	Total N= 157
Food distributors	5.1%[8]		1			1 (.63%)
Food,drink&tobacco processors					1	1 (.63%)
Forest products	1%	1				1 (.63%)
Gov./Mun Services	8%	3	2	1		5 (3.14%)
Health-drugs &healthcare		5	6	3	6	20 (12.58%)

---

[5] Andrews' categories were not open to segregating in as much detail as the Forbes listings.
[6] Listed in Andrews as "rubber products"
[7] Andrews' categories were not open to disaggregation in as much detail as the Forbes listings.
[8] Includes all food and allied products.

Insurance	(in real estate)			1		1 (.63%)
Law (added)		1		1	1	3 (1.89%)
Metals	5.5%	1	1	1		3 (1.89%)
Retailing	3%[9]		1	2	1	4 (2.51%)
Real Estate	Included w/insurance	1	2		3	6 (3.78%)
Transportation	12%			1		1 (.63%)
Not answered			2	1		3

Source: Andrews (1966)

The above data confirm the more general classifications that show the trend toward service and "knowledge" businesses. For example, consulting, financial services, computers and communications, together account for 22% of the people who answered my surveys. Several of the comments coming back from the respondents suggested that the cases deal with small vs. large businesses and service vs. manufacturing businesses, showing a trend that matches the employment switch from manufacturing to service-based and knowledge-based businesses. Table 15 represents years of service. In the Andrews/Powell research, average tenure with corporations was 17 years.

---

[9] Including wholesale.

Number of years of service		%	Total of 157	%		%	Total of 157	%	Harvard % w/ company
<1	0	0	2	1.27	1	2.7	3	1.91	3.1%
1-5	11	29.73	29	18.47	18	48.65	56	35.67	6.5
6-10	11	29.73	33	21.02	7	20.	39	24.84	14.5
11-15	8	21.62	36	22.93	8	21.62	25	15.92	18.6
16-20	3	8.11	37	23.57	1	2.71	23	14.65	21.9
21-25	0	0	9	5.73	1	2.70	6	3.82	17.2
26-30	2	5.41	26	16.56	2	5.41	2	1.27	11.1
31-35	1	2.70	2	1.27	0	0	0	0	4.9
36-40	0	0	0	0	0	0	0	0	1.1
Missing	1	2.70	3	1.91	0	0	3	1.91	1.1
Mean	9.88		12.41		6.71		8.87		
Mode	1		10		1		1		

Table 15 School Blue N= 37

Number of years of service	Time in this Industry	%	Total of 157	%	Time with Company	%	Total of 157	%	Harvard % w/ company
<1	3	8.11%	2	1.27	1	2.70	1	1.91	3.1%
1-5	6	16.22%	29	18.47	12	32.43	18	35.67	6.5
6-10	9	24.32%	33	21.02	8	21.62%	7	24.84	14.5
11-15	13	35.14%	36	22.93	5	13.51%	8	15.92	18.6
16-20	2	5.41%	37	23.57	8	21.62	1	14.65	21.9
21-25	2	5.41%	9	5.73	1	2.70%	1	3.82	17.2
26-30	0	0	26	16.56	0	0	2	1.27	11.1
31-35	0	0	2	1.27	0	0	0	0	4.9
36-40	0	0	0	0	0	0	0	0	1.1
Missing	2	5.41	3	1.91	2	5.41	0	1.91	1.1
Mean	14.37		12.41		9.20		6.71		
Mode	16		10		1		1		

Table 13 School Orange N=35

Number of years of service	Time in this Industry	%	Total of 157	Per cent	Time with Company	Per cent	Total	Total percent of 157	Harvard Study %
<1	1	2.86	2	1.27	0	0	1	1.91	3.1%
1-5	7	20.	29	18.47	13	37.1	18	35.67	6.5
6-10	4	11.43	33	21.02	10	28.57	7	24.84	14.5
11-15	7	20.	36	22.93	1	2.9	8	15.92	18.6
16-20	11	31.4	37	23.57	8	22.86	1	14.65	21.9
21-25	3	8.57	9	5.73	1	2.9	1	3.82	17.2
26-30	2	5.71	26	16.56	2	5.7	2	1.27	11.1
31-35	0	0	2	1.27	0	0	0	0	4.9
36-40	0	0	0	0	0	0	0	0	1.1
Missing	0		3	1.91	0	0	0	1.91	1.1
Mean	13.29		12.41	9.77			6.71		
Mode	13		10	1			1		

Table 15 School Yellow N= 48

Number of years of service	Time in this Industry	%	Total of 157	Per cent of 157	Time with Company	Per cent	Total		Harvard Study %
<1	1	2.08	2	1.27	1	2.08	1	1.91	3.1%
1-5	8	16.67	29	18.47	13	27.08	18	35.67	6.5
6-10	12	25.	33	21.02	14	29.17	7	24.84	14.5
11-15	12	25.	36	22.93	11	22.92	8	15.92	18.6
16-20	10	20.83	37	23.57	6	12.50	1	14.65	21.9
21-25	4	8.33	9	5.73	3	6.25	1	3.82	17.2
26-30	0	0	26	16.56	0	0	2	1.27	11.1
31-35	1	2.08	2	1.27	0	0	0	0	4.9
36-40	0	0	0	0	0	0	0	0	1.1
Missing	0	0	3	1.91	0	0	0	1.91	1.1
Mean	12.25		12.41		9.58		6.71		
Mode	10		10	1			1		

Sixty-two percent of the total sample have been with their company for ten or less years, whereas only 24.1% of the Harvard study had been with their employer for the same amount of time. Respective percentages for this research, with tenure of ten or less years, are:

Green	71.35%
Blue	56.75%
Goldenrod	65.67%
Yellow	58.33%

Reasons for this include downsizing, merging of industries and companies, greater mobility for the generation that was studied, and less loyalty to the corporation. In addition, over 20% of these students paid their own tuition, with reasons that included changing careers.

In the Harvard study, 74.8% had been with their company for more than 10 years. These data showed that only 35.69% of the four schools surveyed had managers with that kind of seniority. In the Andrews/Powell study, it was clear that the programs were not being used as stepping stones; in fact, the average seniority was 17 years. In this research, the average seniority was 8.87 years. School Green had a mean of 6.71 years with the company, while the other three were over 9 years. This information follows along with my proposal questions, which acknowledged the lesser seniority in companies today, and the fact that people may use the EMBA programs as a stepping stone. Ten people, or 41.67% of those I interviewed, had changed jobs after they completed their program. Part of the reason stems from the fact that the Harvard study focused on executives with more average experience. The Table 15 summarizes the age of the participants at the time of the survey.

Table 16 Age of Participants (Question #30)

Age at Survey	Green N=37	Blue N=37	Goldenrod N=35	Yellow N=48	Total N=157	Andrews %
< or = 30 years	3 8.11%	1 2.70%	1 2.86%	0	5 .63%	2%
31-35 years	14 37.84%	2 5.41%	4 11.43%	17 35.42%	37 23.57%	8.3
36-40 years	9 24.32%	18 48.65%	17 48.57%	17 35.42%	61 38.85%	23.9
41-45 years	6 16.22%	9 24.32%	9 25.71%	8 16.67%	32 20.38%	29.3
46-50 years	3 8.11%	4 10.81%	2 5.71%	4 8.33%	13 8.28%	23.1
51-55 years	0	0	0	2 4.17%	1.27%	10.4
> 55 years	1 2.70%	0	0	0	1 .63%	2.8
No answer	1 2.71%	3 8.11%	2 5.71%	0	6 3.82%	.2
Mean	37.61	40.38	38.79	39	38.93	43.3
Mode	34	39	36	35	39	
Median	36	40	39	38.5		

When looking at the ages, it can be seen that 23.1% of the Andrews' sample were between 46 and 50 years of age, while the aggregate number for this research was 13%. Thirty-four % of the Andrews' subjects were 40 or under in age, while over sixty-five per cent of the current participants were in that age bracket. The average age for this research was 10% lower than the Andrews/Powell research. Discussions in the literature review of the recognition of the need to update skills is a partial reason for this fact. It is also a signal to university educators that their target market may be younger than they have previously thought.

The next question, represented by Table 17, asked the amount of tuition paid by the employer. I was interested in this information because of the question about whether people use executive programs to change jobs. If a large number of these alumni had paid for their program themselves, it would help to identify a trend toward self-financing of the 'lifelong learning' experience.

Table 17 Amount of tuition support (Question #3)

	N=	100%	80-99%	50-79%	<50%	None
Green	37	10 27.03%	3 8.11%	4 10.81%	9 24.32%	11 29.73%
Blue	37	16 43.24%	1 2.70%	5 13.51%	5 13.51%	10 27.03%
Goldenrod	35	19 54.29%	2 5.71%	4 11.43%	7 20%	3 8.57%
Yellow	48	19 39.58%	6 12.50%	8 16.67%	4 8.33%	11 22.92%
Total	157	64 40.76%	12 7.64%	21 13.38%	25 15.92%	35 22.29%

We know that 100% of the Harvard survey participants were supported, indeed nominated, by their companies. In the current research, only 41% had their program totally funded by their employer. In a few cases, it was a disagreement over program support that prompted the participants to seek other employment.

The fact that over 20% of the participants funded their own programs is an indication that this kind of education is seen as necessary, whether or not the corporation is willing to pay for it. This may be a signal to universities that their target marketing can include more than corporations; it can include people looking to change careers, unemployed managers, etc. The market is growing and needs re-examination.

One of my research questions was whether people use funded MBA programs to prepare themselves to seek other employment. This question was also part of the Harvard research (questions #12 and #13). Table 18 represents both questions, which asked whether the respondents had changed employers and, if so, if there was a connection with having attended the executive program.

Table 18 Have you changed jobs? If so, is there a connection?(Questions 5 and 6)
(% based on those who did change jobs, not total N for this question)

	N=	Changed jobs	Did not change jobs	Connection (% of those who who changed)	No connection	Not answered
Green	37	19 51.35%	18 48.65%	13 68.43%	5 26.32%	18 48.65%
Blue	37	14 37.84 %	23 62.16%	9 64.29%	9 64.29%	9 24.32%
Goldenrod	35	11 31.43%	24 68.57%	5 45.45%	6 54.55%	24 68.57%
Yellow	48	11 22.92%	37 77.08%	10 90.90%	5 [10] 45.45%	33 68.75%
Harvard	5,775	54.6% within their company	40.5% within their company			
Total	157	55 35.03%	102 64.97%	37 67.27%		

A few comments from the Harvard data:

1) "Almost 94% of the men reporting were still with their companies at the time of the questionnaire (Andrews, 1966,p.129)."

2) "Only 89 men (1.5%) reported any connection at all between the change and their attendance (ibid.)."

3) "The principle significance of this stability is to allay the fears of companies that university programs are used as recruiting grounds in which men may be tempted to greener pastures (ibid.)."

There is a clear difference between the majority of the Harvard men, 54.6% of whom changed jobs within their company, but only 6% of whom actually left their company (of those only 1.6% changed within a year), and this research, where 35% changed jobs. In the Harvard study, only 89 men, or 1.5%, reported any connection between the change and their attendance at the program, while my research found that 67% of those who changed jobs said there was a connection. The answer to the question about whether people use these programs as stepping stones, then, is more difficult to provide in my research than it was for Andrews and Powell. It is obvious that some people, indeed a large number of people, leave their jobs after the program, either because their companies did not make use of their skills, or because their new credentials opened up new opportunities. The next question, represented by Table 19, surveys these reasons.

---

[10] The numbers for whether there was a connection or not do not add up to the total who changed jobs because some people checked both columns even if they did not change jobs.

Table 19, open ended; if there is a connection, what is the connection?

What is the connection?	Green	Blue	Goldenrod	Yellow	Total
N=	14	9	6	11	40
Enhanced skills expanded opportunities available.	6 42.86%	4 44.44%	1 16.66%	4 36.36%	15 37.5%
Current employer attracted to my background.	2 14.29%	0	1 16.66%	0	3 7.5%
Was self-employed; purpose of MBA was career change.	0	0	0	1 9.09%	1 2.5%
Networking and the program helped me decide.	2 14.29%	1 11.11%	1 16.67%	1 9.09%	5 12.5%
Previous employer offered little support or room for growth.	2 14.29%	1 11.11%	1 16.67%	2 18.18%	6 15%
Wanted to use my skills in another way.	2 14.29%	3 33.33%	2 33.33%	0	7 17.5%

These answers showed that only 15% left because their previous employer offered little growth opportunity. The downsizing trend that has struck corporate America may have left little opportunities for some of these people to utilize their skills with their corporation because those jobs were no longer there in the way they were during the 1950's as American benefited from post-war growth.

My next interest was in whether those who stayed with their companies increased their scope of responsibility. Table 20 represents the answer to Question #9.

Table 20 (Question #9) If you still hold the same position, has the scope of your responsibility changed?

	Harvard	Total	Green	Blue	Goldenrod	
Scope of responsibility increased	54.6%	53 (33.76%)	8 (21.62%)	11 (29.73%)	9 (25.71%)	(

The difference between the Harvard number of 54.6% whose responsibility increased, and this group of alumni, where 33.76% had increased the responsibility in their job assignments, should be looked at along with the data showing that 35% of the group had changed jobs, while only 6% of the Harvard group had changed jobs.

What is the message we should take from the above numbers? We don't need them to know that lifetime job security is no longer possible, but they do show that those who pursue advanced degrees, whether or not their companies pay for them, may be more likely to change jobs or careers once their programs are completed. If there were ways for corporations to make some use of what the students have learned, the turnover might be lessened. Given the tightened job climate of today, however, this may be more difficult to accomplish than the companies would like. One of the people I interviewed works for a very large manufacturer who paid for her entire program. She was very clear that she would leave the company if another opportunity presented itself. Yet her Vice President of Human Resources sees the risk as low.

For those who stayed with their companies, the next question asked about the relationship between the attendance at the program and an increase in salary, a promotion, or an increase in responsibility. The results are displayed in Table 21.

Table 21 Relationship between attendance at the program and an increase in salary, promotion, or responsibility.

School	Harvard	Total	Green	Blue	Goldenrod	Yellow
Salary increase		N= 157	N= 37	N=37	N=35	N=48
No change	13%	19 12.10%	6 16.22 %	4 10.81%	2 5.71%	7 14.58%
No relationship	28%	34 21.66%	5 13.51 %	11 29.73%	9 25.71%	9 18.75%
Uncertain of relationship	34%	41 26.11%	8 21.62	8 21.62%	12 34.29%	14 29.17%
Direct relationship	14%	48 30.57%	13 35.14%	10 27.03%	11 31.43%	14 29.17%
Direct relationship (seriously considered)	11%	6 3.82%	1 2.70%	2 5.41%	1 2.86%	2 4.17 %
Missing		9 5.73%	4 10.81%	2 5.41%	3 8.57%	2 4.17%
Promotion		N= 157	N=37	N=37	N=35	N=48
No change	30%	30 19.11%	8 21.62%	6 16.22%	8 22.86%	8 16.67%
No relationship	14%	28 17.83%	4 10.81%	7 18.92%	9 25.71%	8 16.67%
Uncertain of relationship	26%	26 16.56%	7 18.92	7 18.92%	3 8.57%	9 18.75%
Direct relationship	10%	44 28.03%	12 32.43%	11 29.73%	10 28.57%	11 22.92%
Direct relationship (seriously considered ahead)	20%	16 10.19%	1 2.70%	3 8.11%	5 14.29%	7 14.58%
Missing		13 8.29%	5 13.51%	3 8.11%	0	5 10.42%
Increase in responsibility		N= 157	N=37	N=37	N=35	N=48
No change in position	19%	20 12.74%	6 16.22 %	3 8.11%	6 17.14%	5 10.42%
No relationship	15%	22 14.01%	4 10.81%	5 13.51%	7 20%	6 12.5%
Uncertain of relationship	31%	31 19.75%	7 18.92%	10 27.03%	5 14.29%	9 18.75%
Direct relationship	16%	55 35.03%	14 37.83%	12 32.43%	13 37.14%	16 33.33%
Direct relationship, seriously considered.	19%	17 10.83%	1 2.70%	5 14.29%	4 11.43%	7 14.58%
Missing		12 7.64%	5 13.51%	2 5.41%	0	5 10.42%

The following chart, Table 22, compares the number of Andrews/Powell respondents who felt that their increase in salary, promotion, or responsibility occurred because of a relationship to the program with the total of my respondents who answered the same way:

Table 22 Harvard results compared w/current research

	Harvard	Current research
Salary	35%	34.39%
Promotion	30%	38.22%
Increase in Resp.	35%	45.86%

Figure 1 shows the representation of the three areas, salary increase, promotion, and increase in responsibility.

Figure 1

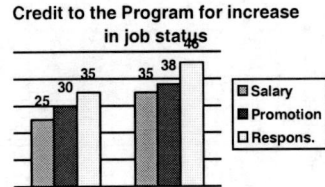

Credit to the Program for increase in job status

The greatest percentage of people in my research credited the program with a change in responsibility. In the Harvard research, 35% credited the program with both an increase in salary and an increase in responsibility. In my research, 35% credited the program with an increase in salary, but almost 46% credited the program with an increase in responsibility. These data are strong indicators of the value of the programs I studied. Question #7 asked their position before they began the MBA program; question #8 asked their present position. The data are helpful in determining a trend toward promotion in those attend EMBA programs. Appendix L lists the actual responses for these questions from each school.

Table 23 depicts the percentage of the participants who held positions at various levels before and after the program. The Harvard percentages are listed on the left. They are compared with the percentages from the total 157 participants in my research and from each individual school. For instance, the Harvard research showed that 38% of the men held senior line or staff positions. The current research showed that 19.11% of the total held senior line and staff positions before they began the program and 25.48% held such positions after completing the program.

Note: I have listed those who described themselves as "self-employed" in senior line and staff.

Table 23 Position before and after the program

N=	Harvard	157 Total	37 Green	37 Blue	35 Goldenrod	48 Yellow
Senior line and staff	38%	30 19.11%/ 40 25.48%	2 5.41% /7 18.92%	8 21.62% /10 27.03	10 28.57% /12 34.28%	10 20.83% /11 22.92%
Functional department head	41%	40 25.48%/ 60 38.22%	5 13.51% /10 27.02%	11 29.73% /12 32.43%	10 28.57% /16 45.71%	14 29.17% /22 45.83%
Lower middle management	11%	54 34.39%/ 25 15.92%	19 51.35% /9 24.32%	12 32.43% /10 27.03%	9 25.71%/ 2 5.71%	14 29.17% /4 8.33%
Professional and non-management	8%	16 10.19%/ 17 10.82%	6 16.22% /6 16.22%	4 10.81% /4 10.81%	1 2.86%/ 1 2.86%	5 10.42% /6 12.5%
Military personnel	1%	1 .64% 1 .64%	0	0	1 2.86%/ 1 2.86%	0
No answer	1%	16 10.19%	5 13.51%	2 5.41%	4 11.42%	5 10.42%
Total	100%	157/100%	37	37	35	48

The progression of position (Table 24), combined with the previous charts, supported the fact that the program was of some significance in the later increase in responsibility:

Table 24 Position before and after the program

	Title at Start	Title Now	Harvard
Senior Line & Staff	19.11%	25.45%	38%
Dept. Head	25.48%	38.22%	41%
L. Middle Mgmt.	34.39%	15.92%	11%
Professional	10.11%	10.82%	8%

The Harvard research tended to focus on men who were sent to the programs because they were deemed to be promotable, so the above results are not surprising for that group. Andrews said that

> the evidence of promotion verifies a kind of harmony between the directors of programs and companies sending participants, in that programs want men who are

to rise in responsibility and companies send men who turn out to fill the bill(p.131).

Although Andrews pointed out that "program directors who have advertised the numbers of their graduates promoted as testimony to the value of the program are thus misguided (p.131)," he also said that "there still may be substantial contribution made by education to subsequent performance, competence, and promotion (p.131)." I found a number of people, mostly with the big corporations, such as Boeing and U.S. West, where the participants had to lobby to be sent to the program. An overall comparison of job titles and credit to the program for some type of advancement would seem to confirm the contribution that the contemporary type of program is making to commerce and productivity.

I was also interested in the number of people who became self-employed after the program, because it supported the notion that people are relying less on corporate America for their livelihood. But, when I added up the number of people who went into their own business after the program, I found that one from School Blue and two from School Goldenrod had listed such a change, for a total of less than 2% of the survey respondents.

Table 25 discusses the use employers made of the skills acquired in the program:

Table 25 Use made of skills acquired (Question #11)

	Green N=37	Blue N=37	Goldenrod N=35	Yellow N=48	Total N=157
Yes, did use my skills; satisfied with their reaction	11 29.73%	13 35.14%	10 28.57%	17 35.42%	51 32.48%
Some, but not enough	11 29.73%	13 35.14%	13 37.14%	17 35.42%	54 34.39%
Made no effort	12 32.43%	10 27.03%	12 34.29%	11 22.92%	45 28.66%
Not answered	3 8.11%	1 2.70%	0	3 6.25%	7 4.46%

This question was not used in the Andrews/Powell study. The results reminded me of one alumnus I interviewed, who said, "30% left their careers, 30% got promoted, and 30% stayed where they were." Those who said that their company did indeed use their skills totaled just over 30%, which would go along with the comment that "30% got promoted." School Goldenrod, with 34.29% saying that their company made no effort to use their skills, had the largest proportion of people with that feeling. However, School Goldenrod was also a location where I heard from several alumni that it was their personal responsibility, not that of their company, to make use of the knowledge gained in the EMBA program.

A total of 66.87% agreed that their corporation had made at least some use of their skills. One could concentrate on those who feel underutilized or the majority who agree that their education is being applied, at least to some extent, on the job.

Question #12a was an open-ended one about what the participants thought the program was trying to accomplish; it is represented by Table 26. It was followed by another open-ended question, Question #12b, that asked what the program actually accomplished; it is represented by Table 27. I found that many people used the word "skills" in combination with "broad " in this research.

In the Harvard research, 54.2% answered that the program was trying to accomplish some sort of broadening of thinking, including an understanding of areas other than their own area of expertise. In this research, less than 40% used the same labels. Sixteen per cent mentioned that they expected to attain skills in preparation for becoming a general manager. This information is also apparent in the promotional literature for the schools. Other than that, it can be seen that the answers were fairly evenly divided. I think you could find more similarities here than differences from what the Harvard participants expected to get from their program and what the EMBA students from the four schools I researched expected to gain from their experience.

In addition to the comments noted in the chart, the following notations were also made in relation to the question "what really happened?":

1) Given today's business climate, not much; 2)Some people attended just to get degrees; 3)Too theoretical (Yellow)

			N=37	N=37	N=35	N=48	N=157
1	Broaden thinking, perspective.	21.2%	2 5.41%	1 2.70%	2 5.71%	1 2.08%	6 3.82%
2	Broaden knowledge of mgmt:produce better businessmen.	14.4%	6 16.22%	1 2.70%	6 17.14%	7 14.58%	20 12.74%
3	Broaden thinking-areas of business other than own jobs.	10.3%	1 2.70%	4 10.81%	0	6 12.50%	11 7.00%
4	Broaden thinking-broaden approach to problems;broaden base of knowledge w/emphasis on analytical thinking and objective approach to decision making.	8.3%	7 18.92%	7 18.92%	5 14.29%	5 10.42%	24 15.29%
5	Broaden thinking-w/reference to moral and ethical response. Of business to society.	7.3%	0	0	0	0	0
6	Develop a sensitivity in dealing with people; human relations.	6.6%	0	3 8.12%	0	0	3 1.91%
7	Broaden thinking-through contact with other executives to develop a mutual awareness and understanding of common problems and procedures in different businesses.	5.8%	4 10.81%	3 8.12%	1 2.86%	3 6.25%	7 4.46%
8	Broaden thinking-general broadening of outlook and knowledge preparatory to accepting more responsibility; broaden middle management horizons w/instruction in top management problems.	5.3%	1 2.70%	4 10.81%	7 20%	4 8.33%	12 7.64%
9	Prepare for successful leadership role.		1 2.70%	1 2.70%	2 5.71%	3 6.25%	7 4.46%
10	Teach skills in accounting, finance, etc.		2 5.41%	1 2.70%	3 8.57%	1 2.08%	7 4.46%
11	Provide skills in preparation for becoming general manager, including global perspective.		3 8.11%	5 13.51%	7 20%	11 22.92%	26 16.56%
12	No consensus on what was to be accomplished.		0	1 2.70%	1 2.86%	0	2 1.27%
13	Revenue and stature for the school		3 8.11%	2 2.70%	0	0	5 3.18%
14	Overview of bus. w/emphasis on international scope &strategic thinking		2 5.41%	0	0	3 6.25%	5 3.18%
	No answer		1	4 (10.81%)	1 (2.86%)	4 (8.33%)	6 (3.82%)

		N= Harvard	N=37 Green	N=37 Blue	N=35 Goldenrod	N=48 Yellow	N=157 Total
1	Varying benefits to different individuals-much to some and little or none to others.	12.3%	4 10.81%	2 5.40%	2 5.71%	4 8.33	12 7.64%
2	Broadening-no elaboration	11.0%	0	0	0	1 2.08%	1 .64%
3	Knowledge of problems of other businesses and ways other firms approach and solve problems attained through exchange of views with other participants	9.1%	3 8.12%	6 16.22%	4 11.43%	0	13 8.28%
4	Objectives attained.	8.5%	6 16.22%	2 5.40%	1 2.86%	4 8.33%	13 8.28%
5	Social and psychological benefits of association, friendship, and fellowship with other executives, many of whom became valued personal friends..	7.0%	4 10.81%	1 2.70%	2 5.71%	1 2.08%	8 5.10%
6	Broadening effect-learned about phases of business and management foreign to their particular specialty and learned the interrelations of all aspects of management.	5.7%	4 10.81%	0	6 17.14%	4 8.33%	14 8.92
7	Very beneficial to other participants.	4.3%	0	0	2 5.71%	0	2 1.27%
8	Broadening effect-flexibility of ideas, acceptance that there may be different paths leading to solution of problems, ability to look at old things in new and different ways.	4.0%	0	0	1 2.86%	1 2.08%	2 1.27%
9	Moderately beneficial to participants who made progress.	3.8%	0	0	0	0	0
10	Broadening effect-modification of attitudes and prejudices toward tolerance and humility.	3.4%	0	0	0	0	0
11	Number of (men) were promoted.	2.9%	0	0	2 5.71%	2 4.17%	4 2.55%
12	Broaden understanding and skill base to move on to greater responsibility.		2 5.40%	0	3 8.57%	3 6.25%	8 5.10%
13	Allow specialists to advance to leadership positions within their specialty.		0	0	1 2.86%	0	1 .64%
14	Learned from each other, practical applications for their jobs.		0	0	1 2.86%	2 4.17%	3 1.91%
15	A number of people switched jobs.		2 5.40%	1 2.70%	1 2.86%	6 12.5%	10 6.37%
16	Learned to work in teams.		0	2 5.40%	2 5.71%	3 6.25%	7 4.46%
17	Personal growth, developed self-confidence, skills enhanced, exposed to new network.		5 13.51%	5 13.51%	6 17.14%	11 22.92%	27 17.20%
18	Program too basic; those without prior bus. Experience gained the most.		0	0	2 (5.71%)	0	2 (5.71%)
19	Missing		7 18.92%	17 (45.94%)	2 (5.71%)	6 (12.5%)	32(20.38%)

As in the previous question, a large percentage (24.1%) of the Harvard participants referred to the "broadening" effects of their program. Only 10.82% of the current participants chose those answers. The largest single group from the current research mentioned the personal growth and self-confidence that they developed (17.20%). The next largest group just said that their objectives were attained. The Harvard percentage for this comment was 8.5%, while the current research chose that comment 8.28% of the time. Other comments included those about teamwork, which was a common thread throughout this research, and the social/psychological benefits of the association. The last comment garnered 8.5% of the Harvard responses, and 5.10% of the respondents to my surveys. However, if the missing numbers are removed from the total, social and psychological benefits actually accounted for 6.4% of the total. It is interesting to see the rank ordering of these comments, as shown by Table 28:

Table 28 Ranking of program benefits

	Harvard Rank	Current Research Rank
Varying benefits	1	4
Broadening-no elaboration	2	14
Knowledge of problems of other businesses...	3	3 (tied)
Objectives attained	4	3 (tied)
Social and psychological benefits	5	6
Broadening—learned about phases of business...	6	2
Broaden understanding and skill base to move on to greater responsibility.	Not included	6
Personal growth	Not included	1
Number of people switched jobs	Not included	5
Total per cent of respondents	53.6%	70.08%

What does this tell us? The current research participants seemed to be focusing more on the networking and personal growth that resulted from their program, but both groups placed high value on learning about other aspects of business. Eleven per cent of the Harvard participants used the word "broadening" with no elaboration, while less than one per cent of my respondents used that designation. This may be because the people who filled out my surveys were more vocal, or because they felt a responsibility to their school to elaborate further. It may also be a signal of the American culture, which tends toward individualistic attainment rather than going along with the group. What interested me the most was the overwhelming number of people who listed personal growth and self-confidence, especially as these designations received little mention in the earlier study for this question. Self-confidence becomes very important in the next question, #12c, represented by Table 29. I have listed the ranking of each comment for the school below the percentage who gave the answer.

Table 29 What do you think happened to you? (Question #12c)

	Harvard	Green	Blue	Goldenrod	Yellow	Total
	5,654	37	37	35	48	157
Broadening effect without elaboration	10.6%	1 2.70%	1 2.70%	0	0	2 1.27%
Rank	1	5	5	--	--	10
Confidence in own ability; assured that performance of duties would undergo marked improvement.	8.0%	5 13.51%	8 21.62%	9 25.71	11 22.92%	33 21.02%
Rank	2	1(tied)	1	2	1	1
Broadening effect-knowledge of problems of other businesses and insight into ways in which other firms approach and solve problems, this through exchange of views with other participants.	7.3%	4 10.81%	5 13.51%	2 5.71%	5 10.41%	16 10.19%
Rank	3	2	2	3	4	3
Broadening effect-learned about phases of business and management foreign to their own particular specialty; learned about the interrelations of all aspects of management.	7.3%	5 13.51%	3 8.11%	10 28.57%	7 14.58%	25 15.92%
Rank	4	1 (tied)	3	1	2	2
Social-psychological benefit-association, friendship, and fellowship with other executives, many of whom became personal friends.	6.1%	1 2.70%	0	2 5.71%	1 2.08%	2 1.27%
Rank	5	5	--	3 (tied)	7	10 (tied)

Table 29, continued	Harvard	Green	Blue	Goldenrod	Yellow	Total
Broadening effect-learned the importance of human relations, became better at managing and getting along with people.	5.4%	2 5.41%	0	0	2 4.17%	4 2.55%
Rank	6	4 (tied)	--	--	6	8 (tied)
Broadening effect-flexibility of ideas, acceptance that there may be different paths leading to solutions of problems, ability to look at old things in new and different ways.	4.7%	0	2 5.41%	0	1 2.08%	3 1.91%
Rank	7	--	4(tied)	--	7	9 (tied)
Broadening effect-modification of attitudes and prejudices toward tolerance and humility.	4.3%	0	0	0	0	0
Rank	8	--	--	--	--	--
Evaluation rather than description of benefit-very beneficial to all participants.	3.7%	2 5.41%	1 2.70%	1 2.86%	1 2.08%	5 3.18%
Rank	9	4 (tied)	5(tied)	4 (tied)	7 (tied)	7

Detailed knowledge of specific subjects of great importance and value.	3.4%	2 5.41%	2 5.41%	0	0	4 2.55%
Rank		10	4(tied)	4(tied)	--	--	8 (tied)
Broadening effect-mind -stretching, enlarging horizons, exploring all facts before making decisions, understanding that managerial problems cut across industrial and occupational lines.	3.2%	1 2.70%	1 2.70%	2 5.71%	5 10.42%	9 5.73%
Rank		11	5 (tied)	5 (tied)	3 (tied)	3	4
The objectives of the program were attained.	3.1%	1 2.70%	0	2 5.71%	0	3 1.91%
Rank		12	5 (tied)	--	3 (tied)	--	9 (tied)
Stimulating desire for further reading, study, and development.	2.5%	0	0	1 2.86%	0	1 .64%
Rank		13	--	--	4 (tied)	--	11 (tied)
Greater acceptance of personal responsibility for own career.		3 8.11%	3 8.11%	1 2.86%	1 2.08%	8 5.10%
Rank	Not used	3 (tied)	3 (tied)	4 (tied)	7 (tied)	5
Company has not taken advantage of what I learned.		0	1 2.70%	1 2.86%	0	2 1.27%
Rank	Not used	--	5 (tied)	4(tied)	--	10 (tied)
"Taught what Prof. Felt was important. Given a degree and set adrift."		0	0	1 2.86%	0	1 .64%
Rank	Not used	--	--	4 (tied)	--	11 (tied)
Broadened and deepened business skills; developed a network of contacts.		2 5.41%	1 2.70%	2 5.71%	1 2.08%	6 3.82%
Rank	Not used	4 (tied)	5 (tied)	3 (tied)	7 (tied)	6
Opportunity to change careers		0	0	0	3 6.25%	3 1.91%
Rank					5	9
Not relevant answers		0	8 21.62%	0	8 16.67%	16 10.19%
No answer		8 21.62%	1 2.70%	1 2.86%	2 4.17%	13 7.64%

Now, by way of comparison to the earlier question about what happened to others, I will rank Harvard's responses to "what happened to you?" against the ranking for the current research (Table 30):

Table 30 Ranking of program effects

	Harvard Rank	Current Research Rank
Broadening without elaboration	1	14
Confidence in own ability	2	1
Broadening-knowledge of problems of other businesses.	3	3
Broadening—phases of business other than their specialty.	4	2
Social/psychological benefits—association , friendship	5	13
Total per cent	39.1	49.68%

Here the Harvard and current research were more in agreement. Self-confidence ranked #2, with 8%, in the Harvard research, while it ranked #1, with 21%, in my research. Self-confidence and learning about other phases of business proved to be common outcomes both for the Andrews/Powell research and my research with EMBA programs. However, as Andrews pointed out, self-confidence was not one of the expected outcomes of the program before they went into it.

An interesting side-note about the Harvard research is that there were a number of negative comments about the programs, even though the overall rating was positive, as it was in my research. These comments included "Make a name for (the school):assist them with their finances in later years (p.150)," and "The courses were so simple that they were boring (p.151)." Again, there continued to be similarities between what people expected and got out of executive education in both the 1950's and today.

The following question, represented by Table 31, asked what the participants thought the program would be like before they enrolled. This question covers the area of what kind of information was available to them before the program, how accurate was the information, and how clear the school personnel were about the elements in the program. Implications for today's programs would be to comment on areas in the program recruitment process which may need updating or modifying. For instance, if most people said that they had a pretty accurate idea of what to expect, the program directors could be satisfied that their recruitment program was an accurate source of information.

Table 31 What did you think the program would be like before you enrolled(Harvard #27a[11])?

	Comment	Green N=37	Blue N=37	Goldenrod[12] N=35	Yellow N=48	Total N=157
1	Challenging, rigorous, competitive	3 / 8.11%	13 / 35.13%	11 / 31.42%	11 / 22.92%	38 / 23.57
2	Knew what to expect through information and research.	6 / 16.22%	3 / 8.11%	3 / 8.57%	4 / 8.33%	16 / 10.19%
3	Had no preconception.	3 / 9.00%	3 / 9.00%	4 / 11.42%	1 / 2.08%	11 / 7.01%
4	More challenging than it was.	2 / 5.41%	2 / 5.41%	4 / 11.42%	1 / 2.08%	9 / 5.73%
5	Intense, but fun.	0	1 / 2.70%	2 / 5.71%	1 / 2.08%	4 / 2.55%
6	Broad based business education.	5 / 13.51%	5 / 13.51%	4 / 11.42%	5 / 10.41%	18 / 11.46%
7	Analytical, quantitative ;narrow skill-based.	0	2 / 5.41%	2 / 5.71%	7 / 14.58%	11 / 7.01%
8	Easier pace of learning than it was.	1 / 2.70%	2 / 5.41%	2 / 5.71%	4 / 8.33%	9 / 5.73%
9	Did not realize how broad the subject matter would be.	0	0	1 / 2.86%	0	1 / .63%
19	Found it more interesting than I had hoped.	0	0	1 / 2.86%	0	1 / .63%
11	More independent work; did not realize there would be so much team work.	2 / 5.41%	1 / 2.70%	1 / 2.86%	2 / 4.17%	6 / 3.82%
12	An easy way to get an MBA	0	0	1 / 2.86%	0	1 / .63%
13	Did not expect high level of camaraderie in class and the study groups.	1 / 2.70%	0	0	1 / 2.08%	2 / 1.27%
14	Academic, lecture, wide range of material covered with theory.	3 / 8.11%	3 / 8.11%	0	4 / 8.33%	10 / 6.37%
15	More in depth than we actually received.	2 / 5.41%	0	0	1 / 2.08%	3 / 1.91%
16	Students would be more qualified than they were.	1 / 2.70%	0	1 / 2.86%	0	2 / 1.27%
17	Prepare me to run a corporation	0	0	0	2 / 4.17%	2 / 1.27%
18	Missing	8 / 21.62%	2 / 5.41%	0	4 / 8.33%	14 / 8.92%

The largest number of respondents, almost 27%, said that they thought the program would be challenging and rigorous. A little over 11% knew what to expect. An interesting 9% expected the program to be more challenging than it turned out to be. From the comments I received during the interviews, both with the corporate sponsors and the alumni, these comments are fairly reflective of the expectations of both sponsors and prospective students. Table #32 will now compare expectations with the reaction at the end of the program.

---

[11] This question was not discussed at length in the published report of the Harvard study.
[12] Here and elsewhere the number in the table may exceed the number of people because some people gave more than one comment. The unit of analysis was comments, not people.

Table 32 Reaction at the end of the program (Question #13b) (Harvard #29)

	N=	37	37	35	48	157
		Green	Blue	Goldenrod	Yellow	Total
1	Intense, stimulating, challenging; increased self-confidence; personal growth, friendships.	4 10.81%	9 24.32%	6 17.14%	11 22.92%	30 19.11%
2	About the same as I expected.	7 18.92%	2 5.41%	3 8.57%	5 10.42%	16 10.19%
3	Filled in gaps of knowledge about business principles.	2 5.41%	5 13.51%	1 2.86%	1 2.08%	9 5.73%
4	Excellent emphasis on group learning; improved learning; helped each other.	4 10.81%	2 5.41%	1 2.86%	2 4.17%	9 5.73%
5	Did not cover enough finance.	6 16.22%	0	2 5.71%	1 2.08%	8 5.10%
6	Not as difficult as I expected	1 2.70%	2 5.41%	0	4 8.33%	7 4.46%
7	Excellent curriculum; very pleased	2 5.41%	4 10.81%	0	0	6 3.82%
8	Broad, not as much detail as expected; fast pace prevented in-depth exploration.	2 5.41%	0	2 5.71%	2 4.17%	6 3.82%
9	More difficult than expected.	1 2.70%	1 2.70%	2 5.71%	3 6.25%	7 4.46%
10	Learned more from classmates than expected.	1 2.70%	0	2 5.71%	2 4.17%	5 3.38%
11	My org. did not use my skills.	1 2.70%	1 2.70%	1 2.86%	1 2.08%	4 2.55%
12	Great deal expended and great deal accomplished.	0	3 8.11%	1 2.86%	0	4 2.54%
13	Glad it was over.	3 8.11%	0	0	1 2.08%	4 2.54%
14	Hard work; excellent adventure; impetus from the course increased my desire for learning.	0	0	0	3 6.25%	3 1.91%
15	Great staff; interesting courses.	1 2.70%	0	1 2.86%	1 2.08%	3 1.91%
16	Full of mediocre players whose companies were willing to pay.	1 2.70%	0	2 5.71%	0	3 1.91%
17	Course work designed for workers in larger corporations	0	0	1 2.86%	1 2.08%	2 1.27%
18	Excellent teaching and class interaction.	1 2.70%	0	1 2.86%	1 2.08%	3 1.91%
19	Missing	0	8 21.62%	9 25.71%	9 18.75%	26 16.56%

There were a large number of missing answers for this question. From reviewing the surveys, it appears that people just didn't write anything if they had nothing to add. They could have written "the same", and some did, but many just left it blank

There were only 20 answers to the above question that were negative about the program, but eight of those, or 40% of the negative comments, had to do with the one school that canceled the second finance class. Taking that comment out, there were only negative comments by 7.6% of the respondents to this question. This percentages parallels with the Harvard answers, where some felt the program was too easy and some felt the quality not as good as they expected.

The following are additional comments, each from only one or two people:

1) Did not cover enough leadership (Goldenrod).
2) Expected more on business strategy than received (Goldenrod).

3) Expect more emphasis on people management (Goldenrod).
4) Course work designed for workers in large corporations (Goldenrod).
5) Students excellent; professors excellent (Goldenrod).
6) Excellent program, but the international program left a bad taste (Yellow).
7) More fun than I expected (Goldenrod, Yellow).
8) Professors not as good as I had hoped (Yellow).
9) Surprised at how analytical it was (Yellow).
10) Learned to manage time better (Green).
11) More technical and product oriented than expected (Blue).

The next question, represented by Table 33, asked their feeling now, in some cases three years after they graduated, about the program. Only answers that made up at least 2%, or three mentions, are included in the table. Some comments required splitting out, so that numbers do not always add up to the number from each school.

Table 33 What is your reaction now? (Question #13c) (Harvard #30)

Comment	Total	Green	Blue	Goldenrod	Yellow
N=	157	37	37	35	48
One of the best learning experiences of my life, would recommend it to others.	35 22.29%	8 21.62%	11 29.73%%	7 20%	9 18.75%
I'm glad I did it, very satisfied, would do it again.	24 15.29%	5 13.51%	6 16.21%	3 8.11%	8 16.67%
Good combination of classmates and motivated instructors. Excellent effort on the part of the program administrators.	10 6.37%	3 8.11%	6 16.22%	0	1 2.08%
An excellent foundation for my career	6 3.82%	0	1 2.70%	2 5.71%	3 8.11%
The networking was very important	5 3.18%	1 2.70%	0	3 8.57%	1 2.08%
Should have had more emphasis on finance and operations management	4 2.55%	1 2.70%	1 2.70%	1 2.70%	1 2.08%
The learning has improved my self-confidence	4 1.91%	1 2.70%	0	3 8.57%	0
Weak human relations, international business.	3 1.91%	0	0	3 8.57%	0
Missing	18 11.46%	7 18.92%	4 10.81%	3 8.57%	4 8.33%

In looking at the surveys, I thought it significant that 17 people, or 10.83%, simply answered this question "the same." When I went back and looked at what they had answered to the previous question, I found that they had expected a rigorous, challenging program and felt that they had received it. The above numbers show that 78 people, or 49.68%, had positive comments about the program at the time of the survey, either about the contents of the program, the networking, or the self-confidence. This information would be in agreement with the Andrews/Powell findings. Some of the less frequent comments included:

- "Would like to have had more career planning (Goldenrod, 2 people).
- "Should have had more current material (Green, Yellow, 2 people).
- Very beneficial. Not using specific skills, but broadening helpful.
- Highly recommend the program, but they must be careful in selecting people (Goldenrod, 2 people)."
- "Everything was a review of what I already knew (One each, Blue and Yellow)."
- "Need more real world (Two from School Yellow)."
- "A few poor professors; the quality of the program is oversold (Two from Goldenrod)."
- "Enjoyed the group learning (One from School Green and one from School Yellow)."

The negative comments about elements of the curriculum totaled 15 people, or 9.55% of the total 157 participants. Given that some of these people were answering the survey three years after they graduated, the long-term positive effects that were mentioned contribute to the rating of the programs in general. In the Harvard research, 84.5% reported a generally favorable level of satisfaction with the program at the time of the questionnaire. Only 3.3% reported an unfavorable feeling, and 12.2% had a mixed feeling.

The next two questions, which were not part of the Andrews/Powell research, help to focus specific program outcome satisfaction. Table 34 reviews both question #13d, which asked for a rating of the program, and question #14, which asked for a rating of faculty teaching effectiveness. They really speak to the main research question, "are executive programs meeting the needs of executive students?" In the analysis stage, I was to find out that the program rating was very definitely influenced by the quality of the faculty.

Relating the results of Questions 13d and 14 to the earlier reaction of people to the program, a case can be made for the continued favorable impact of the programs with the alumni. Table 34 shows that the current respondents actually rated their program higher than the Harvard people did, when scores are equalized. In terms of the faculty, School Yellow was the only one to rate the faculty significantly higher than the Harvard numbers.

Table 34 Rating for the program in general on a scale from 1(no current value) to 5(very valuable)(Question #13d).

Question #14 How would you rate the faculty's teaching effectiveness at your program?(Harvard #33, open-ended question.)* 1=Poor/2=Fair/3=Average/4=Above Average/5=Excellent

Table 34	N=37	N=37	N=35	N=48	Total	Harvard
Numerical rating 1-5	Green	Blue	Goldenrod	Yellow	N=157	Scale = 1-10
1 (no current relevance)	1 2.70%	0	0	0	1 .63%	1-2 3.2%
2	2 5.41%	1 2.70%	1 2.86%	0	4 8.33%	3-4 5.7%
3	3 8.11%	3 8.11%	5 14.29%	1 2.08%	12 25%	5-6 14%
4	21 56.76%	12 32.43%	13 37.14%	13 27.08%	59 37.58%	7-8 35%
5 (very relevant or relevant)	10 27.03%	17 45.95%	16 45.71%	30 62.5%	73 46.50%	9-10 42%
Missing	0	4 10.81%	0	4 8.33%	8 5.10%	
Mean Program Rating 1-5	4.05	4.36	4.26	4.66	4.34	
Equiv. to Harvard Score, using 10 pts.	8.1	8.72	8.5	9.32	8.69	7.71
Faculty Rating	N=37	N=37	N=35	N=48	N=157	
1 (Poor)	0	0	0	0	0	
2 (Fair)	0	0	1 2.86%	0	1 2.08%	
3 (Average)	6 16.2%	5 13.51%	3 8.57%	1 2.08%	15 3.13%	
4 (Above Average)	23 62.16%	22 62.86%	20 57.14%	18 37.5%	83 52.87%	
5 (Excellent)	8 21.62%	10 27.03%	11 31.43%	29 60.42%	58 36.94%	
Missing	0	0	0	0	0	
Mean Fac.Rating	4.05	4.14	4.17	4.58	4.26	
Equiv. To Harvard Score, 7 choices[13].	5.67	5.80	5.83	6.41	5.96	5.68

The next chart categorizes the open-ended responses about the faculty. (Note: I have used the actual number answering this question rather than the total N for the group in order to be more accurate with the percentage of people who gave each answer). Table 35 categorizes the comments received from the open ended question about faculty effectiveness.

---

[13] Index as follows: 1(Most instructors ineffective-7(All instructors good or effective)(Andrews, 1966, p.324). The Harvard score equivalency was obtained in the following manner: First, the current score was converted to a % of 5 (e.g., a score of 4=80%). Then, the % was applied to a 7 point scale (e.g., 80% would be a raw score of 5.6).

Table 35 Comments regarding faculty. Question #14.

Comment	Green	Blue	Goldenrod	Yellow	Total
N=	18	23	27	19	87
Many excellent, most above average, a few fair to poor	5 27.78%	3 13.04%	11 40.74%	7 36.84%	26 29.89%
A couple of notable exceptions, but overall rating good	5 27.78%	3 13.04%	1 3.70%	5 26.32%	14 16.09%
90% of instructors were great; 10% should be replaced-politics keeps them there.	3 16.67&	2 8.70%	8 29.63%	0	13 14.94%
Professional knowledge and delivery were excellent	0	4 17.39%	0	2 10.53%	6 6.90%
Highly variable from instructor to instructor	1 5.56%	0	3 11.11%	0	4 4.60%
Could not have asked for better	0	2 8.70%	0	1 5.26%	3 3.45%
Outstanding, brilliant, but very academic	0	1 4.35%	0	1 5.26%	2 2.30%
Other, not enough to include	4 22.22%	8 34.78%	4 14.81%	3 15.79%	19 21.84%

Other comments rating less than 2% of the total:

a) Some better than others; Staff should pay attention to feedback (Goldenrod)
b) Had never studies business; every faculty member opened new doors (Yellow)
c) Teachers concentrated on those who were interested in learning, but let the others ride free (Yellow)
d) Pulling best instructors from three campuses very good (Blue)
e) Some were great, most average, too many egos (Blue)
f) Wish we could have had more depth (Yellow)

Fifty-seven of the eighty-seven who made comments about the faculty noted that there were some poor faculty. That is 66% of the entire sample who answered that question and 36% of the people who answered the survey. Adding these results to the comments that came out of the interviews show a sizable number of people who felt that the faculty mix in each school contains some people who detract from the learning experience.

Table 36 categorizes the teaching methods preferred by the participants.

Table 36 Which teaching methods did you prefer?
(Note: I have used the actual number of people who answered this question).

N=	28	30	33	42	130
	Green	Blue	Goldenrod	Yellow	Total
Case method	3 10.71%	3 10%	9 27.27%	13 30.95%	28 21.53%
Case study/discussion	1 3.57%	3 10%	5 15.15%	10 23.81%	18 13.84%
Lecture/class participation	1 3.57%	3 10%	5 15.15%	8 19.05 %	17 13.07%
Class participation/group project	3 10.71%	3 10%	3 9.09%	1 2.38%	10 7.69%
Case study/group work	2 7.14%	2 6.67%	3 9.09%	4 9.52%	10 7.69%
Interactive, some lecture	4 14.29%	3 10%	1 3.03%	0	7 5.38%
Group work	4 14.29%	2 6.67%	0	0	6 4.61%
Field study/hands on/real problems	2 7.14%	4 13.33%	0	0	6 4.61%
Lecture/reading	1 3.57%	2 6.67%	2 6.06%	0	5 3.84%
Lecture/case study	0	2 6.67%	1 3.03%	1 2.38%	4 3.07%
Lecture/group	2 7.14%	2 6.67%	0	1 2.38%	5 3.84%
Faculty should choose/they are more important than the method.	3 10.71%	0	1 3.03%	0	4 3.07%
Balance of theory and practice	1 3.57%	0	1 3.03%	1 2.38%	3 2.30%

Other comments that did not represent 2% include:

1) "Less BS and touchy feely" (Green)
2) "Program well balanced" (Blue)
3) "Faculty that push hard." (Blue)
4) "Student presentations." (Blue, Yellow)
5) "Experts from industry."(Goldenrod)

In the Harvard study, Andrews mentioned that the largely participative schools showed the highest response (Andrews, 1966, p.177). It is no surprise, given the type of learning found to be most conducive for adults, that the majority of people liked the discussion style, both the case discussion method and the case study/discussion method. This question requires no further expository comments as the results support the decision of the schools to use the case and class discussion methods in many of their courses for executive programs.

Table 37 discusses Question #15, which asked the participants if, given the choice, they would choose to use the money in one of several other ways. In the Harvard study, the participants were asked to rank their choices by order of preference. Because Andrews stated that "this question would have been more useful if we had included in the ranking the opportunity to attend some other university program (Andrews, 1966, p.82)," it was included in my research survey. The rating given the choice "time off to study individually," ranking near the bottom for both surveys, is another acknowledgment of the value of the classroom learning process vs. on-line education.

Table 37 In which of the following ways would you use the same amount of money? (Question #15)

School Green N=37

	Would not choose this alternative	Would probably not choose this alternative	Would probably consider this alternative	Would definitely consider this alternative	Missing	Mean	Total sample mean
Attending seminars and workshops of professional groups.	12 32.43%	7 18.92%	10 27.03%	3 8.11%	5 13.51%	2.13	2.04
Time off to study individually.	15 40.54%	11 29.73%	3 8.11%	3 8.11%	5 13.51%	1.81	1.74
Scheduled visits to other companies to study their operation.	7 18.92%	2 5.41%	13 35.14%	10 27.03%	5 13.51%	2.81	2.52
Attending the university-sponsored executive MBA program which you actually attended.	0	3 8.11%	5 13.51%	24 64.87%	5 13.51%	3.65	3.81
Attending another university MBA program, other than the one you attended.	5 13.51%	7 18.92%	11 29.73%	8 21.62%	6 16.22%	2.71	2.77
Attendance at a technical course to refresh specialized knowledge.	12 32.43%	6 16.22%	12 32.43%	2 5.41%	5 13.51%	2.13	1.97

School Blue N=37

	Missing	Would not choose this alternative	Would probably not choose this alternative	Would probably consider this alternative.	Would definitely consider this alternative.	Mean	Total sample mean
Attending seminars and workshops of professional groups.	4 10.81%	10 27.03%	12 32.43%	9 24.32%	2 5.41%	2.09	2.04
Time off to study individually.	4 10.81%	18 48.65%	11 29.73%	2 5.41%	2 5.41%	1.64	1.74
Scheduled visits to other companies to study their operation.	4 10.81%	5 13.51%	11 29.73%	12 32.43%	5 13.51%	2.51	2.52
Attending the university-sponsored executive MBA program which you actually attended.	4 10.81%	0	2 5.41%	2 5.41%	31 83.78%	3.83	3.81
Attending another university MBA program, other than the one you attended.	4 10.81%	4 10.81%	5 13.51%	14 37.84%	10 27.03%	2.91	2.77
Attendance at a technical course to refresh specialized knowledge.	3 8.11%	14 37.84%	9 24.32%	8 21.62%	3 8.11%	2.00	1.97

Table 37, continued
School Goldenrod N=35

	Would not choose this alternative	Would probably not choose this alternative	Would probably consider this alternative	Would definitely consider this alternative	Missing	Mean	Total Sample Mean
Attending seminars and workshops of professional groups.	12 34.29%	13 35.14%	7 20%	2 5.71%	1 2.86%	1.97	2.04
Time off to study individually	18 51.43%	9 25.71%	3 8.56%	4 11.43%	1 2.86%	1.79	1.74
Scheduled visits to other companies to study their operation	5 14.29%	12 35.14%	11 31.43%	6 17.14%	1 2.86%	2.53	2.54
Attending the university-sponsored executive MBA program which you actually attended.	0	1 2.86%	3 8.56%	30 85.71%	1 2.86%	3.69	3.81
Attending another university MBA program, other than the one you attended.	5 14.29%	5 14.29%	12 34.29%	12 34.29%	1 2.86%	2.91	2.77
Attending a technical course to refresh specialized knowledge.	15 42.86%	8 22.86%	7 20%	4 11.43%	1 2.86%	2.0	1.97

School Yellow N=48

	Would not choose this alternative	Would probably not choose this alternative	Would probably consider this alternative	Would definitely consider this alternative.	Missing	Mean	Total sample mean
Attending seminars and workshops of professional groups.	13 27.08%	15 31.25%	11 22.92%	1 2.08%	8 16.67%	2.0	2.04
Time off to study individually.	23 47.92%	6 12.5%	6 12.5%	3 6.25%	10 20.83%	1.71	1.74
Scheduled visits to other companies to study their operation.	10 20.83%	14 29.17%	11 22.92%	6 12.5%	7 14.58%	2.32	2.52
Attending the university-sponsored executive MBA program which you actually attended.	0	1 2.08%	3 6.25%	35 72.92%	9 18.75%	3.87	3.81
Attending another university MBA program, other than the one you attended.	6 12.5%	12 25%	14 29.17%	7 14.58%	9 18.75%	2.58	2.77
Attendance at a technical course to refresh specialized knowledge.	19 39.58%	15 31.25%	6 12.5%	2 4.17%	6 12.5%	1.79	1.97

In his book, Andrews listed the average rating given each choice, and ranked them according to those choices. Listed below is the order of the average rating given the choices by Andrews[14] and the ranking based on the current study:

	Harvard	Current Research
#1	Current program	Current program
#2	Attending seminars	Another MBA program
#3	Visits to other companies	Visits to other companies
#4	Attendance at a technical course.	Attending seminars
#5	Time off to study.	Time off to study.
#6	NA	Attendance at tech. course

Attending another MBA program was not an option in the Harvard research, but the rankings using the means do give some interesting information:

1) Most people would choose the same program they attended, by a large margin. The mean for that choice in my research was 3.74. The Harvard research showed that 88.6%, or 5,374 of the 6,068 who completed the survey, would choose the university-sponsored executive development program which they attended vs. being given the amount of money it cost (Andrews, 1966, p.90). This answer is consistent with the motivation behind current executive education programs as well.

2) Time off to study individually ranked very low in both cases. One of the reasons that it has relevance today is due to the proliferation of on-line learning programs However, as will be shown when I reach Question #25, 59% of the respondents were not interested in a program that would be offered on-line. This is no surprise, given the many comments about how much students learn from each other in all of the open-ended questions.

---

[14] 1.0= first choice; 2/0 = second choice, etc.

In terms of the original research question, "are executive programs meeting the needs of their customers," the above information adds to the conclusion that yes, the programs I studied are meeting the needs of the students who attend them. The next question, #16 relates to how well the scheduling fit the student's needs. It is represented in Table 38.

Table 38 How did you feel about the schedule? (Question #16)

	Green	Blue	Goldenrod	Yellow	Tota
N=	37	37	35	48	157
I enjoyed it.	32	34	28	45	139
	86.49%	91.89%	80.%	93.75%	88.54
I would have liked one day a week better.	1	1	1	0	3
	2.70%	2.70%	2.86%		1.91
I would have liked ____ better.	2 Friday &Sat. together bi-monthly;2 hrs 3x wk w/2hrs weekend.	0	4 weekends free;every Friday; Saturday	2 additional ½ day for audit courses.	8 5.10
Did not answer	1	2	2	1	6
	2.70%	5.40%	5.71%	2.08%	3.82

Some of the comments included:
*Going from a Saturday to a Friday allows less time to prepare.
*I selected the program because of the schedule.
*Worked well because employer supported it.

Although the approval level of these programs was high, the almost 90% agreement that the schedule was good should also be good news for the schools involved. What especially interested me was that there was high approval for all schools, even though there are two different schedules: Schools Green, Blue, and Goldenrod meet every week on a different day (Friday or Saturday), while School Yellow meets every other Friday and Saturday. School Goldenrod was the only school to receive comments that requested weekends free. That kind of arrangement would most certainly meet with disapproval by the corporate sponsors, as I was told by the program directors.

The next question asked about other effects, other than they had already mentioned, that occurred from attending the program. It is represented in Table 39.

Table 39 (Question #17) Other than the effects of the EMBA program mentioned above, were there any others that you received from attending the program? (Not in Andrews)

Note: again, I have used the number who answered this question rather than the total N for that school because the percentages are more indicative of the strength of the opinion.

	Green	Blue	Goldenrod	Yellow	Total
N=	32	35	26	46	139
Friendships and business contacts	12 37.5%	22 62.86%	14 38.47%	30 65.22%	78 56.12%
Networking	6 18.76%	5 14.29%	1 3.85%	5 10.87%	17 12.23%
Study group kept in touch.	1 3.13%	1 2.86%	3 11.54%	4 8.70%	9 6.47%
Business partnership	2 6.25%	0	1 3.85%	0	3 2.16%

Other comments, which accounted for less than 2% of the total, included:
1) "If I ever decide to change jobs, I know where to go." (Green,Yellow)
2) "Learned a lot from other students." (Goldenrod)
3) "Being able to succeed in a diverse group." (Green)
4) "Enhanced self-respect and respect for others." (Green)
5) "More than 50% of learning from classmates." (Green)
6) "Self-examination and direction." (Blue)

As noted earlier, when asked what they expected from the program, most people mentioned the expectation that they would broaden their base of knowledge, prepare to accept more responsibility, and develop and analytical approach to decision making. The only difference between the responses to my survey and the Harvard responses was that more of my respondents made specific reference to the preparation for the general manager's role and the accounting and finance skills that they expected to learn. To that end, the acknowledgment, from over 68% of the respondents, that the friendships and networking were important take-aways from the program is strong support for classroom-based education vs. on-line programs as technology makes some of these other options available and marketable.

The next question asked their reaction to each area of study that was included in their program, from an interest standpoint. This was Harvard question #39. The responses are separated by school. It is represented by Table 38. In the Harvard study, "not in program" was rated as "1" for weighting purposes. This study did not include "not in program" in the rating procedure. Thus, I could not compare Harvard's actual mean to this study because they used a scale of 1-6 (from "not in the program" to "very interesting", while I used a scale of 1-5 (from "of no particular interest" to "very interesting").

Table 40 (Question #18) Please check over the following areas of study and indicate for each whether or not it was included in the program and, if so, your reaction to is:

Table 40 School Green

N=37	Not in program	Of no particular interest	Somewhat interesting	Moderately interesting	Very interesting	One of the areas of greatest interest.	No answer	Mean (1-5)	Total sample mean
Human relations.	0	0	3 / 8.11%	7 / 18.92%	18 / 48.65%	8 / 21.62%	1 / 2.70%	3.86	3.52
Labor relations.	22 / 59.46%	2 / 5.41%	2 / 5.41%	7 / 18.92%	3 / 8.11%	0	1 / 2.70%	2.78	2.90
Business policy.	2 / 5.41%	0	2 / 5.41%	5 / 13.51%	15 / 40.54%	13 / 35.14%	0	4.11	4.07
Marketing.	0	1 / 2.70%	1 / 2.70%	5 / 13.51%	18 / 48.65%	12 / 32.43%	0	4.05	4.03
Bus. Economics	0	0	5 / 13.51%	12 / 32.43%	12 / 32.43%	8 / 21.62%	0	3.62	4.17
Finance	0	0	2 / 5.41%	6 / 16.22%	17 / 45.95%	12 / 32.43%	0	4.05	4.18
Legal	0	1 / 2.70%	2 / 5.41%	8 / 21.62%	17 / 45.95%	9 / 24.32%	0	3.83	3.59
Production	0	5 / 13.51%	10 / 27.03%	14 / 37.84%	5 / 13.51%	3 / 8.11%	0	2.76	3.39
Public Speaking	19 / 51.35%	0	4 / 10.81%	7 / 18.92%	2 / 5.41%	4 / 10.81%	1 / 2.70%	3.35	3.20
Strategy	2 / 5.41%	0	1 / 2.70%	7 / 18.92%	16 / 43.24%	11 / 29.73%	0	4.05	4.42
Other			1 / 2.70%		3 / 8.11%	3 / 8.11%	30 / 81.08%	4.14	4.39

N=37	Not in program	Of no particular interest	Somewhat interesting	Moderately interesting	Very interesting	One of the areas of greatest interest.	No answer	Mean	Total sample mean
Human relations.	0	0	3 8.11%	8 21.62%	22 59.46%	4 10.81%	0	3.72	3.52
Labor relations.	9 24.32%	1 2.70%	7 18.92%	12 32.43%	8 21.62%	0	0	2.67	2.90
Business policy.	0	1 2.70%	3 8.11%	3 8.11%	17 45.95%	12 32.43%	1 2.70%	4.0	4.07
Marketing.	0	0	4 10.81%	7 18.92%	17 45.95%	9 24.32%	0	3.41	4.03
Bus. Economics	0	0	1 2.70%	3 8.11%	15 40.54%	18 48.65%	0	4.35	4.17
Finance	0	1 2.70%	1 2.70%	5 13.51%	11 29.73%	19 51.35%	0	4.24	4.18
Legal	0	0	1 2.70%	12 32.43%	14 37.84%	10 27.03%	0	3.89	3.59
Production	1 2.70%	3 8.11%	8 21.62%	7 18.92%	13 35.14%	4 10.81%	1 2.70%	3.20	3.39
Public Speaking	16 43.24%	2 5.41%	4 10.81%	6 16.22%	5 13.51%	3 8.11%	1 2.70%	3.15	3.20
Strategy	1 2.70%	0	1 2.70%	7 18.92%	17 45.95%	9 24.32%	2 5.41%	4.00	4.42
Other						International business(8); operations management		4.88	4.39

Table 40 School Goldenrod

N=35	Not in program	Of no particular interest	Somewhat interesting	Moderately interesting	Very interesting	One of the areas of greatest interest.	Did not answer this question.	Mean	Total sample mean
Human relations.	2 / 5.71%	1 / 2.86%	9 / 25.71%	13 / 37.14%	8 / 22.86%	2 / 5.71%	0	3.15	3.52
Labor relations.	17 / 48.57%	0	7 / 20%	7 / 20%	3 / 8.57%	1 / 2.86%	0	2.88[15]	2.90
Business policy.	1 / 2.86%	0	1 / 2.86%	5 / 14.29%	20 / 57.14%	8 / 22.86%	0	4.17	4.07
Marketing.	0	0	3 / 8.57%	7 / 20%	13 / 37.14%	12 / 34.29%	0	3.37	4.03
Bus. Economics	0	0	0	4 / 11.43%	10 / 28.57%	21 / 60%	0	4.48	4.17
Finance	0	0	1 / 2.86%	2 / 5.71%	18 / 51.43%	14 / 40%	0	4.28	4.18
Legal	3 / 8.57%	1 / 2.86%	7 / 20%	16 / 45.71%	4 / 11.43%	4 / 11.43%	0	3.12	3.59
Production	1 / 2.86%	0	5 / 14.29%	6 / 17.14%	13 / 37.14%	10 / 28.57%	0	3.82	3.39
Public Speaking	10 / 28.57%	2 / 5.71%	6 / 17.14%	8 / 22.86%	6 / 17.14%	3 / 8.57%	0	3.08	3.20
Strategy	1 / 2.86%	0	0	3 / 8.57%	6 / 17.14%	25 / 71.43%	0	4.65	4.42
Other	Info. Tech.				Int. strat./ negotiating	Ethics/ leadership		3.85	4.39

	in the program	particular interest	interesting	interesting	interesting	areas of greatest interest	answer		sample mean
Human relations.	0	0	7 14.58%	19 39.58%	14 29.17%	7 14.58%	1 2.08%	3.45	3.52
Labor relations.	15 31.25%	2 4.17%	9 18.75%	12 25%	10 20.83%	0	0	2.91	2.90
Business policy.	0	0	1 2.08%	10 20.83%	18 37.5%	17 35.42%	0	4.10	4.07
Marketing.	0	0	1 2.08%	5 10.42%	26 54.17%	16 33.33%	0	4.19	4.03
Bus. Economics	0	0	1 2.08%	7 14.58%	19 39.58%	21 43.75%	0	4.25	4.17
Finance	0	1 2.08%	1 2.08%	7 14.58%	20 41.67%	19 39.58%	0	4.15	4.18
Legal	5 10.42%	1 2.08%	6 12.5%	14 29.17%	15 31.25%	7 14.58%	0	3.49	3.59
Production	0	1 2.08%	3 6.25%	12 25%	23 47.92%	8 16.67%	1 2.08%	3.72	3.39
Public Speaking	24 50%	2 4.17%	4 8.33%	7 14.58%	8 16.67%	3 6.25%	0	3.42	3.20
Strategy	0	0	0	1 2.08%	7 14.58%	40 83.33%	0	4.81	4.42
Other	MIS					teamwork; computers; Int. bus;program m theory.	22 45.83%	4.53	4.39

Comments about the answers include the following:

1) The high percentage of people who answered this question may be because it was a way for them to contribute to an important response, or because it was an easy question to answer, requiring nothing more than a check.

2) For School Green, marketing, finance, and business policy proved to be most important.

3) School Blue yielded the highest percentage of respondents who mentioned international business.

4) The significant difference between the mean for human relations at Harvard, 5.3 ("not in the program" was included in the mean calculation at Harvard), and the mean for School Goldenrod, 3.86, can be traced to feelings about specific instructors, as noted in Chapter 9, the alumni interviews. However, the total mean for human relations was 3.45, significantly lower than the Harvard average, even taking into consideration the addition of "not in the program" in the calculations. This is an interesting number that bears further research.

Listed below, in Table 41, is a comparison of the means for all schools.

Table 41 Mean study score for schools.(Question #17)

Mean study score	Total Schools mean study score	Green	Blue	Goldenrod	Yellow
Human relations.	3.52	3.86	3.73	3.03	3.45
Labor relations.	2.90	2.78	2.96	2.89	2.91
Business policy.	4.07	4.11	4.0	4.03	4.11
Marketing.	4.03	4.05	3.84	3.97	4.19
Bus. Economics	4.18	3.62	4.35	4.49	4.25
Finance	4.18	4.05	4.24	4.29	4.15
Legal	3.59	3.84	3.89	3.09	3.49
Production	3.39	2.76	3.20	3.82	3.72
Public Speaking	3.20	3.35	3.15	3.08	3.25
Strategy	4.42	4.06	4.00	4.65	4.81
Other	4.40	4.14	4.89	3.86	4.47

Question #17 can be reviewed in several ways. It can be looked at from the comparison of the importance to the current students vs. the Harvard research, it can be looked at as to how the four schools differed from each other, and it can be looked at from an individual perspective for each school. It must be kept in mind that the class make-up, i.e., the number of people who were in the program from various areas of their business, had some effect on the different means for the schools for each subject. For instance, the number of people who listed their titles as involving areas of finance were two for Green, one for Blue, seven for Goldenrod, and six for yellow. The mean for finance was 4.05 for School Green, 4.24 for School Blue, 4.29 for School Goldenrod, and 4.15 for School Yellow. This statistic is interesting because the mean for finance at School Blue was higher than for School Yellow, where there were more finance managers. In the area of production, the mean for School Green was lower than any of the other schools, and a full point lower than school Goldenrod. Again, this may have to do with the technical careers of the managers in each sample. School Goldenrod also rated human relations significantly lower than the other schools. On an overall basis, however, the ratings of the schools were remarkably similar.

<u>Comparison with Harvard</u>

As explained before, the Harvard study included "not in the program" in their analysis. Because only areas included in the program were used in the analysis of the current study, I cannot precisely compare Harvard's results. The following lists rank the areas as they were listed in Harvard's study and from the mean of the total sample:

	Harvard rank	Current study rank	Current study mean
Human relations	1 (tied)	6	3.52
Labor relations	3	9	2.90
Business policy	1 (tied)	3	4.07
Marketing	6 (tied)	4	4.03
Business Economics	2	2 (tied)	4.18
Finance	4	2 (tied)	4.18
Legal	NA	5	3.59
Production	6 (tied)	7	3.39
Public speaking	5	8	3.20
Strategy	NA	1	4.42

Listed below is a chart outlining the difference between the subject rank in the Harvard study and the study on which I am reporting:

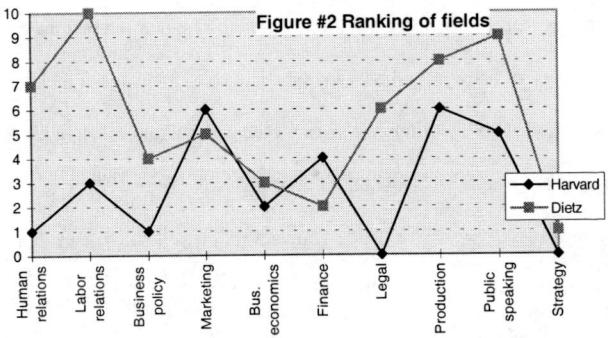

It is puzzling to see the difference in the human relations ranking at Harvard and in my study. Andrews noted that "Human Relations" was a relatively new subject at the time of the Harvard study, and he also noted that one of the Harvard professors, who was "the great mystic of the Harvard program (p. 106)," was responsible for the high degree of interest shown in the human relations area by the program respondents. One of the reasons I find the lowering of interest in human relations surprising is that Training and Development magazine surveyed directors of executive development in 77 companies in the United States and Canada to better understand their plans to respond to future educational challenges. While 22% said there had been a past emphasis on human performance issues, 73% said that there would be future emphasis on these issues(Mann and Staudenneier, 1991). However, the same research predicted that concentration on business strategic issues would increase in emphasis from 23% to 70%. Given that strategy ranked first among the choices in my study, with an overall mean of 4.42 (out of five), this prediction has more than been validated. Even with the many similarities of executives from the 1950's and from my research, the fact that strategy, which was not even a choice in the Harvard research, ranked number one with the current respondents further validates the importance of the subject matter as an integral part of executive programs. In addition, many people commented on the value of international management in the "other" area of Question #18, such that further support for research and innovation in teaching those subjects is important for schools to prioritize.

Given the change in power of labor unions, the change in labor relations is not too surprising, but this score is also lowered by those who said that labor relations was not in the program; forty per cent said that the topic was not in their program.

I expected that marketing would increase dramatically because I remembered how high the support for the earlier programs was from the petroleum industry, where marketing was not so important. In addition, the services business has increased dramatically, as have people in EMBA programs who want to go into their own business and need to know how to market it.

The above information gave a sense of how interesting the topics were. I then wanted to know much the ratings were a reflection of basic interest and how much they reflected the professor's teaching skill or style. That information is reflected in Table 40, which displays the answers to Question #19.

Table 42 To what extent is your expression of interest a reflection of the way in which the different areas were taught, and to what extent is it a reflection of your basic interest in these areas (Question #19):

	Green N=37	Blue N=37	Goldenrod N=35	Yellow N=48	Total N= 157
Mostly basic interest.	13 35.14%	15 40.54%	11 31.43%	14 29.17%	53 33.76%
50/50	2 5.41%	6 16.22%	7 20%	4 8.33%	19 12.10%
Instructor had an influence on my interest.	13 35.14%	8 21.62%	8 22.86%	11 22.92%	40 25.48%
Both correlate highly	4 10.81%	0	3 8.57%	10 20.83%	17 10.83%
Did not answer	5 13.51%	1 2.70%	5 14.29%	7 14.58%	18 11.46%
Biggest factor was the topic	0	3 8.11%	1 2.86%	1 2.08%	5 3.18%
Poor instructors detracted from subject.	0	4 8.11%	0	1 2.08%	5 3.18%

Given that the Harvard research found a large correlation between teaching method and faculty effectiveness, it is no surprise that the instructors played a large part in the ratings the alumni gave to the course material in the current study. A total of 81 people, or 51.59%, gave answers which indicated that the instructor played a part in the effectiveness of the course. Three percent said that poor instructors actually detracted from the subject. The next question, represented by Table 42, asked about the amount of work assigned in the program.

Table 43: (Question #20) Amount of reading and writing assigned in the program.
(Andrews question #41)
Table 43 Reading:

Number for data entry	N=	37	37	35	48	157	6,036
		Green	Blue	Goldenrod	Yellow	Total	Harvard
1	Very heavy	8 21.62%	11 29.73%	13 37.14%	27 56.25%	59 37.58%	48%
2	Heavy	18 48.65%	21 56.76%	15 40.54%	20 41.67%	74 47.13%	38%
3	Moderate	10 27.03%	5 13.51%	7 18.92%	1 2.08%	23 14.65%	10%
	Light	1 2.70%	0	0	0	1 .64%	2%
	Very light	0	0	0	0	0	1%
	Did not answer	0	0	0	0	0	1%
	Mean	2.11	1.84	1.83	1.46	1.78	
	Mode	2	2	2	1		

There is a fairly wide variance between schools on the reading issue. In addition, many more of the Harvard participants said the reading was very heavy than did the participants in my research. This could be because the alumni with whom I conducted the research expected a lot of work, indeed welcomed it. Andrews' also reported that, as the length of the program lengthened (some were 13 weeks long), the amount of reading was seen as greater. Table 44 gives the same information with regard to amount of work, for the written portion of the program.

Table 44 Written

		Green	Blue	Goldenrod	Yellow	Total	Harvard
	N=	37	37	35	48	157	
1	Very heavy	1 2.70%	5 13.51%	1 2.86%	16 33.33%	23 14.65%	1%
2	Heavy	20 54.05%	14 37.84%	19 54.29%	19 39.58%	72 45.86%	4%
3	Moderate	16 43.25%	17 45.95%	15 42.86%	13 27.08%	61 38.86%	22%
4	Light	0	1 2.70%	0	0	1 .64%	28%
5	Very light	0	0	0	0	0	39%
	Missing	0	0	0	0	0	6%
	Mean	2.41	2.37	2.40	1.94	2.26	
	Mode	2	2	2	2	2	

In the Harvard research, 50% said the written work was either moderate or light, while the current research for showed that over 60% felt the written work was either very heavy or heavy. For the corporate sponsors who expressed a desire for rigor, this is most likely what they want to see. The overall schedule ratings tended more toward the "very heavy side," as Table 44 shows.

Table 45 Overall schedule

iber for designation		N=	Green	Blue	Goldenrod	Yellow	Total	Harv
			37	37	35	48	157	
1	Very heavy		3	10	7	25	45	10⁹
			8.11%	27.03%	20%	52.08%	28.66%	
2	Heavy		18	18	18	22	76	49⁹
			48.65%	48.65%	51.43%	45.83%	48.41%	
3	Moderate		14	9	10	1	34	34⁹
			37.84%	24.32%	28.57%	2.08%	21.66%	
4	Light		1	0	0	0	1	2%
			2.70%				.64%	
5	Very light		0	0	0	0	0	1%
	Did not answer		1	0	0	0	1	
							(.64%)	
	Mean		2.36	1.97	2.09	1.50		4%

Andrews reported that "as reported workload decreased, so does favorability (Andrews, 1966, p.115)." The source for the Harvard data is Andrews, 1966, Page 100, Table IV-20. Andrews reported the following:

> when asked to comment on the amount of reading and written work and the weight of the overall daily schedule, the respondents reported the reading very heavy or heavy, written work light, and the total schedule heavy or moderate….The relatively junior men say the workload is heavier than do their seniors (Andrews, 1966, p.101).

The conclusion from the above information is that all four schools administer a program requiring fairly heavy effort in reading and written assignments. The schools can determine from the variances in their scores how they compare with each other. For instance, it appears that School Yellow has a fairly heavy program. The reader might remember that School Yellow administers a program that meets every other week on Friday and Saturday, with lodging provided on Friday night. The other schools meet every week, on Friday or Saturday. It can be wondered whether the schedule had anything to do with the workload ratings. It appears that the workload at the four schools who participated in my research was somewhat heavier than the workload at the residential programs who participated in the Harvard research. Although the students who attended the programs included in my study had been briefed about the workload, it appears that there may have been difference expectations between the two groups, those who attended the programs in the 1950's and those who attended the EMBA programs I was studying.

The next question, represented by Table 46, asked about the personal value to the alumni of the various elements. This was Andrews' question #42. In the Harvard research, it was a ranking question, asking the respondents to rank their choice from one to seven.

Table 46 (Question #21) Please evaluate the personal value to you of the program elements:

School Green

37	No value	Some value	Moderate Value	Extremely Valuable	Harvard mean 1-7, 1= best	Mean 1-4 4=best	Total m 1-4 4=bes
ling for courses	0	2 / 5.41%	18 / 48.65%	17 / 45.95%	3.6	3.41	3.50
mal on-campus ıssions	0	7 / 18.92%	13 / 35.14%	17 / 45.95%	3.2	3.27	3.36
mal social ɛrings	2 / 5.41%	20 / 54.05%	8 / 21.62%	7 / 18.92%	5.4	2.54	2.73
s sessions.	0	0	15 / 40.54%	22 / 59.46%	1.9	3.59	3.77
small study ps.	0	1 / 2.70%	11 / 29.73%	25 / 67.57%	2.4	3.65	3.73
act w/faculty ıbers outside of	1 / 2.70%	10 / 27.03%	17 / 45.95%	9 / 24.32%	5.1	2.92	2.82
national trip.	0	3 / 8.11%	15 / 40.54%	19 / 51.35%	NA	3.43	2.83

School Blue N=37

	No value (1)	Some value (2)	Moderate Value (3)	Extremely Valuable (4)	Harvard mean 1-7 1=best	Mean 1-4 4=best	Total m (1-4)
ling for courses	0	2 / 5.41%	14 / 37.84%	21 / 56.76%	3.6	3.51	3.50
mal on-campus ıssions	2 / 5.41%	2 / 5.41%	11 / 29.73%	22 / 59.46%	3.2	3.43	3.36
mal social ɛrings	3 / 8.11%	9 / 24.32%	14 / 37.84%	11 / 29.73%	5.4	2.89	2.73
s sessions.	0	0	7 / 18.92%	30 / 81.08%	1.9	3.81	3.77
ınized small / groups	0	2 / 5.41%	2 / 5.41%	33 / 89.19%	2.4	3.84	3.73
act w/faculty ıbers outside of	1 / 2.70%	13 / 35.14%	14 / 37.84%	8 / 21.62%	5.1	2.81	2.82
national trip.	1 / 2.70%	4 / 10.81%	8 / 21.62%	23 / 62.16%	NA	3.47	2.83

School Goldenrod N=35

	No value	Some value	Moderate Value	Extremely Valuable	Harvard 1-7	Mean 1-4	Total mean(
ing for courses	0	2 / 5.71%	18 / 51.43%	15 / 42.86%	3.6	3.37	3.5(
mal on-campus ssions	1 / 2.86%	5 / 14.29%	10 / 28.57%	19 / 54.29%	3.6	3.34	3.3(
mal social rings	1 / 2.86%	15 / 42.86%	15 / 42.86%	4 / 11.43%	5.4	2.63	2.7:
sessions.	0	0	8 / 22.86%	27 / 77.14%	1.9	3.77	3.7:
small study os.	1 / 2.86%	1 / 2.86%	6 / 17.14%	27 / 77.14%	2.4	3.69	3.7:
act w/faculty bers outside of	3 / 8.57%	14 / 40%	13 / 37.14%	5 / 14.29%	5.1	2.57	2.8:
national trip.	26=N/A	2 / 5.71%	2 / 5.71%	3 / 8.57%	NA	NA	2.8:

School Yellow N=48

	No value	Some value	Moderate Value	Extremely Valuable	Harvard 1-7 1=best	Mean 1-4	Total m 1-4
ling for courses	0	0	16 / 33.33%	32 / 66.67%	3.6	3.67	3.50
mal on-campus ssions with r executives.	1 / 2.08%	4 / 8.335	19 / 39.58%	24 / 50%	3.6	3.38	3.36
mal social rings	2 / 4.17%	15 / 31.25%	20 / 41.67%	11 / 22.92%	5.4	2.83	2.73
s sessions.	0	0	6 / 12.50%	42 / 87.50%	1.9	3.88	3.77
small study ps.	0	2 / 4.17%	9 / 18.75%	37 / 77.08%	2.4	3.73	3.73
act w/faculty bers outside of	0	14 / 29.17%	23 / 47.92%	11 / 22.92%	5.1	2.94	2.82
national trip. ing=2	0	4 / 8.33%	17 / 35.42%	25 / 52.08%	NA	3.46	2.83

Table 47 lists all of the mean values so that each school can be compared:

Table 47 All Schools mean scores of program elements

	Green	Blue	Goldenrod	Yellow	Harvard[16] 1-7	Total mean 1-4
Reading	3.41	3.51	3.37	3.67	3.6	3.50
Informal on-campus discussions	3.27	3.43	3.34	3.38	3.6	3.36
Informal social gatherings	2.54	2.89	2.63	2.83	5.4	2.73
Class sessions	3.59	3.81	3.77	3.88	1.9	3.77
Organized small study groups	3.65	3.84	3.64	3.73	2.4	3.73
Contact with faculty outside of class	2.92	2.80	2.57	2.94	5.1	2.82
International trip	3.43	3.47	NA	3.46	NA	2.83

′s the ranking of the program elements.

Table 48 All elements ranked in order of mean rating

	Rank	Harvard	Green	Blue	Gldnrod	Yellow
Class sessions	1	1	2	2	1	1
Organized small study groups	2	2	1	1	2	2
Reading for courses	3	3	4	3	3	3
In-formal on-campus discussions	4	4	5	5	4	5
Contact with faculty members	5	5	6	7	6	6
Informal social gatherings	6	6	7	6	5	7
International Trip	NA	NA	3	4	NA	4

As in the Harvard study, class sessions, reading and organized study groups ranked the three highest in the current research as well. School Green was the only place where the International trip ranked higher than the reading for the course. With regard to the Harvard study, Andrews reported that "the most conspicuous feature…is the decisiveness with which class sessions are ranked first in order of value through programs of every length. Andrews, 1966,p.103)." Several points can be made about the above chart:

1) The continued emphasis on classmates, learning from classmates, and class discussions is further confirmation of the value of face-to-face vs. technology-based education.

---

[16] The Harvard question asked for a ranking of the various aspects, so the weighted average is not equivalent to the current study. The Harvard score was computed by (a) multiplying the key numbers by the respective response frequencies, (b) adding the products, and (c) dividing that sum the sum of the frequencies. The lower the score, the higher the favorability (Andrews, 1966, p.103).

2) Two schools, School Blue and School Green, ranked the study groups first. This research is producing confirmation of the value of the study group approach to executive education.

3) The international trip is definitely an experience that the people attending it felt worthwhile.

4) Informal social gatherings received, as they did at Harvard, a lower ranking. Combining this with the interview results from both alumni and corporate sponsors, I can say that these people want a rigorous education and are not looking for social events. Their time with their families becomes too precious while they are in the program to leave much time for extra activity.

Question #22, Experience with the glass ceiling

In the introduction, I mentioned that one of my research questions was "does executive education properly take into consideration differences in cultural background and critical thought?" I added Question #22, which asks whether the female alumni have experienced the glass ceiling, because my own experiences in corporate management have left me with the feeling that the "glass ceiling", or the artificial barriers that exist in business that prevent women and minorities from moving up, is still alive today. I wanted to know what the experience of women in their thirties has been with this issue. I was somewhat gratified to read, in an article about women who received out-placement help when their careers go through derailment, that finally, women executives are getting the same assistance that men get, instead of the 'see you later, alligator' attitude (Lopez, 1992). The same article charted the number of women in management positions in U.S. business, showing an increase from about eight million in 1983 to over fourteen million in 1991. However, the federal Glass Ceiling Commission reported that, although women accounted for just 3% to 5% of senior managers in major corporations, more than 35% of the nation's master's of business administration degrees were being awarded to women.

(Brooks and Groves,1996; Groves, 1996). The report spawned the following comments from Labor Secretary Robert Reich:

> The glass ceiling is not only an egregious denial of social justice...but a serious economic problem that takes a huge financial toll on American business....Equity demands that we destroy the glass ceiling. Smart business demands it as well (Groves, 1996, p.D1).

Another look at the gender issue has been noted by Judith Rosener, a professor at the University of California, Irvine, Graduate School of Management, who teaches and does research in the areas of men and women at work, cultural diversity, and business and government. According to Rosener,

> Ultimately, it will be the inclusion of women—not just their leadership styles— that will create the successful businesses of the future....Tying the two styles together are better than one alone. Women—and their traditional styles of leadership-are an economic resource, not a problem.

Rosener, a Ph.D. graduate of the Claremont Graduate School, details how much of an economic resource women can be in her current book, <u>America's Competitive Secret</u>: <u>Utilizing Women as a Management Strategy</u> (Oxford, 1996).

On the glass ceiling issue, there seem to be mixed feelings, an example of which was articulated by Helen Rheem in an article for the Harvard Business Review. She noted that "the verdict is still mixed."

> One the one hand, the vast majority of female managers surveyed (in 1995)...said that they still experienced unfair treatment and negative attitudes on the job. On the other hand, they cited progress toward equality in the workplace; perhaps most important, many of the respondents said that they had developed effective ways to overcome gender-based obstacles (Rheem, 1996, p.13).

From my research, I knew we were making progress; asking Question #22 of these women would give me a fresh perspective. Table 49 represents the comments.

Table 49 (Question #22) If you are a woman, have you experienced "the glass ceiling?"

	Green	Blue	Goldenrod	Yellow	Total
Number of women who returned the survey	9	9	9	10	37
Number of people answering	8	10	10	10	38
Comments:					
Yes, opportunities are limited, even with more education.	3 37.5%	7 70%	3 30%	5 50%	18 47.37%
No, I have made progress commensurate with my level of education and ability	3 37.5%	1 10%	3 30%	3 30%	10 27.03%
In previous companies, but not at current company	1 12.5%	0	1 10%	1 10%	3 7.89%
Yes, but not due to the causes written about.	1 12.5%	0	0	1 10%	2 5.26%
Yes, to the point where my next job will be my own company.	0	1 10%	0	0	1 2.63%
It if exists, it's wrong	0	1 10%	0	0	1 2.63%
The MBA allowed me to change industries because of it.	0	0	1 10%	0	1 2.63%
How about the male white ceiling?	0	0	1 10%	0	1 2.63%
Not a female, but the class had some who had experienced the glass ceiling	0	0	1 10%	0	1 2.63%

Some of the comments included the following:

- "If it exists, it's wrong."
- "Yes, for the first time. For me, the glass ceiling has been constructed by a fundamentalist. His beliefs are that women, especially mothers, need to be at home. Although nothing has been said, his personal beliefs have retarded my career growth."
- "Absolutely, especially in the area of finance."
- "Yes, the white men want women to succeed so it looks good, but only to certain levels."
- "It definitely exists, maybe because of a lack of role models.
- "Yes, the dominant culture in aerospace is "white men rise to the top."

Did the above information answer my question? Well, yes, it told me that the "glass ceiling" is still a problem in a number of ways, sometimes because of particular managers, sometimes because of the comfort level of male managers, and sometimes because of the company culture. The data also confirmed that women are making progress. Twenty-seven percent of the people who answered this question have been able to use their education and skills to advance in their careers. Further research into this area might concentrate on more micro-management situations, as well as studies of the company culture as a whole.

Question #23, represented by Table 50, asked what suggestions the respondents would make to improve the program. It related directly to my research questions: "Is executive education meeting the needs of the customer?" It read as follows:

Question #23) What suggestions would you make which you think would serve to improve the program you attended? (Andrews question #47)

Because there was such a diversity of answers to this question, I have chosen to list the comments by school. I have divided them into a) positive comments; b) suggestions for the administration, faculty, and admission procedure; c) suggestions for curriculum:

Table 50 Suggestions

School Green

A	Positive comments about the school
1	Good procedure for listening to the students and making changes in the program.
2	It was fine, developed for a wide range of students
B	Suggestions for administration, faculty and admissions
1	Maintain or increase selectivity of students.
2	The diversity of the class required too much catch-up
3	Only more experienced faculty should teach.
4	Calculus as a pre-requisite—no pass, no degree
5	Some classes too academic
C	Suggestions for the curriculum
1	Only one group learning class per quarter.
2	More time to rest before the international trip.
3	Ability to specialize in a given area.
4	More time for group study.
5	Add material on the Internet.
6	Less written cases, more from students.
7	More real life situations.
8	Most of the people in the service business, but the text was heavy in manufacturing.
9	Attention to small business applications.
10	Option of beginning finance.
11	More applications for public speaking.
12	Provide a negotiating class.
13	Visit local companies.
14	More time on personal techniques and style.
15	Get rid of the international trip and go to New York City to visit wall street.

Table 50 School Blue:

A	Positive comments about the school
	Very responsive; have already made some improvements.
B	**Suggestions for administration, faculty and admissions**
1	Omit summer break and run for 18 months.
2	More female professors.
3	Not enough ways for professors to grade individual efforts and skills.
4	Strict evaluation of faculty prior to involvement.
5	Get constant feedback to keep program current and effective.
6	Change study groups periodically to keep certain people from exerting a power base (2 comments like this).
7	Study groups very valuable, but more individual testing of skills.
C	**Suggestions for the curriculum**
1	Have the two classes more in balance (economics and marketing—economics took more time).
2	Plan so major project in both classes not due on the same day.
3	More time for small group meetings, focused on solving problems.
4	More in-depth visits of local businesses.
5	More computer simulation, more diversity training.
6	Less dependent on group project, more on individual effort.
7	More subject matter on technology as a tool of office productivity.
8	More marketing and finance.
9	Some subjects require more than ten weeks, some less.

Table 50 School Goldenrod:

A	Positive comments about the school
1	Well structured and balanced.
2	Business strategy has now been added.
B	**Suggestions for the administration, faculty, and admissions.**
1	Better faculty. More input from business people.
2	Get rid of the 'dead wood' and people who should not be teaching in the executive program.
3	Some of the instructors could have been better.
4	Improve the quality of the weaker instructors.
5	Weed out few bad professors.
6	Better teachers, higher standards for entry and continuation.
7	Better speakers during lunch.
8	Additional assistance for those being introduced to a subject for the first time.
9	Get rid of the poor professors who ranked low.
C	**Suggestions for the curriculum**
1	Add portfolio management theory and practice.
2	More focus on using skills and less on developing them.
3	Emphasize the study of leadership.
4	Spend more time on economics and finance; business to business marketing.
5	More focus on MIS.
6	Better integrated curriculum with course work.
7	Study groups that work.
8	More time on career path development.
9	Mandatory international component.
10	Local site reviews tied to case studies.
11	Courses on running a small business.

Table 50 School Yellow

A	Positive comments about the school
1	Progress was excellent; well thought out and managed.
2	Nothing that I can think of.
B	**Suggestions for the administration, faculty, and admissions.**
1	Smaller class size.
2	Study groups not to exceed four people.
3	Flunk out marginal students.
4	The bottom 20-030% did not belong there.
5	Require preparation course in statistics.
6	Better explanation ahead of time of how courses flow together.
7	Prevent one ethnic group from forming their own study group.
8	Better administrative support, better marketing of the program.
9	Not so lenient with contributors.
10	Like to see professors have more real world experience.
C	**Suggestions for the curriculum**
1	Too much on traditional business as practiced by the conglomerates. More attention to future trends, strategies for business development.
2	More focus on current events.
3	More computer training prior to enrollment.
4	More concentration on finance and how financial decisions are made by the general manager.
5	Expand finance (several comments).
6	More career counseling.
7	Options for electives.
8	More business law and ethics.
9	Study executive behavior—how to manage to be successful,
10	Reduce time in human resources and ethics.
11	I would have liked a legal class.
12	Less on the mechanics of manufacturing; more on speaking, presenting, writing, finance.
13	More focus on leadership.
14	Greater emphasis on operations management and finance.
15	More options for electives.
16	More use of the case method.

On an overall basis, the following common suggestions occurred:

1) Improve weak faculty.
2) Offer courses in public speaking and personal improvement.
3) Offer courses in leadership.
4) Make the international trip mandatory.
5) Provide for individual grading vs. group grading in some areas.
6) Provide for local site visits.
7) Concentrate on smaller business management as well as the large corporations.
8) Provide aid in career path development.
9) Improve admission standards and uphold standards throughout the program.

In the Harvard research, the authors reported strong support for the programs they used. However, with such a large population, they had people with some of the same complaints that I heard from the four schools who participated in my research. The main complaints that Kenneth Andrews found were:

1) Course content and format
2) Faculty deficiencies

3) Administrative problems.

These were the complaints registered by the 97 most unfavorable men, and comprised 83.57% of the complaints from that group. They were, "on the average, younger…than the rest of the population and much more highly educated (Andrews, 1966, p.124)." Thinking about those people I interviewed and the surveys, an analogy can be drawn with those who participated in my survey. One of the respondents who was most negative is a Naval Academy Graduate who is significantly younger than his classmates, but who obviously felt very superior to them.

In line with my desire to determine how well schools are meeting the needs of the customer, the next question asked about the applicability of the course work to their careers. Question #24 is represented by Table 51.

Table 51 (Question #24) How applicable to your career was your EMBA experience?

1= Not very applicable; 2= Fairly applicable;3:Moderately applicable; 4:Very applicable;5= Matched my needs exactly.

	Green	Blue	Goldenrod	Yellow	Total
N:	37	37	35	48	157
Not very applicable at all	1 2.70%	1 2.70%	0	0	2 1.27%
Fairly applicable	3 8.11%	4 10.81%	2 5.71%	0	9
Moderately applicable	6 16.22%	4 10.81%	3 8.57%	5 2.08%	18 11.46%
Very applicable	24 64.86%	18 48.65%	24 68.57%	26 74.29%	91 57.96%
Matched my needs exactly	3 8.11%	8 21.62%	6 17.14%	15 31.25%	32 20.38%
Missing	3 8.11%	2 5.41%	0	2 4.17%	7 4.46%
Mean	3.68	3.80	3.97	4.22	3.93

The majority rated their executive education experience 'very applicable,' again reinforcing the validity of their experience in terms of meeting customer needs. Given the variation in answers for the survey respondents, I found the fact that over 75% of the respondents rated their program as 'very applicable' or 'matched my needs exactly' interesting..

The next question related to the question of meeting customer needs in that it asked about the alumni desire for on-line education, if given the opportunity. Numerous purveyors of higher education are offering bachelor's and master's degrees through distance learning. A number of Fortune 500 companies have signed up for the Executive Education Network, an interactive satellite network "that transmits MBA-level courses from schools like Wharton, USC, Penn State, Carnegie Mellow, and SMU directly to subscriber's offices (Anderson, 1995)." In addition, business schools offering executive education programs via satellite include Carnegie Mellon, North Carolina, Penn State, and Southern Methodist (Byrne, 1995). Both Anderson and Byrne reason that downsized companies cannot afford to lose their managers for lengthy amounts of time. So I wanted to ask this group of alumni what their feeling was about distance learning, now that they were fresh from an intense personal-contact experience that was both time-consuming and rewarding. Question #25 is represented by Table 52.

Table 52 (Question #25) Would you be interested in on-line education for this program?

	Green	Blue	Goldenrod	Yellow	Total
N=	37	37	35	48	157
Yes, for the entire program.	3 8.11%	0	2 5.71%	0	5 3.18%
Yes, for part of the program.	15 40.54%	17 45.95%	7 20%	16 33.33%	55 35.03%
No	18 48.64%	18 48.64%	26 74.28%	31 64.58%	93 59.24%
Missing	1	2	0	1	4

Comments included the following (using only those who chose to make a comment in the total (Table 53):

Table 53 Comments about an on-line option

	N=21	N=24	N=28	N=29	N=1(
	Green	Blue	Goldenrod	Yellow	Tot:
Classroom interaction is critical	12 57.14%	17 70.83%	21 75%	23 79.31%	73 71.5%
Depends on content	1 4.76%	4 16.67%	1 3.57%	2 6.90%	8 10.9(
Might do additional follow-up courses this way	0	3 12.5%	0	2 6.90%	5 6.85
Difficult to get the same level of education with lack of questions.	5 23.81%	0	6 21.43%	2 6.90%	11 15.0%
Some subjects require face-to-face, others could be accomplished.	0	1 4.17%	0	0	1 1.37

These results seem to indicate that, although a definite percentage of the respondents feel that part of the program could be administered with distance-learning, their overall feeling is that classroom interaction is too important to be substituted by video or computer-learning. Preparing foundation courses to be taught on-line for basic subjects might be one way to add this element. The respondents' answers to the above questions were extremely consistent with their comments that their classmates were one of the most important benefits they received from their university education. However, recent business press has featured information regarding schools who offer on-line education as a way to remain competitive. Charles Hickman, director of projects and services of the American Assembly of Collegiate Schools of Business, is quoted as saying "current competition between business schools increasingly is defined by the use of new technology...(the losers will be) schools that don't have the resources to even get involved (Lublin, 1996,p.B1). The article cited features Duke's Fuqua School of Business, where MBA students spend only 11 weeks of the 19-month program in an actual classroom. The rest of the program is spent in a virtual classroom. Problems with on-line communication, many created by technology, will continue to be worked out as schools move to compete in this manner.

The international experience was mentioned as another of the important parts of the executive MBA experience by many of those who responded to my surveys. Because one of the schools who participated in my research does not include an international trip, I was interested in how important a part it really played. In other words, was it fun and a great experience or was it a definitive part of the learning program?

Question #26 asked about the international experience. Table 54 represents the answers.

Question # 26: A number of executive MBA programs today use an international trip as part of the experience. How much do you feel that this experience improved what you took away from this program? (check all that apply)

Table 54 International Trip

		Green	Blue	Goldenrod	Yellow	Total where trip offered (122)	Total 157
	N=	37	37	35	48		
1	It greatly enhanced the educational experience.	25 67.57%	26 70.27%	1 2.86%	34 70.83%	85 69.67%	86 54.78%
2	Enjoyed the trip, but don't think it added anything to the educational experience.	6 16.22%	5 13.51%	0	8 16.67%	19 15.57%	19 12.10%
3	I think it should be a part of all executive MBA programs.	12 32.43%	17 45.95%	3 8.57%	17 35.42%	46 37.70%	49 31.21%
4	I think it should be an optional part of the program.	10 27.03%	5 13.51%	8 22.86%	7 14.58%	22 18.03%	30 19.11%
5	I don't think it should be part of the program.	0	0	1 2.86%	2 4.17%	2 1.64%	3 1.91%
6	N/A, not offered.	0	0	26 74.28%	0	0	26 16.57%

There are probably enough comments that the trip should be an optional part for the schools to do some research into the matter. However, as the program directors told me in the interviews, the logistics of an international trip are so cumbersome that there are bound to be some unhappy people. If the schools made it optional, what would take its place from an educational standpoint? The above data are certainly a strong vote of confidence from the alumni base that the international trip is an integral part of their executive education experience.

Because of my own experience teaching sales management at the college level, where I found that my experience was an important part of my effectiveness, I wanted the respondents' opinion about the credentials they expected for those who teach in executive programs. Would they be willing to accept a seasoned executive who did not have a Ph.D., or did they feel that the entire experience of the 'due diligence' that a Ph.D. requires was also important to the quality of the education? Question #27 gave them a chance to give me their thoughts about this requirement. It is represented by Table 55.

The results are consistent with the remarks made regarding professors who were not current with material. This information can be used to further research what kinds of courses can best be taught by industry practitioners.

By now, the alumni had had an opportunity to comment several times about their executive education experience. Question #28 was their last chance to provide an indication of an area that stood out for them, either positive or negative. Table 56 outlines the major comments, though there were many who left this question blank. Only a total of 98 people answered the question, or 62% of my sample.

<u>Concluding comments:</u>

The research questions introduced in Chapter 3 sought to answer the following:

1) Are schools which are producing executive training at the MBA level meeting the needs of their mid-career students in ways that address their concerns as working professionals?
2) Are the programs affected by lack of security in the workplace today and are people using the executive MBA degree to make a career change?
3) Are the courses relevant to the executives' job needs?
4) Do sponsoring companies make concerted use of the skills learned?
5) Do women continue to have a problem with the "glass ceiling?"

Table 55 Use of experienced practitioners as faculty

	Green	Blue	Goldenrod	Yellow	Total
N=	37	37	35	48	157
Yes	27 72.97%	25 67.57%	30 85.71%	31 64.68%	113 71.97%
No	8 21.62%	10 27.03%	3 8.57%	16 33.33%	37 23.57%
Missing	2 5.41%	2 5.41%	0	1 2.08%	5 3.18%
Comments:					
Need desire to teach	5 13.51%	5 13.51%	4 11.43%	3 6.25%	17 10.83%
Would support hybrid team approach	5 13.51%	4 10.81%	1 2.86%	2 4.17%	9 5.73%
Others could be qualified with experience; would add to the experience	4 10.81%	4 10.81%	1 2.86%	5 10.42%	14 8.92%
Practical experience is essential	6 16.22%	0	1 2.86%	3 6.25%	10 6.37%
Many faculty are out of touch with reality and have a poor work ethic	2 5.41%	2 5.41%	2 5.71%	1 2.08%	7 4.46%
Use as guests	3 8.11%				31.91%

	Green	Blue	Goldenrod	Yellow	Total
N	18	24	22	34	98
Learned, grew and accomplished more than I thought possible.	2 11.11%	4 16.67%	3 13.63%	9 26.47%	18 18.37%
Commitment level of the staff very high	4 22.22%	8 33.33%	1 4.54%	4 11.76%	17 17.35%
Comprehensive and thorough	2 11.11%	2 8.33%	0	3 8.82%	7 7.14%
Study groups put together with care; made for a great experience	2 11.11%	3 12.5%	1 4.54%	2 5.89%	8 8.16%
Do not slow down to let people catch up	0	2 8.33%	1 4.54%	3 8.82%	6 6.12%
Surprised students so uninterested in knowledge and interested only in the diploma.	0	1 4.17%	1 4.54%	1 2.94%	3 3.06%
Uneven quality				1 2.94%	

In addition, I was interested in the level of attraction to executive education programs offered on-line and in whether alumni would support replacing the requirement for a Ph.D. for instructors with a great deal of industry experience.

The answer to Question #1, "are schools meetings the needs...", is yes because the program ratings, the faculty ratings, and the comments support the contention that executive programs are taking into consideration the needs of their customer base. Several levels of analysis allow me to state that there appears to be no major difference in reactions to the questions about effectiveness of programs in the 1990's as compared with those researched in 1959.

The original research question was looking to identify the difference in reaction by executive students to the effectiveness of programs in 1993, 1994, and 1995 vs. their reactions in 1959. Several levels of analysis allow me to state that there is no significant difference in the responses of the two populations:

a) From question #12c, "What happened to you," a majority of both the Harvard group and the current research group mentioned the confidence in their own ability, the broadening effects of gaining a knowledge of business aspects with which they were not previously familiar, and the social/psychological benefits.

b) From Question #13c, which asked for alumni reaction now, while reflecting back, 47% mentioned the positive benefits of the program, with 22.29% stating that the program was one of the best learning experiences of their lives. In the Harvard research, 84.5% reported a generally favorable level of satisfaction witih the program at the time of the questionnaire.

c) Question #13d asked the respondents to rate the program of a scale of 1-5. The Harvard research asked the same question on a scale of 1-10. Numerical equivalencies would show that the current respondents rated the program a mean of

4.34, or 8.69 if using a 10 pt. scale. The Harvard mean was 7.71. This answer would show that the current research group rated the program somewhat higher (12.7%) than the Harvard group. However, given the different scales and lowering of validity when trying to compare two such different groups, I would prefer to state that the experiences were similar in effect.

Research question #2 queried the effect of lower job security on the use of MBA programs to change jobs. Results showed that 35% changed jobs after they left the program, and that 67% of those people agreed that there was a connection with the program. Only 15% of them, however, attributed the change to the fact that their employers offered little support. Most of the rest attributed the change to enhanced skills, which made them more marketable.

Research Question #2, then, would show that some people do use the MBA to change jobs. This is not in conflict with current literature. However, as Chapter 6 will show, corporations plan to continue to support this method of education and do not see the threat of losing employees as restrictive.

Research Question #3, whether the programs are relevant to jobs, would have to be answered in the affirmative. One a scale of 1-5, the mean score was 3.93, or slightly less than "very applicable." This question reinforced the fact that the experience of the alumni met their needs. Anyone reading this dissertation, however, should take into account the negative effect that comments about poorly prepared faculty and lower standards for entrance may have had on overall applicability.

Research Question #4, whether companies use the skills attained from such graduate education, resulted in a split vote. About one-third (32.48%) were satisfied with their company's reaction in that area, one-third (34.39%) said that the company used some, but not enough, and one-third (28.66%) said that the company made no effort to use their skills. This question was not used in the Andrews/Powell survey, but the general reaction would be that there is work to be done in matching job responsibilities with new skills attained through advanced education.

Research Question #5 wondered if the "glass ceiling" was causing the women who answered the survey the same kinds of problems reported in business press. Although there were only 37 in the group who answered the question, 47% reported that the "glass ceiling" still creates roadblocks to advancement for them, while 27% said that their career advancement has been unimpeded.

I was also interested in the interest in on-line programs. The majority of the respondents, or 48.64%, were not interested in it because of the value of in-class discussion, but 40.54% would be interested for part of the program, possibly foundation courses.

Seventy-two percent would support opening up opportunities to industry practitioners without a Ph.D. if the person had excellent teaching skills. This question can be tied to those critical comments relating to poor instructors at some of the schools.

With regard to the international trip, there appears to be considerable support for its use, such that the one school which does not use it might wish to perform further inquiries.

On an overall basis, the survey was helpful in answering my original questions. The interviews of the alumni, covered in Chapter 7, confirmed many of the quantitative results from the surveys.

The next section will review the correlation data that were done on the questions using regression analysis.

Correlation and regression analysis

The following data describe the relationships that exist between some of the variables used in the survey. I chose to analyze the variables with a significance of .05. Table 57 represents the Pearson correlation analysis performed to determine the inter-relationships between some of the variables. The strongest relationships represented those between faculty teaching effectiveness and program rating, years with present company and whether they changed employers, and use of skills with a salary increase.

Table 57 Pearson correlation, 1-tailed significance

	Q30	Q3	Q2a	Q14	Q5	Q11	Q10a	Q13d
Q30	-							
Q3	.009	-						
Q2a	.387**	-.347**	-					
Q14	.212**	.118	-.040	-				
Q5	-.176*	.357**	-.654**	.013	-			
Q11	.024	.010	-.098	-.188*	.142*	-		
Q10a	-.139*	-.158*	-.094	.151*	-.039	-.357**	-	
Q13d	.2009*	-.001	.047	.496**	-.091	-.249	.208*	

*p= <.05
**p=<.01

Q30= age;Q3=employer share of tuition;Q2A=Years w effectiveness;Q5- Changed employers?;Q11= Use of n(increase;Q13D=Program rating.

I wanted to know if the program rating could be predicted by the following variables:

Q30   Age
Q3   Employer share of tuition
Q2a   Years with present company
Q14   Faculty teaching effectiveness
Q5   Have they changed employers?
Q11   Use of new skills
Q10a Salary increase
Q33a Married/Single

Table 58 shows that only faculty teaching effectiveness affected the program rating:

Table 58 Program rating as determined by faculty teaching and "use of new skills."

Dependent Variable	Independent Variable	Beta	T	S
Program Rating (Question 13d)	Faculty Teaching Effectiveness(Q14)	.465	6.28	
	Use of new skills(Q11)	-.16	-2.18	
R=.52				
R^2=.27				
N=141				

About 27% of the program rating could be predicted by the rating of faculty teaching effectiveness. The significance of this finding is that program rating is highly dependent on good teachers, not just on good material or a well-run program.

CHAPTER 5

SCHOOL INTERVIEWS

The four schools that participated in this research were chosen because they were all included in the original 39 programs used in the Andrews/Powell study. They represent four different population bases: Los Angeles, California; Denver, Colorado; Salt Lake City, Utah; and Seattle, Washington. I expected to be able to identify the diversity I was looking for with these cities. I was to find out that the business cultures of the four areas are very distinct in terms of industry emphasis. As an example:

1) In Seattle, Boeing is a major force; 34% of the respondents were from manufacturing or aerospace, vs. 22% in Colorado and 9% in Utah. Southern California, with 28% represented in manufacturing or aerospace, also showed a high concentration of aerospace-related managers.

2) Health care companies are represented by about 15% of the respondents in Seattle and
Utah, but by less than 5% in Los Angeles and Denver.

3) The computer industry, which played no part in the Harvard study, is represented by almost 11% of the respondents in Denver.

4) Services make up the employers of almost 30% of the participants in Utah, while this industry accounts for less than 20% in the other two areas.

Culture, as it is represented by industries, can affect feelings of job insecurity, such as those created by massive layoffs in the aerospace industry in Southern California. It can also represent a positive outlook toward the employment picture, such as that represented by the growing communications business in Denver or the health care business in Utah. Even in Southern California, the entertainment business is growing to make up some of the loss of jobs from the aerospace business. It is difficult to disentangle the corporate culture from the answers of those who filled out the surveys. I finished the interviews with an overall positive feeling about the future of business and the business atmosphere in each city.

My visits to the four schools began with an interview. I had requested this time to speak with each program director, as an addition to the case study information I was compiling. This interview, which lasted from one to two hours, was designed to ask some of the questions included in my research[17]. They included:

1) How has the ethnic/gender make-up of the program changed in the past ten years?
2) Does the school feel that they are meeting the needs of the corporate clients ?
3) How has the change in job security changed the student population and the reasons they come to your school?
4) Has the support from industry changed in the past five years, and, if so, how?

Although some industries, such as aerospace in Southern California, have lowered their employment in that particular marketplace, the corporations themselves have not lessened their long-term commitment to executive education.

5) What is the most critical need for your school to face in order to continue to be competitive as we go into the next century?

Presentation of the interviews will cover these questions in sequence. The four school interviews will be followed by a summary of the general impressions obtained from the interviews.

The University of California at Los Angeles

The Anderson School at UCLA has three distinct programs. They include the following:

1) MBA, for students coming out of undergraduate programs. It is a full-time program that currently has 600 students, 300 entering and 300 in their second year.
2) FEMBA, the fully employed MBA program. The average age is 30, with six years of work experience. The FEMBA program is a three-

---

[17] A copy of the interview is included in appendix H.

year program, meeting either on Saturday or one afternoon and Saturday morning. Two class sections of approximately 65 students are admitted each fall. There are currently 380 students enrolled in the FEMBA program.

3) EMBA, the executive MBA program, for those with more work experience. Most are between 30 and 39 years of age.

The EMBA program is designed for those individuals who want to continue on their career path while securing a prestigious MBA from a top tier business school. I chose the EMBA program because it was closest to the programs at the other three schools.

The EMBA program has been in existence for 40 years. Classes take place on alternating Friday/Saturday combinations. Instruction lasts from 9:30 a.m. to 5:00 p.m. on Friday and from 8:30 a.m. to 4:00 p.m. on Saturday. The program fee for the 1995-96 year was $26,375 a year, including the international trip and a notebook computer. The fee for the 1996-97 year is $27,900. I expected the size and location of UCLA to offer a mix of students that would add to the validity of my results. Table 56 is a profile of students in terms of age:

Table 59 UCLA Age profile

Age	% of Students
30-34 years	22%
35-39 years	48%
40-45 years	23%
Over 45 years	7%

The Andrews/Powell study found the average age to be 43.3, with 76% between 36 and 50. My research received participation from significantly younger people, with an average of 37, almost 15% younger than the original participants.

Listed below, in Table 60, is the current profile of the UCLA students by industry and the industry representation from the Harvard study:

Table 60 UCLA industry profile

Industry	UCLA EMBA Profile	1959 Harvard Study
Manufacturing	28%[18]	46.6%
Retail	3%	2.7%
Entertainment	4%	0%[19]
Government	4%	8%
Computer-related communications	7%	Not included
Services, professions	14%	2%
Real Estate, Development	8%	21%(including mining, oil)
Health care	13%	Not included
Banking, finance	12%	6% (including real estate)

Even though the Harvard categories are not easily translated into the expanded communications categories of today, it is clear from this chart that banking, finance, and health care are major players in the UCLA program. As it turned out, these industries are major players in all of the programs. The switch from a manufacturing based economy to a services based economy is very evident from this comparison of students attending management programs in the 1950's vs. 1996.

On June 8, 1995, The Anderson School officially opened its new seven building management education complex. According to the EMBA 1996 brochure, this addition is "the most technologically advanced business education facility in the world." Every seat in the classrooms, breakout rooms, and the library is wired for use of notebook computers and networked for interactive capabilities. One of the "exceptional extras" highlighted in their brochure is that the UCLA Library System is ranked in the top five among the nation's colleges and universities. The 1996 brochure also states that "the primary goal of the program is to help students become effective leaders and managers in a world marked by uncertainty and change." Seventy people are chosen each year to work together for this intensive 24-month degree program. During the final seven months of the program, the field study allows students to conduct an extensive project for an international firm, and to travel abroad while completing their research.

The Dean of the Anderson School is Dr. William P. Pierskalla. Their new director is Dr. William Broesamle, who came from G.M.A.C. Gary Lindblad, with whom I met, is the Associate Director of the Executive and Fully Employed MBA Programs. Mr. Lindblad has been at UCLA for three years, where he is also pursuing a Ph.D. in Education. His research focuses on the use of the notebook computer in executive education.

I asked about their faculty. Mr. Lindblad said that they use mostly full-time professors, both tenured and non-tenured. They use very few seasoned executives without academic credentials; these people are brought in as speakers. Their professors teach in all three programs.

1) <u>Ethnic/gender make-up of the program?</u>

Part of my research was to query the reaction of a population made up of men and women because the Harvard study included no women. Mr. Lindblad told me that he had seen a picture in their lobby of the first program in the 1950's. There were no women at that time. In the past four years, they have had some increase in female applications. They have been able to get as high as 35% in the Fully Employed MBA Program (FEMBA), where the students are younger. The number is a little lower in the EMBA Program, under 30%. Mr. Lindblad feels that UCLA has been pretty good at putting some successful female students in front of prospective applicants at the information sessions.

Mr. Lindblad also told me that the national percentage of female participants has gone down. There seems to be an increase in female applications to education and some

---

[18] Including aerospace.
[19] Amusement was listed in the Harvard returns, but it garnered only 5 of 6,068 respondents.

other traditionally friendly places for women. The administration wonders if there is communication from women who went through the EMBA program "and it wasn't what they thought it would be …and sharing with younger people who were thinking of going to the program: "It didn't do everything that I thought it would do", or "the glass ceiling is still being experienced." So maybe that created the younger people in business looking elsewhere." In April of 1996, the offers UCLA made put the female participation at 27%.

We also spoke about the ethnic diversity that I expected to find. In terms of funding, Mr. Lindblad said that "there may be funding and scholarships for under-represented groups to go into full-time programs so they may not choose the executive program in the same proportion." Although there is some representation of East Indian, Pakistani and Asian students, African-American and Hispanic applicants are more likely to enter the full-time programs because of the availability of greater financial support.

2) Does the school feel that they are meeting the needs of the corporate clients?

Mr. Lindblad answered this question by stating the following:

> I'm sure there's always some distance between what corporate people want and what we're giving. There's always a distance between what corporate thinks they want and what faculty think is valuable…The thing is, corporate American doesn't think like a monolith, either. One wants people skills and the other wants technical skills. One wants the latest in technology and another wants more functional areas. That's problematic.

He shared that one of the reasons for starting the EMBA Program was to be connected to corporate America. It was felt that the students would help the faculty to refrain from getting too far off the mark. This program is a direct feedback loop from participants. " Twenty-seven thousand dollars a year, that's about as direct as you can get. They are not a shy group. Whatever subject is being taught is probably being taught to five or six people from that profession." According to Gary Lindblad, this reality has been good for the faculty. In addition, the University has taken the following steps to improve relevancy:

1) The office of executive education provides specialized non-degree programs for corporate executives.

2) They use the same faculty and find it a good feedback loop.

3) The Board of Visitors works with the dean's office and meets two times a year to talk about the plans of the school

All of the programs have evaluations. At UCLA, the process is anonymous. The evaluations are read by the faculty and the administration, and they decide whether instructors will be invited back. UCLA has un-invited people.

I asked Mr. Lindblad the same question I was asking of the alumni being interviewed: what advice do you think students would give the school? He responded that students want to be heard and they want what is happening in their business to be incorporated into projects. In other words, they want their professional experiences integrated into the educational experience.

3) <u>How has the change in job security affected your student population ?</u>

Mr. Lindblad said that

> we started seeing, about three years ago, a real increase in both the EMBA and the FEMBA students in their desire to get career counseling and to use career management services. So...we put together a set of readings and what came out of that was a new approach to connecting our students with career services and we hired a 50% time career counselor who works with FEMBA and EMBA because we saw so much traffic. The approach the EMBAs take has to be different. The average salary in the EMBA program is $100,000 a year, $80,000 if you took the doctors out.

One of my questions was whether students use the EMBA as a stepping stone to a better job. I was told that is the case for the "EMBA less so than the FEMBA Program. Students in their late 20's or 30's are more in transition."

4) <u>Support from Industry</u>.

UCLA has seen changes in the past few years, particularly because many of their students previously came from aerospace. One of the nice things about aerospace was that there were very generous and broad reimbursement programs available. Many of the supporting businesses now pinpoint their educational dollars more closely. During the chapter reporting the corporate interviews I conducted, I referred to a survey done by the Rand Corporation, where nearly all of the dozen aerospace firms with a major Southern California presence have slashed more than a third of the workforce in their region since 1989 (Peltz,1996,p.D1). With that being the case, participation from aerospace companies in the research I conducted was still almost 17% of the total from that school. UCLA has noticed the need for some managers in aerospace companies to take some of the skills they have developed and transfer them to other areas of the firm.

Applications at UCLA are up despite the decline in aerospace because other industries have arrived to take its place. This past year, they received 180 applications for 70 spots. In the FEMBA program, they got 420 applications for 132 spots. The entertainment industry is up and biotech is up, so they are receiving support from companies like Disney, Twentieth Century Fox, AMGEN, and other companies in the health care industry. According to Gary Lindblad, there has also been an increase in other professionals, including attorneys and physicians.

5) The most critical need for the school to face

Mr. Lindblad feels that UCLA has been putting its energy into technology, evidenced by the vast capabilities of the new Anderson seven-building management complex. But they need to be sure that they are getting the productivity bump required by the investment into the computer technology.

UCLA feels that a second critical challenge is getting excellent faculty and retaining young faculty, as well as promoting the perception of Los Angeles as a positive place to live.

The third challenge is to focus their advertising, both to relate to a changing sponsor base and to the changing needs of their student base. Some of the changes that have been made in light of the above were outlined for me:

a) The program has changed some with the electives, which are usually chosen by the students. The different make-up of students is starting to drive those changes, which include an elective on the Internet and one on health care.

b) Some of the core courses have fallen out of the core. One approach that they've taken is to integrate some issues throughout the program rather than to teach them as a separate course.

c) Their international field study has been a part of the program for 12 years, so that is where they do a lot of the international integration. In addition, more literature on international companies exists, enabling a further integration into the regular course-work.

d) UCLA has increased their efforts to make sure their students have the appropriate quantitative skills to maximize their participation in the program.

Conclusion

UCLA has been fortunate to have built a reputation which shields them from some of the competition the other executive education programs feel. They have also invested heavily in the technology they see as a stepping stone to the requirements for the next century.

Differences between what the corporate sponsors want, what the students want, and what the faculty feel is important are the same at UCLA as they appear to be at all the schools. However, my interview with Gary Lindblad convinced me that they go out of their way to try to react to student requests for adjustments to their program.

The University of Colorado

The University of Colorado is recognized as the leading university in the Rocky Mountain Region. They have approximately 44,500 students on four campuses, which include the downtown Denver Executive Program, the Boulder campus, the Denver campus, and the Colorado Springs campus. According to their current brochure, their MBA programs boast the following rankings:

1) CU College of Business was ranked in the top 6% of business schools in the country by *U.S. News and World Report* (9/18/95).

2) CU was ranked among the top four universities in the nation among 300 major universities and colleges in the United States by the 1996 *Fiske Guide to Colleges*.

The University of Colorado Executive MBA Program brings together resources from the three CU Business Schools to "create relevant programs for managers (University of Colorado, 1996)." From their 160 full-time faculty, the University of Colorado chooses experienced and committed professionals to develop and teach CU's Executive MBA Program. In the fifteen years since its inception, over 500 managers have participated in the University of Colorado Executive MBA Program. In the spirit of the three-campus system, the "letter from the deans" in their 1996 brochure is signed by the deans of the three business schools as well as by Susan Bunker, the Associate Dean of Executive Programs. The valuable benefits cited by the deans include:

*Investing in the future by developing skills.

*Introducing to the student new competencies and ideas for their companies.

*Receiving a superior education without significant interruption of their career.

Like the other programs, the CU program is a 22 month program. CU is an AACSB accredited institution that combines the resources and strengths of the

University's three Graduate Schools of Business to provide a rigorous program using resources not available to other schools in the region. For the class entering in the Fall of 1996, tuition for the entire Executive MBA Program is $28,480. The tuition covers tuition and fees for all courses, all textbooks, related software and instructional materials, refreshments, lodging for the first year retreat, and travel and lodging for the participant during the international trip.

A key element in the CU program is the use of study groups, which I found to be one of the most important benefits cited by both the people who responded to the surveys and those I interviewed personally. Study groups are composed of five to eight individuals chosen based on desire for diversity of background and geographic proximity for the weekly study group meetings. Classes meet one full day, once a week, on alternating Fridays and Saturdays-thus minimizing disruption of participants' work schedule. During the week-long orientation, teamwork exercises are held. But, as I found out by talking with alumni from all four schools, the study groups do not always work for all members. The University of Colorado administration does not intervene into study group disputes, and the study groups are advised to move around if that works better for them. Ms. Bunker and Mr. Guthrie listen, and negotiate, but they never give a directive to the study groups regarding their situation. As we agreed, you don't become a manager without being able to work with groups of people, and there will always be people you don't get along with. In addition to the orientation week, they have a retreat, which has two functions: 1) To have a wrap-up to the first year and a transition to the second year, in addition to a reinforcement for the significant other in the relationship; 2) To provide a chance for the class to bond with their study groups. In contrast to the social occasions mentioned in the Harvard study, this retreat adds some academic pieces in addition to the chance to move off-site.

Courses in the first year "provide the knowledge necessary to identify, analyze, and solve problems in the functional fields of business....Participants then integrate these functional disciplines in the second-year courses using strategic planning exercises, case studies, and computer simulation games (ibid.)" Participants follow a scheduled program of course offerings, culminating in the international visit, which is integrated into the curriculum and includes visits to plants and headquarters of companies, discussions with foreign managers, cultural activities, and more. Their destinations have included Munich, Stockholm, and Prague.

Classes are held at the University of Colorado Executive Education Center, in Denver. Several of the interview participants told me how nice it was to have their own classroom, and to have faculty come to them, rather than disrupting the already full days with moving from room to room.

The average age of participants is 38. The respondents to my survey were a mean age of 39. They averaged 16 years of work experience. Over 50% of my sample have been with their corporations between six and fifteen years. Seventeen per cent have master's degrees or above. I interviewed several engineers with technical master's degrees, who felt that the MBA was the right addition to their already extensive education.

As with all of the programs I studied, the CU program is heavily supported by the administrative staff, who address aspects such as books and many of the details that make the participants' educational experience more productive. Like the study groups, the support the students receive from Scott Guthrie, the Program Director, and from Susan Bunker, the Associate Dean, adds to their positive evaluation of the program. The alumni I interviewed felt that between 20% and 25% of their program rating is due to the important role that Ms. Bunker and Mr. Guthrie play.

The 1996 brochure states that 50% of participants have their program cost paid in full by their organizations. The numbers coming from my survey statistics were 43.24%. Twenty-five per cent of participants fund their own programs, which comes close to the 29% who answered my survey and stated that they had been responsible for 100% of their tuition.

In addition to their Executive MBA Program, the University of Colorado offers graduate programs in business at their Boulder, Colorado Springs, and Denver campuses. Their Executive Master's Program in Health Administration is offered by CU-Denver, the Network for Healthcare Management. It is an innovative distance-learning program which takes twenty-five months to complete, including ten weeks on campus; the remainder of the curriculum is completed using computer conferencing.

On July 15, 1996, Scott Guthrie greeted me as I arrived at the Denver office of the CU Executive MBA program. He then introduced me to Susan Bunker, the Associate Dean of the program, who had asked to be included in the review of my material.

We started our interview by talking about the backgrounds of the administrators. Scott Guthrie has been with the program for seven years, having previously been a banking operations officer. Susan Bunker was recruited from Boston University, where she started the executive MBA program, three years ago. We spent a few minutes talking about the CU students. Mr. Guthrie said that "the type of student we have recruited lately has reflected the economy of Colorado, which has changed. People feel the need to cover any option that might come up." CU also finds its executive students fairly demanding. In addition, the surveys showed that participants react very positively to the facilities and services provided for them, such as books ready when they get to class, so I knew that this was an important part of the equation. However, the "line between providing a service so that they can attend graduate school vs. a program so that they can dictate what the program consists of (is blurring)." Some of this may be a response to a new trend noted in futurist Faith Popcorn's latest book, Clicking (1996), that of "vigilante customer," where customers can manipulate the marketplace through pressure, protest, and politics. Because the Executive Program receives no state funding, they must disperse their income in three directions, throughout the three universities making up the University of Colorado system. Based on the reactions of the alumni who were interviewed and filled out surveys, this program is reacting to the consumer challenge very well.

1. Ethnic/gender make-up of the program?

I expressed to Mr. Guthrie that I was disappointed not to see more ethnic and racial diversity in the respondents to my survey. He said that "we struggle to have a representation of diversity in the class... I think the number of women in the program has probably remained consistent... But the students we get reflect the students who are in the business community. We know that about 50% of our students have their programs funded, but there are also scholarships available so that financial need should not be an issue for truly qualified applicants."

We talked about the age and marital situation for their students. My survey results showed that 80% of their students were married, higher than the other schools. Ms. Bunker admitted that the program puts stress on a marriage. "As their confidence level goes up, they are anxious to move on things. In that sense, I think the program contributes to that." The class of '96 had four divorces.

In terms of age, their surveys show their average right around 37 or 38, which coincides with my results. This is about five years younger than the mean in the Andrews' research, but Mr. Guthrie said that their participants are getting younger. In smaller companies, they "have 30 year olds with incredible careers; the software industry is an industry with young people who have done very well."

2. Does the school feel that they are meeting the needs of the corporate clients?

Both Ms. Bunker and Mr. Guthrie had comments about this. Ms. Bunker said that "the tricky thing is, who is the customer?....If you have a class that's not just one company—are Lockheed's needs the same as a small company? What possible program could you have? It's just such a complex question." She had the following remarks:

> I have a hard time because I think corporate relevancy is a shorter-term view of things—did those students come back on Monday being able to do something differently? (That is)my impression of what corporate America says to us. I have a view of education that is much longer, and they would argue way too squishy and not outcome-based....When is it you were going to measure that? At the end of the course, at the end of the year, five years out? We get feedback from students that is five and ten years out, that says "It's the way you taught me to think." I believe we help people think differently. Better thinking, better understanding of how to get resources.

With regard to working toward improving the relevancy for corporate customers, both Ms. Bunker and Mr. Guthrie said that they do surveys, they talk with them all the time, and they undergo constant curriculum reviews. Their attrition due to corporate moves this year has been high, so they've been making sure that they change their schedule in some way that allows for corporate moves. In addition, the school has "a fair number of projects that are based in their corporations."

The other component to the relevancy issue is the faculty. As a research institution, faculty are required to maintain contacts with the community. Each of the deans has an advisory council. In addition, there are institutional committees in place that feed information back to the administration at the executive program.

One response to a question interested me. I had been hearing a fair amount about "dead wood" faculty in my interviews with all the EMBA alumni, and the fact that tenure allows some outdated people to remain at a university where they may no longer be contributing. Ms. Bunker said that "faculty do not have tenure with the Executive

Program. If a faculty member does not work out for us, I say to the Dean, "it's not working out.""

Scott Guthrie manages evaluations of every class. The faculty see the comments once they have been typed, so it is a good way of determining if a faculty member needs to make changes.

CU's philosophy is that they are constantly trying to improve. They have trends in terms of what advertising works and whether or not direct mail works. In terms of the curriculum, they have updated it to make it more user friendly for the students. They introduced a brand new marketing program this past year. As these are not short-term decisions, CU is constantly struggling with the time it takes to implement a program vs. the necessity to bring it to market as quickly as possible. I asked specifically how the program has changed in the past ten years, to which Mr.Guthrie answered,

> how hasn't it changed! We've done curriculum issues, little things every year, big things every five. The big things are that the retreat has been incorporated and the international trip has been incorporated. The international trip is a response to the diversity and globalization in the business world.

3. How has the change in job security affected your student population?

Another issue affecting the University of Colorado's Executive Program is the fact that job security has changed greatly in the past ten years. Mr. Guthrie and Ms. Bunker told me that the decision to come to CU is harder for some people because they might not be there long enough. The people they attract are highly motivated, and "could easily move on without the MBA."

4) Support from industry

Support by industry changes the student population as well. Ms. Bunker said that "some companies withdraw support and then come back. Recently, more companies are sponsoring. Coors pays for the whole thing now; there were a couple of years when it was only 50%. Hewlett Packard, IBM, and AT&T participants are still 100% sponsored."

Regarding future enrollment, Ms. Bunker and Mr. Guthrie said that there are two forces: the force of the faculty wanting a class of thirty and the force of the deans wanting a class of sixty. The 1996 target is 45 students, which would, through attrition, bring it down to a little over forty. With relation to frequent corporate moves that seem to heavily affect this program, normal statistical forecasting does not work for CU because one year does not predict the next. This makes it even tougher to settle on a number for admissions that will end up with the optimum class size.

Competition

Denver, unlike Utah and Washington, faces "incredible competition." Denver is the major population center for hundreds of miles. Denver has more AACSB accredited programs than most schools in a similar urban area. The University of Denver is starting a Friday/Saturday program every two weeks, vs. the every week, alternating Friday or Saturday program of CU. In addition, Colorado State, based in Ft. Collins, is opening an executive program in Denver. The result, is that, according to Mr. Guthrie, "unless you hustle, you don't get the quality of students. We are probably battling with the University of Denver for one-half of our students"

5. The most critical need for the school to face.

In answer to this question, Scott Guthrie said that "in my opinion, we have to continue to do what we are doing so that our alums continue to be the main source of our students….That is the most critical need."

Conclusion

I had an advantage during this visit to CU's Denver campus because, unlike the other visits, I had the benefit of having completed most of the statistics from the surveys so that we could discuss specific comments. Ms. Bunker and Mr. Guthrie were delighted to see that their school ranked between 'above average' and 'excellent' on evaluations by the alumni of the program and the faculty. The descriptive comments were important to them because they gave them valid information about what the program is doing right and what the students would like to see changed.

As I continued my interviews into the next day, I consistently heard the comment that "Scott and Susan really went out of their way for us." This element of the participant evaluation of the program should have implications for other schools as they search for program directors who can fill this difficult assignment.

The University of Utah

The University of Utah is situated on 1,535 acres located five minutes from downtown Salt Lake City. The University campus includes 280 buildings and employs 3, 4440 full and part-time faculty. The 17 schools and colleges provide education to 25,868 students. There are 67 undergraduate majors and graduate degrees in 2 disciplines. The student population is comprised of 56% men and 44% women (University of Utah, 1996).

The David Eccles School of Business was founded 20 years ago and is named after a Scottish immigrant whose contributions to the university have been extensive. John W. Seybolt is the current dean. It is accredited by the American Association of Collegiate Schools of Business. The mission statement of the David Eccles School of Business, as published in their current catalog, reads as follows:

The mission of the David Eccles School of Business is to be the acknowledged leader in undergraduate, graduate and executive business education in the Intermountain Region and among the select group of the most respected schools of business in the nation.

Through the synergy of excellent, innovative and visible teaching, research and service, we will build foundations for business leadership with service to students and the business communities of Utah, the region and the nation.

The Executive MBA degree requires a commitment to the intensive 21-month program. It is designed for managers with at least five years of significant work experience who hold a bachelor's degree and a superior academic record.

Classes are held during the regular quarter system one day per week, alternating between Fridays and Saturdays. In addition to courses during the semester, students attend three one-week intensive sessions. The first intensive week is the first week of the program, and the second week is held one year later. Both intensive sessions are held at a local resort area, where the student is in residence during the session.

The third intensive week is at the end of the final portion of the program and encompasses the international trip, where the students are given an opportunity for first-hand learning during visits to businesses in foreign countries. According to Dave Dungan, the international trip has always been at the top of the list for students. The experiences in which the students participate range from political and academic to banks, pharmaceutical companies, and visits to automobile manufacturers such as Mercedes.

The current cost of the EMBA program is $18,500 for the entire 21-month period. The cost is all-inclusive of the costs of the program and covers tuition, fees, parking permits, books, computer time, Friday luncheons, and all expenses relating to the three intensive sessions, except meals on the foreign trip. Maximum class interaction is assured by limiting admissions to a class size of 40 (Ibid.).

David Dungan is the Director, Executive Education Programs. Before he retired from the Navy after 30 years, he was a Professor of Naval Science on the campus of the University of Utah. He retired from the Navy at 51 to take this job, after earning an MA from Webster College. I was able to spend the entire day of April 1st, 1996 with Mr. Dungan, as he showed me around the campus and pointed out landmarks. From my interviews with alumni, I soon learned the Dave Dungan plays a very important part in the reputation of the school among its graduates.

1) <u>Ethic/gender make-up of the program.</u>

"We get three kinds of students," I was told. The first think "I'd better get this" because the competition is very tough. " They don't necessarily come to us thinking that they are going to change careers or jobs, though that happens to more of them than they would think." Because of re-engineering, downsizing, etc., people all of a sudden find themselves out of a job. The second want to move and want to change jobs or careers. "They see this as their ticket." The most amazing group, Mr. Dungan told me, "are the older guys who aren't afraid of losing their jobs and aren't looking for change, but want to be able to perform their job better. They don't even care if they get a degree."

I asked about diversity in the business world. Although there is very little ethnic diversity in their program, Mr. Dungan said that sponsors are always asked the question, "what can we do to diversify." He stated that they have put in a part that is global, an international track, where they teach classes in other languages. They have also aligned themselves with the language department so they can teach business French and business German so the manager can read the Asian Wall Street Journal. "If we've done something really neat, it's our efforts to internationalize. We're getting a lot of help from a grant from the Department of Education. We have as a result of that the center for international education and research. I'm really very proud of that globalization"

<u>Does the school feel that they are meeting the needs of the corporate clients?</u>

One of my survey interests was whether or not companies make use of the skills that students gain from the program. Mr. Dungan said that they do not have the information "in any direct or formal way, and maybe we should. ....We get it back informally by the same people sending us more students. I infer from that that they are satisfied or they wouldn't send us anybody else. We do have a pretty good connect with the business community. Our Dean hears that "this works, this doesn't work." The business community tells us they are looking for more of an emphasis on the people skills, the organizational behavior as opposed to the quantitative kinds of stuff."

I was interested in curriculum review and class evaluation. Mr. Dungan said that evaluations are required at the end, but, also, that "they spend a lot of time with me and they level with me and tell me what's on their mind.....Sometimes I find the informal feedback more accurate than the formal, when these guys write an evaluation." About every three or four years, Dave Dungan goes out to a few classes and asks questions in order to formulate an evaluation. The curriculum review committee meets once a year.

In terms of teaching skills, Mr. Dungan said that "the most critical element is the professor in the classroom." It is critical that they relate the real world to what is being studied. I asked if he would support relaxing the requirement for a Ph.D. for those with a lot of experience. His answer was "yes, if they are good teachers." He said that 90% of the professors bring the best of the theoretical and practical worlds together.

I was wondering about tuition reimbursement. Mr. Dungan said that about 70% of the participants are funded to some degree. This ranges from the total program to just tuition. His prior remark that the third type of student, those who just want the knowledge and don't care about the degree, may just pay for it themselves, was supported by this comment.

The brochure for the Executive Master of Business Administration at the University of Utah includes quotations from past graduates. I was able to interview two of them while I was in Salt Lake. The following comments are representative of those found in the literature:

1987 graduate:

> Two things stand out for me. First, being able to come to the University one day per week and have many of the tools assembled for me was a life saver.....The

second, and most important aspect was my fellow students…..I learned as much from them as from the professors.

1991 graduate:

My experience at the Executive MBA program was unparalleled. Although the two years I spent were two of the most challenging years I have ever had, they were also two of the most exciting, rewarding, and instructive.

Perhaps one of the greatest benefits of the program was the removal of the traditional wall dividing professors from students. I was given the opportunity of engaging in discussions with highly qualified, highly educated, and highly successful teachers who cared about my future and my learning experience.

4) Support from industry.

In answer to my question about changes in corporate support, Mr. Dungan told me that it has changed as industry has looked at this downsizing thing. They feel they have less and less money to spend on these types of things. People who used to send us people just don't. They can't afford to let them go to day programs. But, again, we get more and more students every year. It may increase enrollment because people know that they're going to have to have whatever gives them the edge. ….Maybe they're paying on their own as opposed to otherwise.

5) The most critical need for the school to face.

When asked about changes for the future, Mr. Dungan stated that they will have to look at distance learning, and "at the electronic means (through which) we can deliver some of this stuff." He said that marketing plans are not changing a lot right now, but "if we change our format, the delivery system….more and more stuff using distance learning, using the capability that technology is giving us, I think we can go after a totally different person, one that can be further away, one that doesn't have to be here one day a week."

Conclusion

The University of Utah was the first site visited for this research. I found the needs for competitiveness in the future fairly consistent, however, with the other schools. Utah shares the desire for a more diverse student body, but they also share the extensive steps they take to make sure their program is current and responsive to their sponsors' needs. Continued enrollment is expected based on their large base of sponsors and their work within the community to strengthen their customer base.

The University of Washington

Since its inception in 1983, the University of Washington Executive MBA Program has "set the standard for management and executive development in the Northwest (Bradford,1996)." It has repeatedly received national recognition. Founded in 1861, the University of Washington has sixteen schools and colleges offering instruction in more than one hundred academic disciplines. The Graduate School of Business Administration is accredited by the American Assembly of Collegiate Schools of Business and is a member of the Graduate Management Admission Council. Their programs include the Executive Master of Business Administration, the Master of Business Administration, the Master of Professional Accounting, the Doctoral Program, and Executive Programs. As such, the University of Washington was one of the first schools in the western United States to offer graduate business degrees.

The Executive Master of Business Administration (EMBA) Program is a two-year course of study which "serves individuals who have been identified as potential general managers, as well as those already in senior management ranks (U. of Washington, 1996)"
Enrollment is limited to assure maximum interaction between students and faculty members, but enrollment will increase from 48 to 50 with the opening of the Seafirst Executive Education Center, scheduled for completion in early 1997.

The program meets one day per week, either Friday or Saturday, beginning with a one-week residence week in September. The fee for the University of Washington Executive MBA Program is $17,000 per academic year. The fee includes tuition, books, course materials, residence weeks, parking on class days, meals, and food and refreshments at hosted social functions. The University of Washington does not include an international trip in their program at this time.

On July 8th, 1996, I met with Nina Sanders, the Director of Executive Programs at the University of Washington, located in Northeast Seattle. She has been in this position for seven years, when she left a training and development position in the financial industry to become an educator in the academic discipline. Ms. Sanders holds a Masters Degree in Education from the University of Pennsylvania.

Student Population

Program participants average age 37, with 15 years of work experience and nine years of managerial experience. Currently, there are 180 MBA students and 90 enrolled in the EMBA program. Organizations represented in each class range in size from Fortune 500 companies such as Boeing and Microsoft, to entrepreneurial start-ups and small non-profits. The University of Washington EMBA brochure lists the participation of males as 62% and that of females as 38%. I sent surveys to 60 people, 68% male and 31% female. The actual surveys returned had a representation of 72% male and 23% female, with 2.8% declining to specify gender. This means that a higher percentage of the men who received the survey returned it. In this sense, my population showed fewer females than has been The University of Washington's recent experience.

In terms of industry representation, Table 61 lists the industries their brochure outlines, those identified in the Harvard study, and the actual results of my research:

Table 61 Industry participation for U. of Washington vs. Harvard

Industry	Research participants from the University of Washington.	Harvard Study
Agriculture/Forestry /Mining/Construction /Petroleum	1 2.8%	21%
Manufacturing /Aerospace	12 34%	46.6%
Transportation /Communication	3 8.5%	12.4%
Services	4 11.4%	10.7%
Wholesale/Retail	3 8.5%	2.7%
Finance/Ins./Real Estate	3 8.5%	2.7%
Health Care	5 14.2%	0
Computers	3 8.5%	0

The only area showing a marked difference in expected numbers vs. actual returns was finance, insurance, and real estate, where industry representation is published in the program brochure as 16%, while the representation in my population was 8.5%, or half of what I would have expected. The increase in financial industry participation from the time of the Harvard survey was as I expected, a marked increase from the 6.5% of the participants who came from this industry in the late 1950's.

1) Ethnic/gender make-up of the program.

Participation by ethnic minorities is listed as 12% in their brochure, which means that at least four of my respondents should have listed their ethnic classification as other than Anglo, White. The 33 people who identified their ethnicity all classified themselves as Anglo, White. One of my research questions was to query the increased ethnic minorities that I thought would be included in current executive programs. The participants from the University of Washington did not show the expected diversity. In speaking with Ms. Sanders about the ethnic/gender make-up of the school and how it has changed in the past ten years, she said that they think they draw Asians very well. "We've been disappointed in the number of African Americans. We have done very aggressive outreach and have concluded that there are so few people in the ranks that the executive MBA programs draw from. We're not in control of that....There may be minorities out there that we'd love to have, but, if their companies aren't going to sponsor them, we're not going to get them." She shared with me that this is frustrating to them, but that they are trying to work with it. The University of Washington, however, is very pleased with the participation of women. Ms. Sanders said that "our percentage of women has ranged from 25-40%."

2) Does the school feel that they are meeting the needs of the corporate clients?

The University of Washington administers evaluations after every class. In addition, they do focus group evaluations at the end of each quarter. One representative from each study group is asked to comment on everything from courses to what they are serving at lunch. Ms. Sanders said that the evaluations of the courses parallel the faculty strengths. They use primarily full-time faculty from the University of Washington. While she commented that "yes, we are meeting them", she said that "we're also always checking on that; always asking for feedback, both from the students and sponsoring organizations. We have an advisory board."

The University of Washington feels that it is very important to maintain their standards in terms of getting the quality of students that they want. This is part of their response to the quality of education that the sponsoring organizations expect.

Before students are enrolled, Ms. Sanders said that "we are very strict about the expectations and the rigor." In terms of the study groups that were common to all of my sites, she told me that "our feeling is that we want to provide a valuable experience to our students that will help them be more successful in the business world." She also acknowledged "that doesn't mean that they're going to love everything that they experience because they're not going to love everything they experience out in the business world."

3) How has the change in job security affected your student population?

Ms. Sanders said that this change has affected their students in a couple of ways. Some people are "applying because they are keenly aware that there is no such thing as job security and they want to increase their marketability....Some people change jobs while they are in the program." I found the above to be the case with representatives of all four schools. Ms. Sanders commented that, when a participant changes jobs while in the program, and goes to a company that does not support the program, there are problems. But this was a minor issue for most of the participants. I found that the necessity to upgrade skills and be marketable was the overriding impetus for participants to pursue the Executive MBA.

4) Support from industry.

Boeing continues to be a major supporter of this program, making up 31% of my participants. With regard to Boeing, Ms. Sanders said that "they have had their ups and downs, but it really hasn't had much impact on their participation in the program." They "see this program as something for the long-term for them," and "they continue to send us just about the same amount of people."

About 60% of the University of Washington students have their program funded in full by their sponsors. In my population of respondents, 54% had their programs funded entirely and 5.7% had between 80% and 99% funded.

In terms of the sponsors, Ms. Sanders said that there has been more attempt to keep in touch with sponsors over the past few years. Also, the curriculum is evolving in response to input from sponsors and students alike.

5. The most critical need for the school to face.

Ms. Sanders told me that "the school needs to be concerned with the quality of the faculty and whether they can teach executives. Whether they can continue to provide a curriculum that is academically substantive........(We need to) keep the curriculum evolving to meet developing needs. " My surveys and interviews for the four schools brought out several complaints about professors who should not be teaching but who, because of the tenure system, were allowed to maintain their position. Because the University of Washington uses faculty from their regular MBA program to teach in their executive program, if someone chose not to teach in the executive program, it would not leave space for an entirely new faculty position. Providing good teachers as well as good scholars is an ongoing commitment for the University of Washington.

Another challenge is to "incorporate new technology." This was shared by all the schools. The need to get funding to add technological abilities such as on-screen projection always raises the problem of the trade-offs inherent in project financial support.

Conclusion

Nina Sanders was specific about the ways in which The University of Washington is working with their sponsors to respond to their needs and to prepare for future needs. They are fortunate in being able to attract high quality people each year and they realize that they must continue to upgrade their program to meet the needs of, not only future managers from current sponsors who will be coming, but also those from emerging high-tech industries who will expect the University of Washington to meet their needs as well. Maintaining high quality faculty and current educational programs are at the top of their list for responding to the needs of this program as we near the next century.

Chapter Summary

In response to the five main questions that made up my interview, the following general observations resulted:

1) In response to the query about a change in ethnic make-up, the program directors were as frustrated as I was that there is not more diversity in the EMBA classes. The consensus seemed to be that the ranks from which executive MBA programs draw do not yet include a large representation of ethnic minorities. This was in addition to the possibility that full scholarships are available for some of these people; thus, they would attend a full-time MBA program rather than one designed for working managers.

2) Matching student level of ability to course work continues to be a problem. As the program directors knew, I received a number of responses complaining about a lower level of ability than was expected of one's classmates. The general response from the program directors was that some people are particularly good in accounting and finance, while some people are better at managing people. The programs do offer remedial courses in math and quantitative skills before classes start. Great effort is made to place people in study groups such that there is an appropriate mix of the specific skills that will be covered in the program. In addition, efforts are being made in the selection process to raise the level of quantitative skills possessed by the entering classes.

My interviews with both program directors and students confirmed that the study groups are an important element of the program.

3) The change in job security has had a definite impact on why people choose an Executive MBA. The people I interviewed who had masters degrees in other fields still felt that they needed to have skills to make them marketable in a variety of ways. This was the consensus of all of the program directors. In addition, many of the participants

are changing careers in their mid-forties, so the MBA was critical to being current and being marketable in a new career. The numbers of attorneys and physicians in my population support the benefit of a general MBA for advancing one's career in a number of directions. Factors combining to encourage the addition of further academic credentials include the movement in the health care industry towards managed care, the saturation of people in some professions, and the corporate downsizing that continues to influence employment patterns.

4) Even though industry support has changed in several ways, all of my interviews confirmed that corporations are continuing to fund executive education programs as a long-term investment.

5) The most critical needs for these schools as they go into the next century include several:

> a) There were numerous complaints in the surveys about faculty who are outdated or not qualified to teach executives. The University of Colorado seems to have a good solution to this problem, where the faculty are not tenured in the executive program, while they may be tenured on their respective campus. Their 3-campus system makes this solution workable. However, the political problems and the problems that tenure creates have no current solutions.
>
> b) Incorporating new technology, in the right amount and at the right time, is an issue that all four schools face, especially the ones who are self-supporting.
>
> c) Finding the right balance between student requests for program revisions and school objectives continues to be a balancing act.

Other conclusions

a) The importance of the program director and his/her relationship with both prospective and current students was made clear during both the survey comments and the personal interviews.

b) Continued funding for executive programs does not seem to be in jeopardy, as new industries are replacing the ones, such as aerospace, where downsizing is occurring. Literature references to the concept of 'continuous learning', combined with the proportion of professionals seeking to leave areas such as medicine and law to accept business training, combine to assure this area of education a lucrative future. The only threat would be if they do not remain current in curriculum or stray from listening to their student/corporate advisors with regard to program adjustments.

CHAPTER 6

CORPORATE INTEVIEWS

The interviews with representatives of corporations who support executive education were held between January 17, 1996 and July 11, 1996. The ten interviews were conducted on premise as well as via phone, with a fax sent ahead to alert the participant to the nature of the questions. I obtained the names of these people through networking among current colleagues and classmates. I found that access to people at this level usually requires a contact, as my overtures to interview people from corporations such as Marriott Corporation and Microsoft, where I have no contacts, were met with no response. However, in every instance, the people I did interview were gracious about their time because they feel that support of executive education is one of the keys to future competitiveness. Table 62 provides the list of those interviewed.

Table 62 Corporate interviews

Corporation	Position	Date
Aerojet	General Manager	April 17th
Deloitte & Touche	Regional Managing Director	June 24th
Goulds Pumps	H. R. Director.	June 19th
McDonnell Douglas	Dir. of Ethics Compliance and Exec. Development	March 4 (Phone and fax)
Rainbird	Director of H.R.	June 5th
Southern California Edison	V.P., Human Resources	March 14th
Towers Perrin	Director of Success. Planning&Recruiting	March 19th (Phone & fax)
Xerox	Human Resources	July 11th
Toyota	National Manager	March 21st
Wellpoint	Exec. V. P.	February 20th

I used a similar format for interviewing each of the participants. The three areas on which the interviews focused include:

1) The current workplace.

2) Are courses relevant to needs?

3) Training expenditures.

I was interested in whether the corporations were getting their money's worth from the investment, whether they plan to continue investing at the same level, and what changes are being made in planned course content due to competitive or future economic situations. The following information reflects the feelings of these people, not necessarily the official position of their corporations. In every case, the information I used has been reviewed and approved by the executive interviewed.

As will be shown in the close of this chapter, the following conclusions were drawn from the interviews:

1) Corporations plan to spend more money in the future on training. Some of the literature suggests that this is also intended to improve employee loyalty. After "a decade of downsizing that left many workers traumatized, some American companies are cautiously trying to put words like "security" and "commitment" back into their relationships with employees (White, J.B. & Lublin, J.S., 1996, PB1)." For some of them, that means extending their in-house university and for some it means adding to management training programs.

2) Corporations are satisfied with the general skills being taught.

3) Corporations see a low risk that employees will use the financial support they have been given to seek other employment.

4) The greatest growth in hiring will be for people with specific skills, much of them gained through technology.

5) There is currently little in the way of programs to make specific use of the skills gained during the program.

6) Corporations are looking for rigor and intensity in the programs they fund, not a resort vacation.

I will start with an overview of the companies who participated in the interviews. I will then report their responses as they related to the three areas mentioned above: the current workplace, relevancy of course work to their needs, and corporate training expenditures, both now and in the future.

Corporate participants

The corporate participants were comprised of representatives of the aerospace business (Aerojet and McDonnel Douglas), manufacturing (Goulds Pumps, Rainbird, Xerox, and Toyota), consulting (Deloitte & Touche and Towers Perrin), utilities (Southern California Edison), and health care (Wellpoint). As the above comments relate, I was interested in the many ways in which these companies are similar when it comes to executive education.

1) **Aerojet**.

Aerojet, based in Azusa, California, is one of a dozen aerospace firms in Southern California who have slashed more than a third of their work forces since 1989 (Peltz, 1996, p.D1). California's aerospace industry has three main goals: lower costs, greater efficiency and better use of information technology. For Aerojet, I interviewed, Dr. Bob Culver, their former General Manager. The interview took place at The University of La Verne.

The Los Angeles Times reported, on March 17, 1996, that even where there is hiring, the jobs are in fields that frequently involve computer and scientific engineering skills, not "metal benders." GenCorp's Aerojet, a $1.8 billion aerospace company, saw it's employment drop from 2,400 in 1990 to 1,200 in 1995 (ibid.).

2. **Deloitte & Touche**

At Deloitte & Touche, I interviewed Bob Wetzel, the Regional Managing Director for the Deloitte & Touche Consulting Group. A private partnership, Deloitte Touche Tohmatsu International ranks among the 500 largest private companies in the US, with revenues estimated at over $5 billion (Boon, R., Jr. et. al., 1995).

As one of the world's top accounting, tax, and consulting firms, they offer a wide variety of services (Deloitte & Touche, 1996). According to company literature, among the top 500 companies, Deloitte & Touche clients generate over 20% of the group's revenues—a greater market share than that of any other firm.

The hiring program at Deloitte & Touche invoves recruiting from top rated schools, including the Claremont Colleges, and putting them to work for several years before sending them off to business school, where the education is funded by Deloitte & Touche via a tuition reimbursement program for those employees who excel.

3. Goulds Pumps, Incorporated.

At Goulds Pumps, I met with Jacqueline Kent, the Human Resources Manager for their Vertical Products Division, located in the City of Industry, California. Since their founding in 1848, Goulds Pumps has remained an important factor in the development of mining, agricultural, ranching and manufacturing industries. A public company since 1964, their sales in 1995 were $718 million, a 23% increase over 1994 (Goulds Pumps, Inc, 1995). Their many divisions and plants are housed as far away as Venezuela and The Peoples Republic of China. Goulds has 2,775 employees in the United States and 2,125 in international locations.

The imperatives, as listed in their 1995 annual report, include the following:

1) Improve profitability.
2) Drive internal growth.
3) Pursue external growth.
4) Optimize use of assets.
5) Create a new culture.

4. McDonnell Douglas

At McDonnell Douglas, I conducted the interview with Jac Meacham, the Director of Ethics Compliance and Executive Development at their headquarters in St. Louis.

McDonnell Douglas is a $14.3 billion player in the aerospace and defense industry, has 161,800 employees and ranks #1 in sales per employee in a Forbes industry analysis (Banks, H., 1996).

In the aerospace industry, 1995 profits were an estimated $4.5 billion, down from a record $5.65 billion in 1994. Employment is expected to decline for at least another three years (ibid.). McDonnell Douglas will be hiring fewer managers than they have in the past five years.

5. Rainbird

At Rainbird, I interviewed Licia Ramos, one of their directors of human resources. Rainbird Sprinkler Manufacturing Corp. is the largest manufacturer of irrigation systems in the world. They are a privately held company, based in Glendora, California, with six strategic business units and one international company.

Rainbird believes that training represents a critical element in giving people the knowledge and skills they will need to continue to excel with Rain Bird. To that end, their educational reimbursement program provides for 50% reimbursement with a "C" or better for approved programs. In addition to their educational reimbursement program, Rainbird offers a variety of in-house developed management courses and technical training to its employees. These include empowerment and front-line leadership. Rainbird's plans for hiring in the next five years are to increase recruiting on an overall basis.

6. Southern California Edison

Dr. Emiko Banfield is the Vice President of Human Resources at Southern California Edison, as well as a Vice President of Edison International. SCE Corporation, a public electric utility, reported sales of $8.3 billion for 1995 in the January 1, 1996 issue of Forbes. Dr. Banfield shared with me some of the challenges that affect the electric utility business in the new, uncharted world of competition.

According to Thomas R. Kuhn, "competition is coming swiftly to the electric power industry. Given the critical role that electricity plays in every US home and business, it is essential that deregulation of the industry benefit all electricity customers, not just large customers at the expense of small businesses and residences (Kuhn, 1996)." The debate continues to rage over who pays the costs associated with the investments the utilities have made under the traditional regulatory system. With that problem, and with comopetition in mind, Edison will be hiring more people, in order to infuse new and different skills into their company. Many of the people they are hiring tend to be more highly educated, with the business skills they need to help with the changes taking place because of the introduction of competition as their business mode.

7. Towers Perrin

At Towers Perrin, I interviewed Bea Lalla, their Director of Succession Planning. Towers Perrin is a $868 million privately owned multinational management consulting and risk management firm with corporate offices in Stamford, Connecticut (Kitchen & McCarthy, 1995). They have approximately 5,700 employees and 70 offices in 66 cities across 19 countries.

Towers Perrin will be hiring fewer managers in the next five years than in the past, but is continuing to experience excellent business growth and has been adding to its worldwide employee population on a steady basis.

8. Toyota Motor Sales, USA

Toyota Motor Sales, USA , is the $26 billion US division of Toyota Worldwide, whose sales are $ 110 billion (Flint, 1996). As I interviewed Mike Morrison, in the Office of the President, he told me that the current labor market for managerial jobs is only fair, but will be good in the future. Toyota's hiring plans for the next five years are to hire less than in the past give years, though Mr. Morrison sees the availability of talent as better in the future than it is now.

In terms of rank in the automobile industry, Toyota's size puts them third, behind General Motors, at $167 billion, and Ford Motor, at $136 billion (ibid.). Latest analysis by auto analysts predicts that Toyota's redesigned 1997 Camry could allow them to grab 27% of the market by late 1997 (Bremner, 1996).

9. Wellpoint

My interview at WellPoint Health Networks was with Jack Shaw, Executive Vice President, Office of the President, of this $3.1 billion provider of health services. WellPoint Health Networks is the largest publicly traded managed health care company in California and one of the largest in the nation. WellPoint was incorporated in 1992 to own and operate the managed care business of Blue Cross of California. The company serves the health care needs of more than 2.8 million medical members and approximately 10.4 million dental and pharmacy benefit members.

The 1996 goals for WellPoint include delivering more value to the customer, investing in people, becoming a national company, increasing shareholder value, and continuing to demonstrate the quality of networks and services. Their strategy involves building their core competencies, which will require that they make the best use of education that is available for their managers and executives.

10. Xerox

My interview at Xerox was with Raleigh Steinbach, Human Resources Manager for Xerox Production Systems. Xerox is a $16.6 billion public company, which has 85,900 employees, 45,900 of whom are in the United States (Xerox, 1996).

The Xerox 1995 Annual Report reflects their support of research to continue to push the frontiers of document technology. Xerox believes that, by helping their customers navigate and manage the world of documents, they can help them improve their productivity and grow their business (Xerox, 1995). Their key objectives are productivity and growth. Throughout the interview, Mr. Steinbach's comments reflected Xerox' support for continued management training.

Corporate interviews

As outlined above, I will go through the three sections of the interviews on which I focused: The current workplace, relevance of course work to need, and training expenditures. The actual interview covered 45 questions: 30 objective queries covering amount spent on education, preference for training location, etc., and 15 open-ended questions asking what the corporations expect to get from the education they are paying for and what they actually get in terms of productivity, loyalty, etc. Table 63, on page 196, outlines the responses to the questions in key parts of the interview.

The current workplace

In this section, I wanted to know the outlook for both the current and future workplace, in terms of availability of talent and availability of jobs. I also wanted to know how diversity affects productivity in the workplace. The general consensus about the current labor market, as outlined in Table 63, was that it is fair, but expected to get better in the future. Comments included the following:

- From Deloitte & Touche, for those people who have a track record of progress and are able to move from one company to another, managment jobs are fairly plentiful. Deloitte & Touche is looking for the following in those who return from business school: "interpersonal skills, the ability to work in teams, to rapidly come up to speed in a situation that's unfamiliar to them, to handle unstructured, unfamiliar problems, and to be articulate about describing problems and potential solutions" to clients.

- Licia Ramos, of Rainbird, felt that the current and future labor markets are fair, with a good availability of talent. Diversity has affected Rainbird in a positive way because "you get a comprehensive and broader perspective with people who have a multi-national background."

- Although Dr. Emiko Banfield, of Southern California Edison, felt the current labor market is middle of the road, many of the people they are bringing in tend to be more highly educated, with business skills to help with the changes taking place because of the introduction of competition to Edison's business needs.

- Bea Lalla, at Towers Perrin, characterized the current labor market for managerial jobs as fair to good. She also said that diversity has improved productivity, because "by having a diverse workforce when going out into the market, we are able to represent views that reflect a more diverse client base and we can very quickly get to the root cause of the problem."

- Toyota's Mike Morrison thought that the current labor market for managerial jobs was only fair, but will be good in the future. He does not know what impact diversity has had, but said that "I would like to think that it's had a positive impact, because....we are filling the pipeline with a lot of outstanding women."

- On the negative side, Jack Shaw, of WellPoint, said that there are fewer classes of managerial jobs after the flattening of the corporations in the early 1990's. However, he also thought the job market will improve in the future.
- Raleigh Steinbach, at Xerox, said that the market at Xerox is good mainly for people with certain technical skills.

I was also interested in future plans for hiring, given the current labor market in talent and availability of jobs. Of the ten companies interviewed, four plan on hiring more managers, one the same, and five plan on reducing the hiring in certain areas. This means that 50% of the executives who participated in my interviews said that their companies would be hiring fewer managers. Many said that they will be looking for specific skills that currently require more education:

- Dr. Culver, from Aerojet, said that Aerojet will be hiring fewer managers, partly because of their marketplace, but that increased diversity of workers has increased productivity.

- Deloitte & Touche is in a business that "is experiencing explosive growth, resulting in much greater demand for qualified and experienced people." They are looking for people who can bring value, who can easily work in teams, and who can contribute based on what they personally can add, not necessarily how many people they manage. In addition, while Deloitte & Touche plans to hire more people in the future, some of them will come from industry backgrounds as opposed to fresh from MBA programs.

- Jacque Kent mentioned that Goulds Pumps will keep hiring steady in the future, but that executive ability is better than it was five years ago. Although they had a significant cutback a year and a half ago, turnover remains next to nothing.

- McDonnell Douglas' future hiring patterns reflect their marketplace. Jac Meacham told me that they will be hiring fewer managers than they have in the past five years. He feels that current availability of talent is "fair," and that diversity has increased productivity in the workplace.

- Rainbird intends to increase recruiting on an overall basis, but Licia Ramos also told me that turnover at Rainbird is very low, partly because Rainbird has shown a concern for the development of the employee. They are looking for "good leaders, be they individual contributors or managers. We also look for people who can think strategically as general managers."

- Edison "will be in the hiring mode to infuse new skills, different skills, into our company." Their plans are to increase the hiring of managers over the last five years.

- Even though they are part of the fast growing consulting industry, Towers Perrin will be hiring fewer managers in the next five years than in the past, but is continuing to experience excellent business growth and has been adding to its worldwide population on a steady basis.

- Even though Toyota's Mike Morrison sees the availability of talent as good, about the same as it was five years ago, their plans for the next five years are to hire less than in the past five years.

- As opposed to the aerospace industry, which is experiencing slower or no growth, the health care industry is growing rapidly, even though, as Jack Shaw told me, there are fewer classes of managerial jobs after the flattening of corporations in the early 1990's. However, he also told me that, even though WellPoint will be hiring more managers than in the past five years, his feeling is that executive ability is worse than five years ago because many skills are not appropriate for current needs.

- Even though Xerox has gone through a reduction in force, Raleigh Steinbach told me that me that they are hiring now, in small numbers, mainly people with certain technical skills. Even though he feels the resources coming off the college campuses are good, Xerox tries to groom people from the inside whenever possible.

The consensus about the current and future workplace, among these ten people, was that the current job market is fair or poor, and that the future market will be good. Though 50% of those I interviewed will be hiring less managers than in the past five years, they all pointed out that the skills they are looking for are different.

Are courses relevant to jobs?

I asked short questions, such as "are you satisfied with the results of the training," and longer ones, such as "Do you feel that these programs are relevant to the jobs being done?" As Table 63 (p.196) points out, all ten of the corporate participants in this study said yes, though some qualified their answers:

- Aerojet's Dr. Bob Culver said that many students seem unable to apply what they have learned because they look for "rules" and "laws" for success. But, he did say that the programs are relevant. With regard to the professors, he said that the professor has more to do with what is learned that does the institution. This information was borne out by my research.
- Bob Wetzel, from Deloitte & Touche, said that the programs are better now than they were. He believes the programs are stronger, the admission standards are higher, and the rigor of the programs is better than it was. He said that schools are also demanding that people be more team oriented and somewhat less theoretical than they used to be. The use of the team approach among students is a large part of the

programs at the four schools used for this research, and proved to play large part in the positive results cited in the alumni interviews.

- Jacque Kent, from Goulds Pumps, felt that people come back from executive programs with better problem solving skills and better presentation skills, but she was not sure that their people skills are enhanced. She also said that "I know they are making major efforts in trying to link business with the curriculum that's being taught."

- Jac Meacham said that McDonnell Douglas is "somewhat" satisfied with the results of the training they support, a six on a scale of one to ten. However, he said that "core competencies need to be more specific,"50% of the training they support does not reflect the current global perspective of business, and is not a good value for the money. However, Mr. Meacham also said that "much can be adapted if they look for ways of utilizing what they've learned."

- Rainbird's Licia Ramos felt that the universities have made progress in this area, and that most universities have become more flexible in a general sense. Like Jac Meacham, she added that "my sense is that university programs can be lacking in real world applications…I personally feel that good business practitioners who have had a good business background are suited to be educators rather than academicians who don't have business experience."

- Southern California Edison has a new corporate structure, which is likely to affect how executive education programs are evaluated for funding. To that end, they have enlisted the University of Southern California to put together programs designed to target the specific skills on which Edison wants to focus. With regard to satisfaction, Dr. Banfield said that "yes, I am (satisfied). I believe that all of these programs and the experiences benefit the individual." She would like to do more with leveraging that knowledge back at the workplace.

- Bea Lalla, from Towers Perrin, said that the programs are applicable to real business situations, reflect action-learning principles, and contribute to the growth and development of its people. However, with regard to external development offerings, she sees some weakness and continued need for improvement with respect to practical application of the course offerings.

- Toyota's Mike Morrison said that they are satisfied with the programs their managers attend. The most consistently high feedback they get is from Pepperdine because it provides a real-world education with a strong faculty. Skills developed include management and leadership competencies that people don't necessarily develop on the job.

- It is important to WellPoint that their programs fit their needs, because their investment into executive education is part of their competitive advantage. According to Jack Shaw, the companies who invest in education are "world class companies." He felt that, on an overall basis, there is some weakness in practical applicability, but the skills the managers are attaining are worthwhile for their purposes.

- Raleigh Steinbach said that Xerox is satisfied with their return from the programs they support "specifically because we focus the kind of training….secondly, it gives them the opportunity to network with a lot of people from other companies."

The wish-list for programs included more global programs, more leadership training, more diversity training, and greater emphasis on communication skills. Given that many of the participants in the surveys stated there was no training in public speaking, the area of verbal communication appears to be one that is overlooked by many programs.

I was interested in whether the corporations were looking for loyalty after investing a large amount of money in executive education. Two corporations said yes, two said yes, but they wanted skills first, and the rest said that loyalty is not expected.

Another interesting outcome from the interviews was that corporations, and specifically the executive students themselves, are looking for rigorous programs, not off-site resort experiences. This point was made in both the corporate interviews and the interviews with the EMBA alumni.

The general conclusion about course work was that, while it provides a good background to the students, there is some lacking in real-world applicability, especially where the professors have no practical experience.

Training expenditures

Most of these companies have a 100% reimbursement policy for programs such as an EMBA. As cited above, support for educational programs will increase for most companies, even if their hiring is not slated to grow. As an example, Southern California Edison will make more investment in the next five years with regard to training. A downturn in revenues will not affect their support because they see training as an investment rather than a cost. More companies, including Aerojet, Xerox, and Towers Perrin, are reconfiguring their executive education programs to make sure that the courses relate to the succession plan the employee is on. Succession planning works to recognize the future career path planned for the employee by and with the corporation.

In addition, there was heavy emphasis in my interviews on the new and different skills that employers are expecting. Corporations like Deloitte & Touche, who used to expect their consultants to have a fair amount of knowledge already, are developing programs designed for the special needs their consulting contracts are demanding.

Are there any rewards provided to those who pursue advanced degrees? Most of the corporate representatives said that the tuition reimbursement was the reward. What about accountability for what they learned and a program to make use of those skills? Again, most of the corporate representatives said that there are no specific programs for making use of the employee's new skills. Gould's Jacque Kent mentioned that this is an area where she feels emphasis will come in the future and Edison's Emiko Banfield said that there is no systematic program to use the skills, thought it does happen. At Edison, evaluating managers on their role in providing opportunities for their subordinates is left to the individual discretion of the department.

Because of the size and complexity of the corporations, it was hard to compare their training expenditures. Some examples follow:

- Towers Perrin spends about $2.3 million on training programs of the sort I was researching, divided as follows: 27% for academic programs such as MBA's, 33% for off-site programs, and 39% for on-site programs.
- McDonnell Douglas invested $2.8 million in executive education programs in 1995. Fifty-three percent went to academic programs such as an MBA, 18% went to off-site programs, 21% went to on-site programs run by their internal training department, and 7% went to on-site programs run by consultants and universities.
- Toyota Motor Sales, USA spends about $3.5 million on training when everything is lumped together. They also make use of an in-house program, where up to 40 courses are listed in their catalog.

A chart showing the expenditures as a percentage of total income would be misleading because the reporting responsibility for the programs is often split among many different departments.

Many of the corporations use a combination of in-house programs, consultants, custom university programs, and programs such as the Harvard Advanced Management program. Preferences revealed the following pattern:

- Aerojet's Bob Culver prefers university professors and then on-company consultants, followed by a team of professionals in the prescribed area.

- Deloitte & Touche is starting to hire professional trainers to come in and deliver programs. Columbia and Northwestern are their partners in this endeavor to help enhance the overall capability of their partners.

- Gould's Jacque Kent said that her choice for delivering programs would be, first, consultants in the area of interest; second, custom university programs; third, university programs, such as an MBA; and, fourth, university programs open to the public, other than an MBA.

- Southern California Edison receives the greatest leverage from custom university programs. They also use university programs open to the public, MBA programs, and consultants in the area of interest.

- Toyota Motor Sales prefers consultants and university/corporate cooperative programs.

- In many cases, Xerox uses their own employees to deliver training. Raleigh Steinbach said that all of their choices, including the long-term programs at Smith College, in Northampton, Massachusetts. and the use of consultants for in-house training, have provided good experience.

There are a variety of choices available to companies with regard to the logistics and timing of training programs. Some of these logistics are made more difficult by the down-sizing that has trimmed the number of managers available to provide short-term replacement for those undergoing training. In the interview, I asked the preferences of the corporations with regard to off-site vs. on-site programs, and day vs. overnight programs. Forty percent of the executives preferred off-site programs, some as day only programs and some as overnight. Comments included the following:

- All of Deloitte & Touche's programs are delivered off-site, overnight.
- Goulds Pumps' Jacque Kent prefers off-site weekend programs, followed by on-site during the week, and off-site full week. Off-site training is done to avoid the interruption of phone calls. This was a common reason for the choice of off-site locations.
- Jac Meachem, from McDonnell Douglas, chose off-site full week programs, followed by off-site overnight, off-site day only, and on-site.
- Rainbird's Licia Ramos specifically mentioned that their people can't afford to go away for long periods of time. Each of their business managers chooses the schedule that works best for them. Ms. Ramos chose short programs, over a longer period of time, to meet the needs of most of their managers.
- Dr. Banfield, from Southern California Edison said that "if the objective is to bond, overnight helps." If it is a matter of just being educated, she prefers to make it day only, off-site. She said that "it is virtually impossible not to be distracted physically as well as mentally if you are on-site."
- Towers Perrin's Bea Lalla also picked off-site programs, weekly first and then overnight. On-site programs were rated last.
- Jack Shaw, from WellPoint, prefers on-site programs that are customer university programs planned with the corporation.
- For Xerox, the preferable way was on-site, short duration, not overnight.

Although the answers tended to heavily favor off-site training, it was interesting that size of corporation did not make a difference; in other words, Xerox, a $16.6 billion corporation, preferred on-site programs, while Towers Perrin, a company of less than $1 billion, preferred off-site. The answers seemed to have more to do with specific objectives, facility availability, and manager's schedule. My own experience with Delta Faucet, a $650 million corporation, has been that, although they built a brand new training facility in 1995, they have continued to use their off-site training locations in order to lessen distraction.

Suggestions for improvement

After establishing the degree of satisfaction with the executive education programs they were supporting, I wanted to know what suggestions these executive would have to further improve the programs for the future:

- Deloitte & Touche is looking for more team-building skills, the ability to be responsive to unfamiliar situations, and the ability to be flexible in adapting to different environments.
- Goulds Pumps is looking for more emphasis on communication and interpersonal skills. They feel that the good programs are real world.
- McDonnell Douglas is looking for "real people from industry and business as part of the faculty to tell their stories." They want ready-to-use skills via a process.
- Bea Lalla, from Towers Perrin, sees some weakness and continued need for improvement with respect to practical applicatioin of course offerings. Case work should be practical and relevant.
- Mike Morrison, from Toyota, feels that the programs need some updating. He said that the theory needs to be applied to the real-world applications resulting from it. His message to send back to universities: "get real."

These managers are looking for quantifiable skills in the managers they support more than they are looking for loyalty. Many of them feel that people come back from programs expecting a formula to use, when, in most situations, that does not exist. The business world of today requires even more flexibility and creativity from its managers than it ever did.

Table 63 lists the feelings of the participants about many of the issues the research was addressing. These interviews provided a good and consistent view of how corporate American views current and future executive education investments. The following were the general observations relevant to my questions about whether the corporations are getting their money's worth:

1) Corporations will be spending more on training, regardless of the business atmosphere. Some of the companies would adjust to a downturn in revenues, but, in general, there are plans to increase rather than decrease such investments. However, recent moves by the Federal Government may put more financial pressure on corporations with regard to the tax benefits they get from assisting their employees with their education. Graduate-level courses that began after June 30, 1996 are not included in that tax-break. Future actions by the government are unsure at this moment (Capell, K., 1996).

2) Corporations are satisfied with the general skills that their employees bring away from executive programs. They would like for them to be able to think more strategically and rely less on a blueprint that they learned in school, but they are satisfied that they are getting their money's worth.

3) Corporations are looking for rigor in these programs, and for real-world examples for students to be able to apply on the job. These areas are their most common complaints.

4) Corporations are not concerned about turnover due to diversity. They feel that diversity has increased productivity, and will continue to, for many reasons, including the breadth of outlook provided by employing people from a variety of backgrounds.

Table 63 Corporate interviews

Company	Aerojet	Deloitte & Touche	Edison	Goulds Pumps	Rainbird	McD Dou
Size	$1.3 billion	$5 billion	$8 billion	$718 million	$350 million	$14.
Current Labor Mkt	Fair	Fair	Good	Fair	Fair	Fair
Future Labor Mkt	Good	Good	Good	Good	Fair	Fair
Future plans for training exp.	More	More	More	More	Same	More
Future plans for hiring mgr	Fewer	More	More	Same	More	Fewer
Satisfaction with the relevance of courses	Yes	Yes	Yes	Yes	Yes	6 on scale
Avail. of talent	Good	Fair	Good	Good	Good	Fair
1st choice for training location	University program	In-house or Custom University	Custom university programs	Off-site consultants	Depends	Cust univ prog
Risk of employee leaving	Low	Low	Low	Low	Low	Mod
1st choice for schedule		Off-site, overnight	Off-site, day only	Off-site weekend	Shorter, for a longer period of time.	Off-s week over
Add programs	In-house		Leadership	All sources	Variety	Univ outsi
Wish-list:						
Global Ec.						Yes
Diversity						Yes
Leadership			Yes			Yes
Other				Communication skills, interpersonal skills		
Objectives	Skills	General skills	More effective in doing their jobs.	Skills, affective commitment	Good leaders, thinking strategically	Core comp
Weakness	Come off looking for a blueprint.				Lacking in real-world application.	Lack real- appl
Expect loyalty	No	Yes	Yes	No	No	No

Table 63, continued

Company	Towers Perrin	Toyota	WellPoint	Xerox
Size	$767million	$26 billion	$3.1 billion	$16.6 bi
Current Labor Mkt	Fair	Fair	Poor	Good
Future Labor Mkt	Fair	Good	Improve	Good
Future plans for training exp.	Same	More	More	More
Future plans for hiring managers	Less	Less	More	Less
Availability of talent	Good,> 5 yrs ago	Good	Fair	Good
Relevance	Yes	Yes	Yes	Yes
1st choice for training location	Off-site full week	On-site, consultants, custom university.	On-site, custom university	On-site, universi consulta
Risk of leaving	Low	Low	Low	Low
1st choice for schedule	Weekend lecture	Day	No choice	On-site, overnigl
Add programs	In-house and external.	Leadership development	All types	Leadersl
Wish-list:				
Global Ec.	X			
Diversity	x			
Leadership		x		x
Finance	x			
Other	Strategic Mkt.		System dynamics	Tailored individu
Objectives	Broaden perspective, increase leadership skills.		Critical thinking skills.	
Weakness	Rigor, current topics	Real-world application.	Practical applicability	
Expect loyalty	Not mentioned	Yes, but skills first.	Yes, but skills first.	

1) There is little in the way of specific plans to use skills that employees bring back from executive courses. Corporations do take them into account when promotions are being considered, but the skills that are improved are what they expect to contribute to the future success of the manager.

2) Corporations see the risk as low that employees will use their support to get an advanced degree and then seek other employment. The people I interviewed felt that it was the responsibility of the corporation to provide an atmosphere of growth for the employee. Several of the corporations do require that the employee be on a succession

plan before they will sponsor the program, but more of them recognized the future importance of this type of planning even though it is not part of their current management development activities.

3) The greatest growth in hiring will be for people with the technical skills expected to continue to grow in demand, e.g., up-to-date knowledge of the latest CAD-CAM technology (computer assisted design and computer assisted manufacturing).

4) Affective commitment is important to these managers, but the skills and overall contribution of the manager are more important. They would like loyalty, but rarely is it the first result expected from the financial support to attend an executive program.

5) The employment market will continue to be good for the right people, who have the right skills. Corporations are starting to work very hard to identify the right people to hire, narrowing the market for those who have not spent the time keeping up with the skills they will need for the future.

6) With the flattening of the corporation, executive education decisions are being moved from the human resources department out into the field, where each manager uses his or her budget to choose the most appropriate training for their employees.

The "continuous learning" revolution that has received support from such books as

Peter Senge's The Fifth Discipline will continue to gain strength. The message I carried away from the ten interviews I conducted with key managers from major corporations was that people entering and expecting to move up in the workplace of tomorrow need to take personal responsibility for keeping their skills current and for taking advantage of educational opportunities, whether or not the corporation is funding them. If they do, corporations are ready to reward the attendant value-added package with great opportunity. If they don't, the labor market will continue to squeeze them out.

CHAPTER 7

ALUMNI INTERVIEWS

The proposal for this research contained plans to interview a selection of the alumni who returned the surveys. The desire for a random sample required that I choose the interview participants in a manner that did not detract from that objective. When the surveys came back, I chose every other one, as I had the labels for the original surveys. In the case of Utah, I made the trip to Utah before the surveys actually went out, so interviewing non-random alumni was approved by my committee chair. I was then able to interview one of the Utah graduates in Los Angeles. In the case of UCLA, I followed my procedure of selecting every other survey to choose six to interview. In the cases of Washington and Colorado, I called the selected people about two weeks before my trips to those locations. I requested about 45 minutes and re-affirmed that the interview would be anonymous. If the person called was not available or did not return my call after three attempts to reach them, I went to the next survey in the sequence of every other returned survey. I interviewed a total of 24 people, six from each school. The interviews lasted from 45 minutes to 1 ½ hours. Each interview was tape recorded to assure accuracy of transcription. Before the interview started, I re-affirmed to the participant that their name would not be used in the final document.

Ten of the interviews were conducted by phone because the participant was either not available in person or was too far away to allow the interview to take place. In terms of gender, marital status, amount of support for the program, industry, and ethnicity, the nature of the sampling process created the following mix:

GENDER: There were 14 men and 10 women, or 58% men and 42% women. The actual surveys returned covered 72% men and 23% women (the missing 5% are those who declined to specify gender).

ETHNICITY: As with the survey sample, the vast majority of the people I interviewed are white. I interviewed two men of Hispanic origin and one African American woman. The surveys returned were 87% Anglo, 1.9% Hispanic, and 1.9% African American. Comparing this to my interviews, the people I interviewed were 87% Anglo, 4% African American and 8.3% Hispanic.

SUPPORT: Fifty-four percent of those interviewed had their entire program paid for, vs. forty percent of the survey population. Twenty-nine percent, or seven people, paid for the program themselves vs. twenty-two percent of the entire survey sample.

EDUCATION: I did not ask about previous education in the surveys, but was struck with the extent of those who had earned previous graduate degrees (or the equivalent), as noted by Table 64:

Table 64 Advanced degrees held by interview participants

Designation	Number
MD	1
Masters in Accounting	1
Attorney	3
Masters in Engineering	3
CPA	3
Masters in Communication	1

This means that 50% of the people I interviewed held other advanced degrees or professional certifications. Only one of the people I interviewed did not have a bachelors degree when entering the program, but was accepted based on business experience. Year of graduation represented by those interviewed are represented in Table 65:

Table 65 Graduation year of alumni interview participants

Year	1992	1993	1994	1995	Other/missing	Total
Number Interviewed	2 8.33%	5 20.8%	5 20.8%	9 37.5%	3 12.5%	24
Number in entire sample	2 1.27%	42 26.75%	44 28.03%	60 38.22%	9 5.73%	157

When they sent me the labels to use in sending out the surveys, the schools did not separate them by year, so I cannot identify the original sample by year of graduation. However, the schools accept the same number of students each year, so it can be hypothesized that 33% of the original sample who received the surveys came from each year. In other words, of the total of 44 surveys sent to alumni from School Green, about 15 represented each of the years 1993, 1994, and 1995. The reason some of the people who responded put "1992" is unknown. It is clear that those interviewed from 1995 were the largest percentage, but those interviewed and those who responded to the surveys both constituted about the same percentage of their respective populations. Apart from specific complaints, such as regarding an international trip that occurred in 1995, and about specific professors who are no longer there, I found the comments to be fairly well spread out among the respondents.

Table 66 depicts the interview participants with regard to gender, age, occupation, marital status, and ethnicity:

Table 66 Characteristics of alumni interview participants

Interview #	Gender	Ethnicity	Industry	Married	Children	Program support
1	M	WH	Consulting	Y	3	100%
2	F	WH	Aerospace	Y	1	100%
3	M	WH	Medical	Y	2	0
4	F	WH	Attorney	Y	1	0
5	F	WH	Manufacturing	N	0	100%
6	M	WH	Aerospace	Y	2	100%
7	F	WH	Environmental	N	0	100%
8	M	Hispanic	Manufacturing	Y	2	100%
9	M	WH	Manufacturing	Y	2	100%
10	F	AA	Telecommunications	N	0	100%
11	M	WH	Retail	Y	2	0
12	M	WH	Environmental	Y	2	0
13	F	WH	Software	N	0	100%
14	M	WH	Telecommunications	Y	2	100%
15	M	WH	Aerospace	Y	0	100%
16	M	WH	Distribution	Y	1	0
17	F	WH	Software	Y	0	100%
18	F	WH	Finances	N	0	80-99%
19	M	WH	Aerospace	Y	3	100%
20	M	WH	Attorney	Y	2	0
21	F	WH	Health Care	Y	2	<50%
22	F	WH	Health Care	Y	0	<50%
23	M	WH	Banking	Y	2	0
24	M	Hispanic	Health Care	Y	0	100%

The industry classification of the interviewed alumni vs. the entire sample and the Harvard study is represented by Table 67:

Table 67 Industry breakdown of interview participants

Industry	% in interviews	% in entire population	% in Harvard study
Manufacturing	29.17%	28.03%	46.6%
Consulting	4.17%	4.4%	NA
Communications	8.33%	7.64%	12.4%
Computers	8.33%	7.64%	0
Government Environmental	8.33%	12.10%	21%
Finance	8.33%	10.83%	6.5%
Health care	12.5%	8.92%	0
Law	8.33%	Not included	0
Retail /Wholesale	8.33%	4.17%	2.7%

Aerospace/Manufacturing, Finance, and Computers contain close parallels between the interview population and the total surveys returned. Health Care had a higher percentage in the interviews than it did in the survey sample, but I do not believe that this fact decreased the validity of the interviews. The text of the alumni interview is contained in Exhibit 2, on page 41.

Interview participant rating of the program and the faculty

One of the areas that interested me was the rating of the faculty and the rating of the program. I was interested in whether those who were supported financially would rate the program higher or lower than those who did not received the same level of financial support. Table 68 represents the alumni who were interviewed and how much tuition support, if any, they received from their employers.

Table 68 Tuition support for those interviewed

Interview #	Age	% Support from company	Program Rating	Faculty Rating	Gender
1	34	100%	4	5	M
2	36	100%	5	5	F
3	54	0	5	5	M
4	39	0	5	5	F
5	34	100%	4	3	F
6	46	100%	5	5	M
7	39	100%	5	5	F
8	39	100%	5	4	M
9	43	10%	5	5	M
10	35	100%	4	4	F
11	42	0	5	5	M
12	39	0	5	5	M
13	33	100%	3	4	F
14	39	100%	5	4	M
15	43	100%	4	4	M
16	30	0	4.5	4	M
17	41	100%	4	4	F
18	32	80-99%	4.5	4	F
19	37	100%	4	4	M
20	39	0	5	4	M
21	35	<50%	4	4	F
22	32	<50%	4	4	F
23	39	0	4	4	M
24	33	100%	4	4	M
Mean	38.04	2.41 (1=100%, 5=0)	4.45	4.33	
Mean of Total	39.93	2.71	4.33	4.26	
Mean of Men	39.78	2.71	4.60	4.42	
Mean of Women	35.6	2.1	4.25	4.20	

The following section describes the ratings as they relate to my questions regarding gender, support, and age.

The people who were interviewed rated the program slightly higher than the total of the returned surveys, but not by a significant amount. They also rated the faculty slightly higher than the sample as a whole.

1) Age. The average age for those interviewed was 4.73% lower than the average for the total of those surveyed, or about 1.5 years. Table 69 represents the ages and program ratings:

Table 69 Rating of interview participants

Age (# that age)	Program Rating Mean	Faculty Rating Mean
< 33 (2)	4.25	4
33-36 (7)	4	4.14
37-40 (8)	4.75	4.37
41-44 (4)	4.5	4.5
>44 (2)	5	5

Those from under 33 years of age to 38 years of age rated the program with a mean of 4.13 and rated the faculty with a mean of 4.16. Those from age 39 to greater than age 46 rated the program with a mean of 4.73 and the faculty with a mean of 4.65. It would appear from this, as it did from my interviews, that the younger people are more critical and more demanding of the program and of the faculty. Perhaps it is because, to some of them, the topics are not as new to them as they are to, say, a 54 year-old surgeon to whom each subject is challenging and exciting.

2) Gender. The women were less likely to receive financial support than the men interviewed; their average program and faculty rating were also lower than the men interviewed. However, their faculty rating was the same as the average of the survey population.

3) Area of emphasis. I noticed that those with a strong quantitative background seemed to be more likely to complain about those in the program with lower quantitative skills and more likely to suggest that classes in finance or quantitative areas be added to the

program. There were 12 people in the group of those interviewed who had a technical background. I looked at these data from the interview population and got the results shown in Table 70:

Table 70 Mean program rating of interview participants

N=	12	12
#	Technical background	Non-technical background
Program Rating Mean	4.29	4.54
Faculty Rating Mean	4.33	4.25

These data appear to suggest that those from a non-technical background gave the program a higher rate, but the faculty a lower ranking. However, there is a difference of only 5% in the program rating and less than 2% in the faculty rating.

4) Financial Support

The following data, shown in Table 71, relate financial support to the rating of the program and faculty:

Table 71 Financial support and program rating

N=	15	2	7
Amount of Support	80-100%	<50%	0%
Average program rating (5=best)	4.37	4	4.78
Average faculty rating (5=best)	4.27	4	4.57

Although this was a fairly small sample, it would indicate that those who financed the program entirely on their own gave both the program and the faculty a higher rating than those whose education was mostly or entirely financed by their employer. Table 72 represents the correlation of the variables considered in Table 71.

Table 72 Correlation matrix of questions 3, 13d, and 14[20].

	Question #3	Question #13d	Question #14
Question #3	1.00	-.001	.118
1-tailed significance	---	.494	.070
Question #13d	-.001	1.00	.496
1-tailed significance	.494	--	.000
Question #14	.118	.496	1.00
1-tailed significance	.070	.000	---

Of the variables tested, amount of tuition support, program rating, and faculty rating, the only variables which showed significance at the $p=.001$ level were Question #13d, the program rating, and Question #14, the faculty rating. Tuition support was not a statistical factor in the program or faculty rating.

Interview Results

Once I transcribed all of the interviews, I categorized their answers with respect to each question, such that similar answers could be grouped in the text. The schools are not separated in the text of these results. I feel that the mix of gender, occupation, company financial support, and year of graduation are sufficient to offer a broad mixture of opinions that should approximate the entire sample of those who returned the survey and, in turn, the total population of EMBA graduates from these specific schools.

Question #1 : From your recollection of the survey, can you think of anything that the survey left out?

I grouped the answers into the following areas: need to be consistent about entrance requirements, the amount of learning that occurred, and the study group effects.

a) Need to be consistent about the entrance requirements, or even raise them. The comments here included:

> "Make sure everyone enters at the same level (female, age 41)."
>
> "If you had a sponsor that was willing to shell out the dollars, you could get in.(female, age 32)"
>
> "Need to be diligent about the entrance requirements (male, age 42)."

b) Comments that focused on how much they learned, such as:

> "It taught us that we no longer have to be competitive (54 year old male)"
>
> or
>
> "You have to take personal responsibility for what you get out of the program (male, age 39)
>
> and
>
> "I learned as much from the other students as from the program (male, age 37)."
>
> or
>
> "I had years of experience in health care, but I needed to be marketable in other areas (female, Age 35).
>
> A 38 year-old female attorney said that "I always missed the grounding in the business area."
>
> A 46 year-old engineer, who also had a law degree when he entered the program, summed up many feelings when he said that " I gained confidence and an understanding of concepts." Another, a 39 year-old chemist, recounted that "they learned people skills."

c) Comments that focused on the study groups. Although most of the comments in the interviews regarding the study groups were positive, all of the study groups were not harmonious, resulting in a certain amount of shifting around during the first year. The program directors confirmed that this happens and that they encourage the students to bond with people they are most comfortable with. One 37 year-old female shared

---

[20] Question #3 asked amount of tuition support provided; Question #13d asked a program rating; Question

with me that she "had the most dysfunctional study group in the program." Although I did not hear the same type of stories from most people, she assured me that personality problems occurred frequently.

Comments on Question #1

Most of these people were very favorable about their programs and just made comments regarding the challenge of the program. My main research question was "Is executive education meeting the needs of the customers?." Consequently, this question was uppermost in my mind as I conducted the interviews. The positive nature with which the participants started the interviews gave me a clue about the overall results.

Question #2, What was your first reaction to the program?

Again, the answers were divided into major categories:

a) The first reaction, at the orientation session or week, was often an exclamation of some sort:

> " It was overwhelming, a lot driven by the people in it. More of a reaction to who would be my peers (female, age 34)"

> "It was very exciting. Being independent cusses, the hardest thing to learn is team participation (male, aged 54)."

> "It was wild. The whole environment of the caliber of people, the journey they laid out for on what we would learn, the magnitude….(37 year-old male)."

> "I was really excited about getting started. I wondered what I had gotten myself into because I was already working 70 hours a week (female, age 40)."

> "I was nervous. These were really smart people. I was nervous and really excited. There were doctors (in the program) (female, age 41)".

> "It was exciting and overwhelming. It was good to get back into the classroom (male, age 39)."

b) Comments about the workload:

> "I thought, this is going to be more work than I even had readied myself for (male, age 42)"

"I was overwhelmed when they talked about how much family life was going to change (male, age 39)."

"They told our spouses that we would be able to have sex during the two weeks at Christmas."

"I thought, holy s____, what have I gotten myself into…..I needed a 30-hour day (female, age 37)."

"I was nervous. You start wondering if you've done the right thing. After getting a few papers back, that settles down pretty quickly. I like that challenge. I like education (male, age 39)."

c) The last group commented about the study groups as part of their first reaction to the program:

"It was an intense group process. I knew it would be time consuming (male, age 39)."

"The study group was tremendously helpful. Good relationships (male, age 45)."

Comments on Question #2

I continued to hear mostly positive comments about the study groups. One person felt she was stuck with "a bunch of mental lightweights….from a rigorous, academic standpoint, they could not cut it." One person also mentioned that the financial material scared him in the beginning; again, however, the vast majority of the alumni wanted more rather than less rigorous financial classes. The teamwork required in the program stood out as one of the most important benefits to the alumni.

Question #3. Apart from what the program intended, what do you really think happened to those who attended?

Answers to this question fell into four groups: a) those who mentioned the broadening effect of the education; b) Those who mentioned the study groups; c) Those who mentioned the teamwork focus of the education, and; d) Those who were critical of the experience. Comments fell into the groups as follows:

a) those who mentioned the broadening effect of the education:

"Each person received a foundation outside their area of expertise. I became more confident in my abilities as a manager (male, age 36)."

"I was able to take personal responsibility...I opened a day-care business with my wife, where I needed the confidence to write a business plan (male, age 39)."

"I do projects for the head of the lab when they need presentations....People higher up are looking for my help...they listen to me (male, age 39)."

"We were really in it to learn the tools of managing a business and almost all have moved on to higher positions (male, age 37)."

"Looked to broaden my horizons, get out of the rut of technical... Getting into the program and being able to interact with people from all different backgrounds was stimulating and stimulated more of my thought processes....(female, age 40.)"

"A basic set of skills and understanding of business principles; it also introduced me to the key people in the community (male, age 34)."

"I was able to apply work experience and see it in a more academic light...It offered certain resume enhancing benefits (male, age 39)."

"It taught us to be a learning organization, in a way. I think that was successful (male, age 54)."

"Friendships, networks, gained in areas (I was) not expecting; I see things differently, I think differently (female, age 34)."

"Many received promotions; 50% relocated. I received a promotion (female age 32)."

b) Those who mentioned the study groups

"The study groups were a big plus; it opened my eyes to things I had known, but forgotten (male, age 39)."

"The study groups were great. We stayed up until 2 a.m. the first week (female, age 33).

c) Those who mentioned the teamwork focus of the education

"There was an emphasis on teamwork (female, age 33)."

"The curriculum emphasized team-building exercises....I was really impressed with the caliber of the people...there were no slackers (male, age 46)."

d) Those who were critical of the experience

"It was a watered down program, but it added $80,000 to my paycheck, so it met that objective (female, age 32)."

Comments on Question #3

By now, I was starting to see the pattern of the very few who were critical of the program. There were one or two from each of the four groups who felt the curriculum was not challenging enough or the standards high enough. About 2 of the 24 people I interviewed, or under 10% of the total, felt that the program lacked some important elements to be totally satisfactory.

Question #4. Can you tell me a little more about the best parts of the program?

Knowing what was best about the program was important to my finding because, in order to answer the question "is executive education meeting the needs of the customers," I needed to see a strong pattern of positive responses from questions such as #4. Answers fell into the following areas: a) Other class members; b) The study groups; c) The international trip; d) Quality instruction; d) "thinking outside the box;" and ; e) the classes and thought processes.

a) Other class members:

"The type of people in the class, the exposure to different subjects (female, age 33)."

"The knowledge that other class members brought….I liked having the real world, people who could say 'that's good on paper, now let's talk about what really happens (female, age 37)."

"The people, exposure to a lot of different subjects I had no previous exposure to. The people exceeded my expectations….(female, age 41)."

"The interaction with other people, the lunch-time presentations, speakers…(male, age 37)."

"Opportunities to have debate and dialog with my classmates, to hear about experiences (female, age 35)."

"Relationships and professional relationships that I wouldn't have had. To be able to do brainstorming and share common interests (male, age 39)."

b) The study groups.

"Good job of splitting it up that way, with groups (male, age 39)."

"Having one group for two years….got to think like other people (female, age 36)."

"Group processes. The emphasis on research and not accepting without research (male, age 39.)"

"We went through with the same group of people. The study groups helped each other (female, age 32).

c) The international trip:

"The international trip, to Helsinki, the communications class, some professors (female, age 34)."

"The international field trip (Paris). It was long enough that we got to know the industry and the company, even some personalities (female, age 38)."

"I enjoyed the international trip (Hong Kong) (male, age 39)."

d) Quality instruction:

"The class size. The professors came to us. The professors had a nice style (male, age 39)."

"Very notable faculty. Macro-economics was world class, the material was really good….usefulness as a reference library (female, age 32)."

"Felt like the instructors were genuinely concerned about my future and willing to do things to help me (male, age 34)."

"The high caliber of professors. It doesn't mean all were that caliber. But, for the most part, the fact that they enjoyed the program, did not treat it as just another lecture, that kind of thing. I felt like I got something from each of those characters. Our class was run by Scott and Susan as a classy organization… (everything was) always arranged, planned…..they realized the value of time (male, age 42)."

"Bill Alberts (was) very interested in our learning (male, age 36)."

"The quality instructors, the overall quality of those in the class (male, age 34)."

e) The classes and thought processes:

"Having access and gaining knowledge; also, relationship building, connections made (male, age 46)."

"Thinking outside the box...people, networking, interaction (female, age 40)."

"The highlight was the industrial psychology class, an incredible experience about how to organize and prioritize (male, age 33)."

Comments on Question #4

As the interviews continued, I remembered something Susan Bunker, the Associate Dean in Colorado, had said, which was "we change the way they think." I had the opportunity recently to have a conversation with one of the senior professors in the Colorado program, who came to Colorado after many years with General Electric. He also said, "we change the way they think...they are more comfortable in different surroundings." The feeling that this program had changed their outlook on many areas of their lives, both professional and personal, continued to be a strong thread throughout all 24 interviews.

Question # 5. What about the less useful parts of the program?

The less useful parts of the program seemed to fall into comments that included poor professors, standards less than desirable for entry, study groups, and comments about the finance program. Other, unrelated comments will be covered at the end.

a) Poor professors

"The ethics course was a joke. We didn't need to be told that there are hard questions out there. The professor was not good at giving feedback. We were also slowed by people who were not qualified (female, age 38)."

"A couple of instructors were (not very good); one is not coming back this year (female, age 40)."

"Some instructors should not be teaching in these programs (female, age 37)."

"Professors that should not be teaching in a graduate program. The leadership class did less with such rich material than I would have thought possible. He came to class unprepared (male, age 36)."

"They need to be careful about some of the instructors. One, in particular, shouldn't have been there (male, age 34)."

"Some of the instructors could have been better (female, age 37)."

"Lackluster presentations. Low level of interest in the students (female, age 32)."

"A couple of weak professors, or new and not prepared (male, age 54)."

"Finance, by far my biggest disappointment. I always assigned that to the professor. This guy got awards in the regular program, but gets ridiculed in our program. A classic academic. A classic lecturer, doesn't want feedback.....What I needed was the thinking, the analysis of the situation. I don't feel like I heard much at all (male, age 30)."

b) Standards for entry:

"The pace was slowed by people who did not have certain prerequisites (female, age 38)."

"Were the standards high enough? A lot of people could have been dinged harder (male, age 39)."

"They should add prerequisites for quantitative areas...more computer. Once you paid your money, there was no way you would flunk out (male, age 34)."

c) Study groups:

"I did not get much out of the study groups. I was used to learning on my own. My job pressures did not decrease at all, in fact they increased throughout this thing....was more than I really wanted to do when I was capable of doing it myself (male, age 42)."

"At times, I grew to resent the amount of drain some members of the study group would do on others. I know that some members of the program managed to get out of the program without knowing much more about finance than they started with (male, age 42)."

"The study group was a disaster. We had a token minority, the first in ten years....bent every rule...did not get it (female, age 32)."

d) The Finance program:

"Not enough finance, too much soft skills. At this level, you should not have to learn to work with people (male, age 34)."

"They took off finance and the marketing was lean (female, age 34)."

"A heavy emphasis on finance. Exposure is good, but several quarters is just silly (male, age 33)."

"Didn't give a sound basis in finance...really needed to know how to crunch numbers (female, age 38)."

"Bring the finance back, more marketing (female, age 34)."

e) Other:

"Some of the luncheon meetings were a waste of time (females, age 36)."

"During residence week, the classes were taught with no follow-up and no introduction (female, age 41)."

"During residence week, the small classes were fillers(female, age 33)."

"The program should have more of a responsibility to continue our corroboration with each other and the school (male, age 34)."

Comments on Question #5

The alumni continued to complain about the few professors who did not meet their standards, or who made it difficult to learn. From my background in sales, I know that a very small portion of an offering (in this case, one or two professors in a program) can poison the perception of future customers when word-of-mouth is effective. Although some people told me that the school seemed to listen to them and not invite the most ineffective professors back, this was clearly not always the case. From my interviews with the alumni and the program directors, I got the sense that politics and power play a large part in the selection of program elements. For instance, at the school where several people complained about too much finance, that particular professor controls many of the decisions relevant to the program schedule.

Question #6 Can you expand on your answer about how well the corporation used your skills when you finished the program?

Fifty-one people, or 32.5%, said in the surveys (Question #11) that their employer had made good use of their skills. Thirty-four people, or 34.5%, said that they employer had used some, but enough. And 45 people, or 28.7%, said that their employer had made no effort to use their skills (4.5% did not answer this question). The answers to this question in the interviews followed much the same pattern, with about 30% agreeing that their companies made a basic effort to utilize their skills. Some changed jobs or careers for this reason, and some concentrated on what the MBA did for their marketability:

a) The company did make an effort:

"I'm now on a special assignment to the Vice President of Human Resources (male, age 46)."

"I am a change agent; a lot of companies want change, but don't want to have to change anything to get it (female, age 39)."

"We are looking at how to market. I am making presentations for the boss (male, age 39)."

"I am always on someone's task force. It would appear that my recommendations are really sought out (female, age 35)."

"The frame of reference is designed to prepare people for general management. (the program) covered a broad spectrum. How I apply it is my responsibility."

"Very well. I was promoted to corporate director. It is a matter of the individual making use of their own skills (female, age 32)."

"Being here, I've taken advantage of quite a bit….a Vice President in two years. It shows in my salary (male, age 39)."

"I have conducted a number of marketing studies and taken advantage of the faculty (male, age 33)."

b) Changed careers or frustrated and looking to change positions:

"I returned from the program with the decision to get out of medicine (male, age 54)."

"I'm at a new place where my skills are being used (female, age 39)."

"They did not acknowledge it one way or the other (female, age 33)."

"They still haven't. There is no indication that having a degree made any difference. I am frustrated to no end (female, age 34)." Note: This person had her complete program paid for, but is looking for other employment opportunities because of the company's lack of recognition.

"Candidly, no. The firm has a couple of key people and those key people have a pretty good idea of what they want (male, age 39)."

"For a company like ours, I really think they would have more of a succession plan. Their expectations for me should be higher (male, age 39)."

"You have to be quite a ways up to be really involved in ....decisions that cross different functions (male, age 37)."

c) The MBA added to their marketability:

"I would not have gotten this job without the MBA (female, age 35)."

"People in management all have MBA's (female, age 32)."

Comments about Question #6

I continued to hear a few people complain that their new skills were being wasted, but I heard just as many explain that they expected to chart their own destiny, even if it meant changing careers or employers. The trend of comments about "personal responsibility" continued. Earlier, I mentioned the book Danger in the Comfort Zone, by Judith Bardwick (1995). In it, she explores the trend toward entitlement in this country. The people I interviewed for this research, however, had mostly undertaken the education to be marketable, whether or not they stay with their current employers. They also expressed the commitment to taking personal responsibility for making sure their skills were used to the best advantage.

Question #7, What would you most like to see schools do to improve this program?

The answers to Question #7 followed the earlier comments regarding raising academic requirements, reducing faculty who do not contribute to the program, listening to students, and updating real-world experiences for the students. There were also comments about adding finance to a program where one of the courses was taken out. By way of clarification, School Yellow cut out one of the finance courses, while School Green has more than one semester of it. That is the reason for the diverse opinions, where some people (from School Green) have suggested that there is too much finance and some people (from School Yellow) have suggested that the finance program there is lacking.

a) Raise the requirements and provide prerequisites:

"Make sure this program is not only tough to get into, but tough to get out of. I want it to not in any sense of the word by a diploma mills. I want to be proud an the only way I can be proud is if I know they're making it tough on people (female, age 35)."

"I don't advocate reducing the quantitative aspects....If you don't have at least a quantitative background in business and economics, it is very difficult to have good decision making (male, age 39)."

b) Attract and retain quality faculty:

"There were a couple of ineffective professors(male, age 43)."

"Get rid of the dead wood. Two professors should not be teaching (there) (female, age 41)."

"There were a couple of ineffective professors. They were new and not prepared (male, 54)."

"Make sure they are keeping pace with the rapid changing world of business. Attract and retain quality faculty (female, age 32)."

"Need to be careful about some of the instructors....There was one instructor that, because of his standing, was able to pick the program that he wanted to teach in but I 'm not sure that he was the best teacher for the course (male, age 39)"."

c) More real world applications:

"Get out of the classroom and into the real world. We only had two exercises where we would actually go out and visit a factory. Real world is a high priority item to make a program good (male, age 39)."

d) More finance coverage:

"Get the soft skills someplace besides an MBA program. More development in finance (male, age 30)."

"Add a second finance class (male, age 46)."

e) Program integration and addition of independent courses of thinking:

"A more integrative approach for areas that complement each other (male, age 39)."

"Room for independent courses of action …..more options for the international trip.(male, age 43)."

"A lot of thinking is independent....Not sitting around in a circle holding hands (female, age 32).

"More focus on planning and organizing on the social/psychological aspects of business. Balance more with finance and accounting (male, age 33)."

f) Input from students:

"Do a better job of getting input from the students during and after the program, and using the input to adjust....(male, age 37)."

"Listen to the customers....input on the foreign trip (male, age 42)."

Comments about Question #7

There was one comment from a 39 year-old male on the fear that the schools "may inappropriately use technology to the detriment of future students...There are too many options to get there quickly." He is afraid that short-cuts may lessen the rigor of higher education. There was also a comment that there are a lot of chauvinistic attitudes out there and that there should be some diversity training.

When the alumni talked about more flexibility in the international trip and "listening to students," I recalled my discussion with Susan Bunker, the Associate Dean at the University of Colorado EMBA program. She shared with me the difficulty to being able to please everyone, both the corporations and the students. Although the benefit of the international trip was confirmed by this research, the operational challenges posed by it continue to be a challenge.

In general, however, the comments about what the schools could do to improve followed the general theme of improving classroom quality, better balance between finance and social skills, and more input on electives or other areas from the students.

Question #8 When you returned from the program, did you feel you did your job differently?

The answers to Question # 8 fell into three categories: Yes, it taught me to think differently and improved thought processes; no; "it was nice to have the ammunition to make points."

a) Yes, it taught me to think differently:

"I had a vision of what was happening in health care. My priorities were changing (male, age 54)"

"I viewed my job differently. I had a better understanding of the numbers(female, age 38).".

"Yes. It reflects on my comment that I think differently. My background was engineering. I was technically focused. Now, I think, what does it mean to the business? (female, age 34)."

"The critical skills help where the company is; I would like to have had it earlier (male, age 46)."

"Yes, I thought about things differently. Thinking outside the box more. I did not do that before (female, age 40)."

"I saw where actions may affect other decisions (male, age 39)."

"Yes, I had a narrow focus. Now, I have a greater appreciation of decisions that are made at the executive level (female, age 37)."

"Night and day. I see the value-added of sales, and supporting key functions (male, age 30)."

"Yes, I look for every opportunity to apply general theories that I have learned. I now use marketing skills...(male, age 39)."

"Yes, before, I would look at the engineering technical aspect of our decisions; now, other things come into play. I've done a better job of stepping back and thinking, how does this affect our customers, finance, as well as the technical part (male, age 37)."

(The above comment came from an engineer at Boeing, and was to prove a very common outcome for the technical people.)

"I'm broader in thinking. I try to incorporate more facts into each decision (female, age 32)."

"I take a different approach to problem solving. I did not assume that I knew the answers and was willing to rethink...(male, age 39)."

"I had a fund of resources I could turn to to find methodologies to approach particular problems (male, age 33)."

It has been helpful with relationships with clients, understanding their problems better." (This comment came from a 34 year-old male attorney)

b) No:

"I don't feel I did my job differently...I'm beginning to atrophy (male. Age 42)."

c) It was nice to have the ammunition:

> "There is a direct relationship between the program and an increase in salary (female, age 35)."

> "The job used the skills. It is nice to have the ammunition to make points (female, age 36)."

Comments about Question #8:

The answers here constitute an important part of the answer to the main research question. As with the Harvard study, the vast majority of the lives and professional behavior of the attendees were improved. Quinn McKay, in writing his dissertation about those who had not filled out the original Harvard survey but agreed to be interviewed later, quoted one wife in saying

> Oh, the program really changed John. He was always what one would call a typical skipper—tough, demanding, and always brusque and to the point....When there was an oversight, John would storm right into the dispatcher and without giving him a change to explain would bawl him out and dress him down....But after he returned from the program, he always called in the head dispatcher and talked things over with him (McKay, 1960, p.31/32).

If we go back to Kenneth Andrews' original 1966 published account of the 39 executive programs that were included in the Harvard survey, the subject of impact also receives a stamp of approval:

> We know that he had rendered a favorable verdict because he thinks that what he learned will make a contribution to better performance. The knowledge he has of this relevance is knowledge born of experience. Within its subjectivity, it carries conviction (Andrew, 1966, p. 126).

Of the 24 people I interviewed, 66.66% answered question #8 with an affirmative relation to their job performance of the material learned in the program. Measuring the question of meeting the customer's needs quantitatively was as difficult for me as it was for Kenneth Andrews, but the Harvard results come very close to my own : the vast majority of people claim to have changed their job performance because of the program.

Question #9 Can you cite a specific incident as an example of doing your job differently?

The answers to this question clustered around the teamwork skills that had been learned at the program, working with several levels of management, and a different way of approaching projects:

a) Teamwork and communication skills:

> "I put together some business teams (male, age 34)."

> "I'm doing teaching about marketing and sales, conducting a survey...I'm able to draw on resources (male, age 33)."

> "Being able to work outside the company with people who have a different style...The study group approached things differently. It was good (female, age 34)."

> "In environmental clean-up, they tend to look at options they have always used. Now, I say, "why not talk to the regulators and see what they are willing to do (female, age 40)."

"One of the things I did when I took over was say, "let's talk about these things and why we make the decisions we do (female, age 37)."

b) Working with several levels of management:

> "I have prepared information on topics for guys two and three levels above...(female, age 36)."

> "Everything I do, my boss seems to comment that I am getting much more done (male, age 46)."

c) Approach problems differently:

> "I was able to look at pooling overhead costs and how they may have a bearing on total costs (male, age 39)."

> "Looking at the work we do and making sure we are doing it right; applying Porter's value chain...pulled out the book for the group (male, age 36)."

> "Feeling I had the tools necessary to rebuild the finance and statistical basis (male, age 39)."

Comments about Question #9:

The original Andrews/Powell work found that a majority of the participants said that "it broadened me" in one way or the other. In the McKay dissertation, this impact was expressed in the comment that "the testimony of the executives showed that broadening was the greatest single effect resulting from the program (McKay, 1960, p.52)." I did not hear the work "broaden" quite as much, but approaching problems differently, thinking in a different manner, and using teamwork skills learned in the program obviously had great impact. As we can trace this effect back to what the executives expected to get out of their experience, 21.2% of the Harvard participants had expected the program to "broaden their thinking and perspective." The greatest number of my research sample, however, (24 or 15.38%) answered the same question with a direct referral to an emphasis on "analytical thinking and objective approach to decision making." The responses to the surveys and the interviews, then, confirm that more finely tuned analysis skills were important to the outcomes of my research, while they were not as specifically chosen by the Harvard participants.

Question #10 From the company's point of view, do you feel it was worth the investment in your time and the company's money to send you to this program?

Most of those being interviewed agreed that the investment was worth the money; Some people said that time would tell if the results were worth it, some said that the benefit was meant as a reward, and a few said no:

a) Yes, the investment was worth the money:

"Without a doubt; I felt I got a tremendous value for the money (male surgeon, age 54)."

"Yes, as more affirmation, my husband is now doing the program (female attorney, age 38)."

"Yes, even though they are not using it (female, age 34)."

"Yes, they got a great return. In senior management's eyes, I'm more marketable; they know what type of person they have (female, age 37)."

"There was not a single week that I didn't put in at least 40 hours, so they continued to get their money's worth (male, Boeing engineer, age 36)."

"Yes, now that I have the opportunity to use what I learned (male, age 37)."

"It was the best investment I ever made (male, age 30 who funded the program himself)."

b) Time will tell:

"Time will tell, So far, I think it is. I'd like to think I'm going to pursue more opportunities with the company (male, age 46)."

c) Used as a reward:

"For (my former company), no, because the benefit was meant as a reward....and then I left (male consultant, age 34)."

d) No:

"Probably not, because I know I did not give the company my best work performance (female, age 32, in the securities industry)."

Comments about Question #10

Fourteen, or 58.33%, of the interview participants, made a direct affirmative comment to this question. All of the seven people who funded the program entirely by themselves felt the investment to have been worth it. Those seven people covered all four schools. So, if we stretch the customer question of "did the programs meet the needs of the customer" to "was it a good value for the money?" there is a growing trend that confirms the worth and validity of the executive MBA programs, whether or not corporations are paying for them.

Question #11 Was there anything about the program, favorable or unfavorable, which particularly stands out in your mind?

Again, several people mentioned the study groups, in a favorable light. They also mentioned the international trip, the excellence of the program, and the family support they got.

a) Study groups:

"The study groups were well designed....lifelong relationships were created (male, age 36)."

"I really liked going through as a class. It would have been disastrous to change study groups (male, age 39)."

"Friday nights at the guest house...study groups, real camaraderie, really good. (female, age 34, School Yellow, where the program was every other Friday/Saturday).

b) The International trip:

"The international trip...There was some discussion about whether it was really helpful...For me, yes, very helpful to build keen assets (male, age 39).

"The international trip was key. It greatly enhanced the program. People need to understand that culture change..(female, age 35)."

"The international experience (female, age 34)."

"The trip to eastern Europe; we went to BMW. Also, the retreat in mid-summer (male, age 39).

c) Excellence of the program:

"I was impressed with the excellence of our program. Also, the international trip was extremely useful. There was a lot of focus on international aspects (female, age 36)."

"Being treated as an adult. They were strong in strategy courses (male, age 54)."

d) Family support:

"I was lucky that I had a good spouse to lighten the workload (male, age 37)."

e) Other comments:

"Association with fellow students (female, age 32)."

"Lunch-time speakers (male, age 30, School Goldenrod)."

"Really good relationships (male, age 46)."

"Some people were a deadly combination of not much experience and age....acted liked they had never traveled before (male, age 42)."

"There should be structure for more quantitative courses (male, age 34)."

"Take student evaluations seriously (female, age 37)."

Comments about Question 11

Those who had negative comments about a lacking in the program, such as enough finance courses at School Yellow or the need to listen to the student's evaluations, continued to express them. The international trip continued to get high marks, such that the school that does not use it may want to revisit the possibility. I did not see as many comments about the relationships developed in this question as previously, but I think that is because it had already been covered and the participants were trying to come up with things they had not previously mentioned.

There was only one comment in response to this question about family support, but my discussions with the alumni confirmed that family support was very important. Many of them said that, without the support of their spouse, they would not have been able to complete the program.

Question # 12 How do you feel about the length of the program?

Most people felt that the length was "just right," and should not be lengthened or shortened. But, their comments fell into five areas: a) Good, don't change it; b) Wondered if having the summer off didn't cause some breakdown at the end; c) Two days together would have been better; d) If they change it, they would have to lengthen it. Only one school, School Yellow, has a program that meets every other weekend (Friday and Saturday). Comments:

a) Good, don't change it

"Excellent, don't see how they could do it any other way. Couldn't shorten or lengthen it (female, age 36, School yellow)."

"Good, fine. If you change it, make it three years (male, age 54, School Yellow)."

"Don't change. I couldn't imagine shortening or lengthening it. There is just enough time to read and absorb (female, age 34, School Yellow)."

"Fine, not longer. Leave it alone (male, age 46, School Yellow)."

"Could have squeezed in a little more, but I don't know how much. You could get rid of the summer(male, age 39, School Blue)."

"About right. The summers off are great. Every Friday would be better. Sometimes, Saturday was difficult (male, age 39, School Goldenrod)."

I was certainly ready for it to be over at the end of two years(male, age 36, School Goldenrod)!"

"Fine, covered a lot in a short time. Some aspects could be shortened or lengthened (male, age 33, School Green)"

"It was just about right. People were starting to reach core meltdown at the end (Male, age 39, School Green)."

"Just right. Any less, would have been giving us a piece of paper. Any more, we could not have handled it (female, age 35, School Green)."

All right. If it had been longer, would have had higher burnout(female, age 32, School Green)."

"Not sure you could shorten it and make it work (male, age 37, School Goldenrod)."

b) The summer took away from the program:

"Wondering if the summer off didn't cause us to break stride (male, age 36, School Goldenrod)."

c) Two days together would be better:

"Would be better to have two days together (Female, age 32, School Goldenrod)."

d) Would have to lengthen it:

"Not longer or shorter. If it were going to change, they would have to lengthen it (male, age 34, School Yellow.)"

Comments about Question #12

Sixteen (66.66%) of those I interviewed said the length was good. This was further indication that the vast majority of the alumni undertook the EMBA program with rigorous expectations of a challenge. Although it seemed that there was a desire for a weekend program like School Yellow, where every other weekend is off, only one person actually mentioned that. Those I interviewed and asked about a Friday/Saturday

218

combination seemed to feel that it would cause problems with either their employer or their family. Because some of these programs have been in existence for up to 20 years, it appears that the schedule is something that has been studied with some regularity.

<u>Question #13. What methods of instruction were employed at the program you attended? What is your reaction to this type of instruction? Would you have preferred more lecture or more discussion type of instruction?</u>

All of the programs used a combination of lecture, discussion, case study, and projects. Most alumni liked the mix of types of instruction. Their answers ranged from an affirmation of approval for the methods their specific school chose, a wish to add a little more to the case studies, to a desire for fewer group projects. The answers of the alumni confirmed that the method the instructor chose was a function of his or her comfort level, and when the method was criticized, it was usually because that particular instructor was not using a method that fit the material.

a) The variety was useful:

"It was interactive; overall, the mix was good (male, age 34)."

"It was excellent; these were really world class people, on the cutting edge of things. They made an extra effort to be available (male, age 54).

"I liked it very much; it was similar to law school, very valuable (female, age 38)."

"It was done pretty well. Each professor had a different way; some were more difficult than others to figure out (male, age 36)."

"Seemed pretty useful: case studies, reading, exams (male, age 39)."

b) Liked case study:

"Liked case study; would like to have had more closure to the cases (male, age 42)."

"The case method and immersion were most effective (male, age 33)."

"I got excited about the cases. They were very worthwhile for me (female, age 35)."

c) Fewer group projects:

"Would have preferred less group projects (male, age 42)."

I then asked if they preferred more lecture or more discussion type of instruction. The answers were very strongly skewed toward an interactive format, especially for this kind of experienced student :

a) Preferred more discussion

"the audience did not warrant pure lecture (female, age 33)."

"would not have preferred more lecture to discussion (male, age 39)."

"Some classes had too much lecture....Sometimes, the lecture was too theoretical (male, age 37)."

"It depended on the class. For the most part, the instructor did a good job of combining lecture with class discussion (male, age 36)."

"The more we worked as a team, the more we realized that we were actually learning more than we wrote down on our own. I liked more discussion (male, age 54)."

"More discussion type (male, age 37; male, age 34; female, age 33)."

b) It was a good balance:

"good balance (female, age 36)."

c) Some people needed "air time (male, age 34)."

Comments about Question #13

As expected, most people felt that a lot of work had gone into devising the best teaching methods for the executive program. They felt that the discussions and case studies added relevance to their education. The only negatives were the instructors who expected too much memorization, used a poor balance of lecture and discussion, and the students who needed "air time." By this they meant the few participants who had to have their say about every issue, and tended to use valuable time in doing so. These types of classmates were in every school. Seven of the twenty-four, or 29%, specifically mentioned the importance of discussion classes.

Table 73 shows the following ranking for classroom elements:

Table 73 Personal value of program elements (from surveys).

	Program Element	Mean score, 1-4, 1=no value, 4= extremely valuable
1	Class sessions	3.77
2	Study groups	3.72
3	Readings	3.50
4	Informal discussions	3.35
5	International trip	2.83
6	Conversations with faculty	2.82
7	Informal social gatherings, parties, dinners, etc.	2.73

In the survey results, the class sessions remained the most important part of the program experience. The 24 interview participants concurred with the above findings, that the classes and study groups were the most important parts of the program.

Question #14a, How would you evaluate the effectiveness of the faculty?

The alumni either acknowledged that the faculty were one of the strongest parts of the program, or they felt that there was some variation in quality of faculty members:

a) One of the strongest parts of the program:

> "one of the strongest parts of the program (male, age 34, School Yellow)."

> "excellent, really world class people, made extra effort to be available to us (male, age 54, School Yellow)."

> "very good. Very effective in being able to figure out what your needs are. Very available….home phone numbers, etc. (female, age 38, School Yellow)."

> "generally responsive to comments (male, age 46, School Yellow)."

> "seemed to bring a lot of experience in…well respected. Held our attention (male, age 39, School Blue)."

b) Some very good, some not so good:

"Reflective of the fact that some were very good and some not so very good....two useless, one gone (female, age 34, School Yellow)."

"Some instructors were better than others. Overall, they were wonderful. (female, age 40, School Blue)."

"Those who had been part (of the program)since inception were probably the most effective ones. A couple weren't prepared and relied too much on discussion instead of delivering a lecture (male, age 39, School Green)."

"Overall, they were excellent; one or two were ineffective. They were really motivated to help us get through the program (female, School Green, Age 35)."

"Statistics teacher only teaching for two years (female, Age 32, School Goldenrod)."

Comments about Question #14 a.

It can be seen from the comments that every school had top notch teachers and every school had a few who were not so well accepted. However, the complaints about those "who need to go" did not contain themselves to one or two schools. This appears to be a common problem, made worse by the high expectations of executive students.

Forty-six percent of the surveys returned rated the program a 5 out of 5, 5 being excellent. The average rating for the program was 4.34..

Question #14b, "Thinking specifically about the instructor you felt was most effective, what attributes and characteristics did he or she demonstrate that a made him or her most effective from your point of view?"

There were numerous words that were common to the answers to this question. They fell into three general categories: strong mix of industry and academic credentials, enthusiasm and an animated teaching style that showed an interest in how the students were learning, and instructors who had rigorous expectations of themselves and came to class prepared for good discussions.

    a) Strong mix of industry and academic credentials:

"A strong mix of both industry knowledge and academic knowledge. They pushed people into having to do something if they didn't have the financial knowledge. They would stick around to eat dinner with the class, and be available for outside assistance (male, age 34)."

"Very complex…the ability to take myriad considerations and to approach and get their arms around it and present it in such a way that we could digest it. Very laudable (female, age 39)."

"It was so obvious they were independent thinkers. They knew their material, did their own research….there was mutual respect….they were interested in picking our brain (male, age 42)."

"Their knowledge, and ability to facilitate the class with real world humor, real world examples. They really seemed to enjoy doing this….they wanted you to have a meaningful experience (female, age 37)."

"The ability to relate the theory to real world situations, the ability to lead a good class discussion (male, age 37)."

"An easy teaching style, the ability to explain; people who were involved with business on the side (male, age 45)."

b) Animated teaching style:

"Enthusiasm. They cared about the topic and about learning more than one point of view (female, age 36)."

"Jose de la Torre went out of his way to make sure he was teaching to the entire class, to make sure that people really benefited from class (male, age 46)."

"The common thread was enthusiasm for the material. They had an interest in using a learning, teaching style that was fun (male, age 36)."

"Bob Brown and Rocky Higgins….entertaining, a good job of relating to the cases (male, age 39)."

"Good presentation, crystal clear, animated (male, age 54)."

c) Rigorous expectations:

" Those who knew how to reach adults, were thorough, and knew that some people had experience (female, age 33)."

"Very discussion oriented; good at applying cases to business, in touch with business (female, age 34)."

"Used case studies. Very demanding, expected a lot. The level of commitment and level of support. He was working as hard as we were in the program to make this a quality experience (female, age 32)."

"The ability to cause us to solve problems that were the curricula of that class. The ability to get the class to figure out what it was that was essential to know, and to teach ourselves (male, age 33)."

"Great knowledge of the subject matter; many years of experience. Real interest in applying it and making sure we understood what we were talking about (male, age 34)."

Comments about Question #14B

The tie-in of industry experience and the ability to teach was clear not only in this question, but in the survey answers to Question #27, whether they would support changing the requirements to something other than a Ph.D. for people with extensive industry experience. The students as customers got the most value from instructors who had a thorough knowledge of their field, could relate it to modern business practices, and presented the material in an interesting way that got the students involved.

Question #15 Can you give me a brief account of your previous experience; that is, prior to entering the program, what types of jobs had you held?

As would be expected, the experience held by the 24 people I interviewed was indicative of a pattern of achievement. Examples include:

1) Naval Academy graduate.
2) MA in Math, taught high school
3) Attorney working in environmental consulting (now in aerospace).
4) Big Six accounting firm in New York, Brazil, and Houston.
5) CFO of a financial services company.

All of the backgrounds of these alumni showed a pattern of movement in a direction that capitalized on their strengths and interests. As seen from previous comments, several told me that the EMBA enabled them to get their current jobs.

Only one of the alumni I interviewed did not have a college degree before entering the program. He runs a family retail appliance store, which is open seven days a week. He shared with me the story of how his building burned down and he knew he needed an education to build his business back up. He credits the EMBA with the skills and the outlook that he needed to gain.

Question #16a. What has been your experience since finishing the program, but way of promotion, salary increases, and increase of responsibility?

One of the alumni said that "30% changed jobs, 30% got promoted, and 30% stayed where they were." There seemed to be that kind of breakdown in the answers to this question, which covered the following areas: a) A salary increase and promotion; b) Nothing direct, but have obtained more respect and responsibility; c) Changed jobs, with the MBA as a factor; d) Increased level of credibility and special assignments.

a) A salary increase and promotion

"Improved my case analysis. My moves in consulting have doubled my salary (male. Age 34)."

"I received a salary increase and promotion. I don't know if it is relevant to the program.(female, age 36)."

"I was promoted from first to second level manager at the end of the second year. It is directly related to the program (male, age 37)."

"A significant promotion after a year. I'm making more than I ever made (female, age 32)."

b) More respect and responsibility.

"People respect me because of my persistence; they wish they could do it, too (male, age 54)."

"My boss probably gives me more responsibility, knowing that I have been through the program (male, age 39)."

"There has been a definite increase in responsibility and diversity. It has made life more challenging and rewarding (male, age 46)."

c) Changed jobs; the MBA was a factor:

"I changed jobs. The MBA was a factor in getting the job (female, age 38)."

"I left my job and started another-it is partially attributable to the program (male, age 33)."

d) Increased level of credibility and received special assignments:

"I was given special projects because of my education (male, age 39)."

"Internally, there is a level of credibility; professionally, it's a good seal of approval (male, age 39)."

Comments about Question #16a

The variables that contributed to the answers to this question included opportunity, that is the proper opportunity at the right time for the person who just finished the program, change in interest or motivation of the person during the program (such as one person who decided that he really liked finance better than engineering, but there were no opportunities for him), and other competition in the form either of other people or other priorities for the corporation or the individual. This is why it is hard to promise a prospective applicant that any EMBA program will specifically accomplish a raise or promotion within a given time frame.

Question 16b If there has been a change in the attitude of other people toward you, can you describe this change of attitude?

There were four different responses to this question: a) there has been no change in attitude; b) there are comments about my performance; c) it took some time in coming; and, d) yes, they do pay better attention. Because the program was a continuous two year process, it was hard for people to recognize specific changes in attitude. They did have some interesting comments:

a) "No, not that I'm aware of."

"No (male, age 34, consulting)."

"I don't think so (male, age 42, manufacturing)."

"Not that I'm aware of (male, age 34, health care)."

"Not really (male, age 37, aerospace)."

b) Comments about performance improvement:

"Yes, the boss has commented any number of times that he's thought I've come to a whole new level. (The change is due to) me changing my attitude (male, age 46)."

"A little more professional respect, a little more value (male, age 39)."

c) It took some time:

"It took some time in coming. Being a woman had something to do with it (female, age 36, aerospace)."

d) Yes, they do pay attention:

"It started as soon as I started the program. One of the people would say, "when you say something, Pete really pays attention."

Comments about Question #16b

As I have reviewed the backgrounds and prior degrees of the people I interviewed, it has become clear that they sought the MBA for their own reasons, to give themselves the credentials they needed for whatever the future brought, and that the attitude of other people was secondary to their mission. This question was not one that received much response one way or the other, again confirming my feeling that a change in attitude of other people was not necessarily what people were seeking.

Question #17 With regard to coverage of issues important to you, how do you feel about that?

With the level of positive response to these programs, I expected mostly approval of the issues taught in the program. As during the other questions, however, I found a vocal complaint here and there that coincided with comments made earlier in the interview. There were five categories of responses: a) Good coverage; b) Not enough finance (related to School Yellow); c) Too much emphasis on soft skills; d) More human relations-type courses, more electives; d) More Information Science, and, e) Don't combine the operations and marketing courses (this related specifically to school Goldenrod, where that was done).

a) Good coverage:

"Not being in business, everything I picked up interested me (male surgeon, age 54)."

"Very good coverage (female attorney, age 38)."

"Good job. Would definitely do it again (female, age 34)."

"The issues I was really interested in were covered really well (male, age 39, manufacturing)."

"Everything was covered really well (male, age 39, male, age 39, male, age 33)."

"Yes, especially marketing and finance. Good organizational development (male, age 37, aerospace).

b) Not enough finance:

"More finance, less soft skills (male, age 30, electrical distribution)."

"Did not spend enough time on how to invest (female, age 40)."

"Extra finance class, more electives(male, age 46)."

c) Too much emphasis in soft skills:

"Less soft skills (male, age 30, electrical distribution.)"

Too much soft skills (male, age 34, consulting)."

d) More information sciences:

"More IS—the professor didn't even know how to use excel (female, age 33, banking)."

"Really light on any of the computer modeling; use of technology weak (female, age 32, finance)."

e) Don't combine marketing with operations management:

"Operations management combined with marketing....Spent 80% of the time working on flows and little on marketing (male, age 39,)."

Comments about Question #17

Nine people, or 37.5%, felt that the issues were covered very well. The isolated comments could be attributed to specific problems that might have been one semester in duration, and to the varying interests of the alumni. For instance, the two comments about the excess of human relations courses came from men, both under 35 years of age, who felt that quantitative issues were more important. The person who wanted more HR skills works in aerospace, and is significantly older than the two men who felt the HR emphasis unnecessary. Several people had mentioned offering electives in the other parts of the interview. Although I would take this information into consideration when planning courses such as finance at School Yellow, where there is an obvious desire, from both the surveys and the interview, the overall evaluation from those interviewed was very positive.

<u>Question #18 Were there other results of this EMBA program, such as social relationships, networking opportunities, that stand out in your mind?</u>

This was the respondent's last chance to make comments about the program. Some used it to reiterate the impact that the people in the program had, some talked about the impact of the program, and some talked about career decisions.

<u>Comments about relationships:</u>

1) "The overall business understanding and networking (male, age 34)."

2) "A different outlook on business, a higher level; it makes us stronger political consumers; great tools that no-one can take away from us (male, age 39)."

3) "Definitely building networking opportunities(male, age 42)."

4) "I have availed of the professors; they treated us as an exclusive class (male, age 36)."

5) "Very, very , good social relationships with people in class (female, age 38)."

6) "Being able to call on people in the community and ask their advice, networking, finding services(male, age 33)."

<u>Comment about business plans</u>

7) "I actually will go into business for myself one day (female, age 36)."

<u>Comments about credibility</u>

8) "I would not have had the credibility without it."

9) "The main things were the tools(male, age 37)."

10) "I am much happier with the result than I expected....would do it again in a heartbeat(male, age 34)."

11) "The degree had an impact on getting the job at Microsoft (female, age 41)."

Other comments about the program

12) "Very pleased with the course overall; response to customer input...learning how to deal with different people, see how customers can be (male, age 46)."

13) Broadened my horizons (female, age 40)."

The International trip

14) "The trip to Munich and Prague (female, age 40).".

15) "I learned a lot from the international trip (male, age 39)."

Negative comments

16) "The glass ceiling is still there (female, age 40)."

17) "Some classes were "dummed down". The statistics class was not good (female, School Goldenrod)."

18) "They let people in who were not going to be able to sustain the level of workload required (male, School Goldenrod)."

19) "They are institutions. As far as vision is concerned, they are slow to change ....did not feel like the customer (female, School Goldenrod)."

20) "The problem professors are out of touch...not appreciating the fact that this is a group of people who were highly efficient in their business and did not have time to just be doing busy work (female, School Green)."

Comments about Question #18

This was a good opportunity to see how strongly the alumni felt about some of the issues they had expressed earlier. The same issues, those of relationship building, the international trip, credibility in the work force, a change in the way they look at issues, came through again. This final comment is a chance for the four schools to review them and take any action they may deem necessary.

Relation to the Research Questions

I was able to comment on the research questions, both after completing the survey research and the 24 interviews. From the perspective of the interviews, the research questions garnered the following general responses (italics for emphasis):

The research question that serves as the basis for the sub-questions is:

> **Are the schools that are producing executive training at the MBA level meeting the needs of their mid-career students for programs that address their concerns as working professionals?** *The comments, program and faculty ratings of the alumni would offer an affirmative response to this question. With the exception of a few comments about poor faculty or courses, the rating of all elements of the programs were above average.*

Several sub-questions and hypotheses were developed using an inductive approach:

a) In relating to the Andrews/Powell survey, the first hypothesis states that there is no difference in reaction by executive students to the effectiveness of programs in 1995 vs. their reactions in 1965.

With regard to the Harvard rating, by equalizing the rating to the seven choices offered in the Harvard study, the overall rating for the faculty was .84 vs. Harvard's .81. If this is accurate, it would mean that the current program faculty were rated about 3.7% higher than the Harvard faculty. Based on the many variables involved, however, I would take this analysis to accept the fact that there is no difference between Harvard ratings and the ratings of the programs in the current research .

In addition, several other questions were be added to the material I used from the original Andrews' survey in order to ask the following:

b) Do these programs effectively address ethnic and gender differences today? *I did not specifically ask this question because, when it got down to sending the surveys out, I did not feel (and my Chair agreed) that this question would add to the worth of the research. There were several comments about the need to run* diversity training, so the answer here would have to be that there remains some need for further work on diversity training.

c) Are the programs affected by the lack of security in the workplace today and are people using the Executive MBA degree to make a career change?

The lack of security in the workforce most definitely has affected the desire of the participants to enhance their skills so that they are marketable. Also, unlike the Harvard participants, who were mostly career men, these people have embraced the opportunity to change careers in their mid-40's. The EMBA has given them the security they needed.

d) Are the courses relevant to the executive's job needs? Do they help him/her do the job better or are they too academic?

In a few cases, the courses were too academic. However, the ratings given the program and the attendant comments leave one with the answer that the courses are relevant to the needs of the students and that the schools continue to work on maintaining that relevance.

e) Do sponsoring companies make concerted use of the skills learned?

About 30% of the companies make specific use of the skills. However, the comments did not seem to reflect a feeling that the lack of use meant that the investment was not worth it for the long-run. I would answer this question in the affirmative.

f) Do women continue to have a problem with the "glass ceiling" even after attaining the skills that the programs produce?

The women I asked agreed that the glass ceiling still exists, but also that they have been able to become and remain successful in spite of it. They know it is there, but work hard to get around it.

Conclusion

The 24 people who invested, or whose companies invested, up to $50,000, in their executive education, felt that they got their money's worth, that the skills they learned enabled them to think differently and improved their job performance. They also felt that there were improvements in their relationships, both personally and professionally.

The overall evaluations of the programs pointed out weaknesses in the area of some faculty and programs, such as finance, that could be strengthened. I will leave it to the schools who so graciously participated in this research to review the comments as they might relate to their specific programs.

Schools are in a difficult position with regard to competitive programs and institutions. They are beholden to the industries who support them and must set their acceptance criteria accordingly. If they set them too high, they might not get the students they need to finance their programs. If they set them too low, there are complaints from other students.

My feeling is that the schools who participated in my research are doing everything they can to maintain high standards, but issues of criteria for acceptance continue to be difficult.

Academic rigor is a plus for these programs. From my corporate interviews, I learned that corporations are looking for rigor, not country club schools. For the most part, these programs met the students' desire for an academic program that challenged them. The study groups contributed to that challenge and to the take-away of other points of view that they experienced.

The 24 interviews tended to confirm, rather than differ from, the survey material. I would have preferred to interview a few people who were representative of more ethnic and racial groups, but I'm confident that this group of alumni represented those who enroll in executive MBA programs today, both those who are fully funded and those who are funding their own education.

CHAPTER 8

DISCUSSION

and

CONCLUSIONS

The Andrews/Powell research, which surveyed 10,000 men who had taken residence management programs at 39 schools, concluded with implications for both university and company action. This chapter will begin with a review of those implications. I will then discuss the elements learned from the triangulation elements of my research as they relate to my research questions and to future strategic plans for university executive education programs.

Discussion of the Andrews/Powell research implications

The Andrews/Powell research noted the following conclusions from their research:

a) Implications for University Action

Andrews noted the following as "the common elements in all programs which appear to be the real sources of participant satisfaction (Andrews, 1956, p.187).":

1) *Instruction without condescension.* This element received a number of comments from the alumni I interviewed, so it is safe to say that it is an important element in today's programs as well.

2) *Full-time use of the mind.* "The satisfaction of protracted thought, never solitary but constantly stimulated by the thinking of others, outweighed the frustrations of a novel social-intellectual climate (ibid., p.188). It is safe to conclude that the expectation and approval of a rigorous and challenging program is a common element in both of these research projects.

3) *Immediate relevance.* In my research, there were a few who made comments that they were disappointed that they were not able to use the knowledge immediately in the workplace, but the majority commented about the methods of seeing problems in new ways and the benefits of a team to look at situations from several different perspectives.

4) *Pleasure in association.* Throughout my research, I found references to the wonderful classmates and life-long friendships that resulted from the EMBA programs I was studying. My research, then, would be in agreement with the Andrews' comment that "it is unnecessary to say more about this universal source of satisfaction (ibid., p.189)."

5) *Self-respect.* The entire Andrews comment is important in that it so closely mirrors my results:

> As indicated in the figures which show that gain in self-confidence is the most frequently reported effect, the discovery that a man's own powers and experience compare favorably with others....must be centrally important in the favorable judgment rendered so often (ibid., p.189).

Andrews also mentioned that the men had not predicted this outcome. In my surveys, the expectation of an increase in self-confidence was also not mentioned.

6) *Respect for occupation.* The research I am reporting on would parallel the former in the contribution that it makes to a worthwhile educational experience.

b) Implication for company action.

Andrews mentioned that companies must take into consideration the characteristics of the program, the course content, the level of responsibility and diversity of participants, the faculty and teaching methods, and the length of the program. My research found many parallels to the above needs, but it did find some differences.

For instance, Andrews found that " a man should normally not be sent after he is 55 years of age (ibid., p.217)." One of the men I interviewed, and one of the most vibrant of the group, falls into this age bracket, paid for the program himself, and was using it to improve his skills so that he could change his field of work. If anything, age limits no longer apply in the world of continuous learning and in the expanding field of executive education.

The need for good and innovative faculty received more than slight mention in my research. In fact, the vocal minority produced an unexpected focus on the importance of retaining good faculty. In one of the program director interviews, the difficulty of attracting and retaining qualified faculty was mentioned as the greatest challenge in the coming years. Andrews did not mention the problem that tenure brings to the employment of faculty, but my research found that the one school where faculty in the EMBA program were not tenured(in that program) seemed to get the best overall ratings from students, who commented that poor professors were simply not there the next semester.

I found in my interviews with corporate sponsors that they are increasingly giving consideration to the succession plan of the employee before commitments are made to send them to executive management programs. The stated purpose, course content, and level of responsibility of the prospective student are being more closely monitored. If nothing else, the downsizing of large corporations would require that their executive education budgets be scrutinized to assure the most for their money.

In general, I found agreement with the Andrews' conclusions regarding what universities and companies need to do in order to ensure a quality experience that returns benefits to the corporation for the money they have invested, and to continue to attract increasing numbers of people who are willing to finance the programs themselves as an investment in their future.

I will now discuss the implications that were drawn from the research done using the four campuses, the corporate sponsors, and the program directors.

Implications of the current research

The advantage of triangulation is that it allows the researcher to follow threads of reasoning from one method to another. I was able to see the following areas of commonality in the survey results, interviews of alumni, and interviews of corporate executives:

1) Today's customers are looking for rigorous programs, whether they themselves are paying for them or not. The days when executive programs were viewed as rewards and opportunities for social interaction are over. The very few in these programs who did not pull their weight were heavily chastised by their classmates and, in some cases, dismissed from their study groups because of it. Companies are looking for a financial justification in order to fund these programs. It was very obvious to me that the participants felt the need for that justification as well, because they knew the value of their time. They were outspoken about poorly qualified faculty as well as classmates.

The original Harvard research reported on social activities because these longer programs tended to have more time for social activities than the programs I was researching. With regard to alcohol consumption, "drinking, as a phenomenon of executive programs, was judged…..halfway between "moderate and "heavy" at a long program. (Andrews, 1966, p.97). Program directors might be concerned "lest preparation for class should be submerged by conviviality. (ibid., p.99)" However, the men in the Harvard research reported that drinking and social activities did not interfere with the pursuit of the program elements. From a general sense, the research I pursued convinced me of the fact that my participants knew they were making a very large commitment of time and effort to attain a goal that they themselves set; thus, they were not interested in letting social activities or drinking lessen the number one purpose of the activity they were pursuing. An actual comparison of social activities in the Harvard research to my research is impossible because the lengths of programs are different and the earlier research dealt with residential programs, but the Andrews/Powell research reported that social activities were less important than the course work to their participants.

2) Because corporations are using succession plans to make decisions about sending people to programs such as the ones I was researching, the competition is tough. But, the corporations I interviewed plan to continue that investment into executive education. They view it as an important investment not always tied to revenues in a specific year. They realize that there is a risk the employees will leave once their program is done, but they do not see it as a major risk.

By the same token, there were a number of alumni who used their EMBA program to advance or change careers. Some of them, however, felt more loyalty to the corporation because of the financial support provided.

3) Executives need a different kind of instruction. When I asked the question "would you support lowering the requirement of a Ph.D. for someone with a lot of experience," the overwhelming comment came back that the most important thing was to be able to teach. The Ph.D.'s who were strong on theory and weak on practical application got the poorest marks. In all four cases, the alumni were pleading with the administration to listen to their complaints and, tenure or no tenure, get "rid of the dead wood." I would suggest that the tenure issue may need to be studied anew. Major changes in industry today include downsizing, different ways of measuring productivity, and explosive

competition. Universities are no different in their need to survey and react to the competitive situation.

Table 2, on page 17, lists the major negative comments that I discovered in doing research on executive education. In listing the comments from the Johnson, et. al. Research (1988), the following were noted:

a) Increased responsiveness is needed to student course content needs.
b) Less academic, more practical content is needed.
c) Appropriate training for instructors is required.

Even though alumni are, in general, satisfied with their executive education experience, the above comments remain as complaints from those who participated in my research. In addition, the following conclusions can be drawn:

1) Yes, EMBA programs are meeting the needs of their customers, both the sponsoring corporations and the students who are increasingly investing in these programs themselves. There continues to be evidence that the schools are making important changes. As an example, a poll in 1995 found that 38% of the MBA students at Washington University's John B.Olin School of Business (in St. Louis) were dissatisfied with the administration's responsiveness. This year, that number dropped to 3% (Leonhardt, 1996). In addition, the current annual <u>Business Week</u> rating of the best business schools notes several references to the importance of teaching, among them "last year, a Wharton prof was yanked off a core finance course after student complaints of poor performance" and "Stanford dropped to seventh from fourth because of student complaints about the quality of the teaching (Byrne, J.& Leonhardt, D., 1996)."

2) The need to continue "lifelong" learning is being heard by the populace. Both the fact that 50% of my interview subjects had previous advanced degrees and the comments of the program directors that people get EMBAs to protect themselves and prepare for an uncertain future corroborated the observations from the literature review, where Peter

Drucker, Peter Senge, and others were quoted as acknowledging the need to be prepared to keep up with and continue to learn new skills. In addition, over 20% of the participants paid for their programs themselves, which is a target-market signal to the universities who put on these programs.

3) The program directors play a number of roles. They include recruiter, house-mother(or father), confidant, sergeant, go-between, planner, and punching-bag. Although some of the alumni confirmed that they see the program director in primarily an administrative function and do not ascribe any of the responsibility of the program to him or her, more of them made comments that the program would have received a higher grade if the program director had been more positive or that the program director was definitely at least 20-25% responsible for the positive feelings the particular alumnus had about the program. One comment, from a woman who was 35 when she graduated:

> What I didn't realize until Dave came along was that that position could be so much more. Dave was incredibly organized, very focused, very task oriented. He added a discipline to it that we hadn't seen before. He was very clear on what was and wasn't possible.

Another comment from a 39 year-old graduate of the same program:

> Dave Dungan is a jewel. From the day I first contacted him, he pulled me into it and was a lot of m y reason for wanting to do it. He was our advocate, he was one of us."

In some cases, the program director has more input into course selection than in others. Regardless of this fact, however, the importance of having someone in that job who is consumer-focused, a great (not good) communicator, a great listener, and very organized was very clear from the research I conducted.

4) Managers are looking to improve their human relations skills. There was less a mention of "broadening" in this group than in the Andrews/Powell research. This group wanted definite skills to improve their competitive abilities and to enhance their ability to manage and lead.

5) The 1959 survey noted a large concentration of managers from the manufacturing and oil industries. Current industry concentration has tended to be in service industries, such as finance, health care, and consulting. These industries include those managed by the "knowledge workers" that Peter Drucker began talking about early in the 1990's (Drucker, 1992). At that time, he said that

> knowledge is *the* (emphasis his) primary resource for individuals and for the economy overall. Land, labor, and capital—the economist's traditional factors of production—do not disappear, but they become secondary. They can be obtained, and obtained easily, provided there is specialized knowledge.

Some of the comments about improving the programs suggested that the schools concentrate less on big manufacturing companies and more on small business, service businesses, and non-traditional kinds of companies. In this respect, all four schools might review their curriculum for the next few years in light of where their students are working now, not where they were working in the late 1980's, before there was a major shift in employment that covered sectors from the aerospace giants to AT&T.

6) The impact of good teachers on students of all ages is an area of varying emphasis in the educational community. In his recent book "Aptitude Revisited," David E. Drew states that

> there is no question that the degree to which faculty are oriented toward working with students is very strongly related to students' satisfaction with their college science experience (Drew, 1996, p. 108).

This research confirmed that there is a strong correlation between the rating of the faculty and the rating of the program. The participants were extremely vocal, both in the surveys and in person, in pointing out that the "dead wood" drag down the school's reputation. For that reason, the one school that does not grant tenure to professors in its executive program seems to have found a workable solution to that problem. I realize that the tenure issue is beyond the scope of my research and that its history contains many more elements than this discussion can cover. However, the fact that students expect to get their money's worth from each and every professor and course, and the fact that this research treated those students as customers, raises the question of whether the tenure issue should be revisited.

7) In what ways is this research like Andrews and in what ways is it not?

    a) Marital status and company seniority were different, as expected. Fewer people were married, and the company seniority was decreased.

    b) Satisfaction with the program was very similar to the original research. This helps to dispel the criticisms of university programs that they are not current.

    c) Satisfaction with the professor has an impact on the program satisfaction for both the Andrews and current research.

Suggestions for further research

1) Because of the correlation between the rating of the professors and the rating of the program, it would be interesting to do further research linking each subject interest with the professor evaluation. This information might help schools to deal more effectively with courses where the subject matter requires excellence in teaching.

2) On the whole, human relations garnered lower interest, as measured by the mean score, in this group than it had in the Harvard research. The mean for Harvard was 5.3 (of 6), while the mean for this group was 4.48, 15.47% lower. This difference bears research to find out why, in an era when good management is increasingly involving human relations skills, this group of alumni would rate it of lesser importance than most other areas.

3) Tenure

The issue of whether to grant tenure to professors, giving them lifetime job security, arises from this research because job security in most other industries has declined markedly over the years. Countries such as Japan, who once used lifetime employment as an advantage in productivity and security for employees, can no longer afford such a promise. US companies such as IBM, whose reputation was in part based on the acknowledged job security of their many thousands of workers, have seen their ranks fall victim to the corporate ax as well. The question, then, remains: is tenure hurting long-term productivity of professors and creating a roadblock to better teachers? Are there better measures to ensure continued quality in teaching? The tenure issue is one that definitely deserves further research, specifically into the following questions:

a) Is tenure meeting the same needs that originally caused it to come into being? (Here, we might draw analogies with some of the programs developed by FDR which are now being revamped to meet the current society's needs).

b) Does tenure cause damage in any way to a school's quality of education?

c) What are the alternatives available, such that academic freedom is protected, given the answers to the above?

The tenure issue was addressed by David Leonhardt in the 1996 rating of business schools for <u>Business Week</u>. He noted that "tenure provides little incentive for faculty to do anything outside their narrow spheres of expertise" and "Many (B-school deans) see tenure…as an outdated system that drives up costs and lessens accountability (Leonhardt, 1996, p.130)." He also reported that no area in the annual rating showed less improvement than teaching.

4) The question about the "glass ceiling," while limited because of the small number of women in my sample, yielded a strong finding that there remain barriers to women in business, both culturally and personally. Further research might look at large and small companies to assess their current climate with regard to the financial benefit they expect

from the performance of their employees when they are assigned positions commensurate with their abilities.

5) The executive student

Andrews commented, and my research confirmed, that the executive student expects to be treated differently. Indeed, in the classes where the professor expected memorization and did not differentiate from his or her daytime MBA students, the evaluations and comments were more often negative.

There has been much research regarding the adult learner. The results from my interviews and the surveys would lead me to want to know in specifically what areas present schools need improvement. With regard to content, I noticed that they wanted less 'big company' cases and more attention to the emerging small business explosion. However, in terms of how they learn, other than the frustration of those who needed remedial training in quantitative issues (and the attendant frustration of those who felt the first group should have been prepared for the quantitative issues), I saw very little complaint that the programs were not addressing specific learning styles. Both my research and the Harvard research confirmed that discussion style learning is preferred by this audience. With the current growth of on-line education, there may need to be further research into how these options are affected by adult learning.

6) Funding

The financial benefit to corporations for sponsoring executive education includes the tax consequences for the corporations. Recent literature points to a possible end to the ability to deduct expenses incurred in the process of this type of education (Capell, 1996). Further research might produce findings on how this circumstance will affect current executive education programs.

Conclusion

Business schools are businesses, even if somewhat different businesses than those that foot the bill for the executive management programs. The schools must attract customers, create a product, finance expansion, and update their resources. Herbert Simon, in his landmark study of decision-making processes in organizations (1976), discussed some fairly specific correlations between business schools and businesses themselves. He found that business schools themselves were interesting fields of research for organization theory. His suggestions included the following:

1) Business schools must "understand the business environment, the nature of the managers tasks and problems, and the skills and techniques employed by successful managers and successful business organizations (Ibid., p.337)."

2) Business schools must have access to information and skills within the sciences that are relevant to the improvement of professional practice. Simon recognized the difficulty of attracting and retaining qualified faculty who also possess business experience. He sought to avoid hiring those who see the academic profession as semi-retirement and a chance at "telling the boys how I did it (Ibid., p.343)." Simon also mentioned the necessity of providing the less experienced faculty member with access to the business environment.

3) The professional school must be vigorous in research as well as teaching.

4) Departmental structures must not be allowed to develop in the professional business school.

5) "What is important is that the administration of the professional school take the lowering of barriers as a major goal of its policy (Ibid., p. 352)."

Simon felt that business schools and businesses have much to teach and to learn from each other. This research was a confirmation of Simon's objectives because it cited problems of communication between faculty and students, and problems of communication between corporations and business school administrations. Both works recognize the need for better communication among all elements of business schools. Business schools must look at their programs the way a business looks at a product: will it sell, and is it what the customer needs? A persistent research result is the need to reduce departmentalization in which one area of the school dominates the other because of strong faculty. Decisions concerning whether to use the lockstep method of moving students through the program together or giving them choices of courses such that their experience is more varied should be looked at anew; this research reported the value of study groups that were created, in part, by the lockstep method. Where are barriers most stripped away, where are research and practice most allowed to coexist? Now is the opportunity for schools to use this information in dissecting each element of their program to decide if it meets both the school's purposes and objectives and the changing needs of the students.

This research identified some of the ways that executive education has changed in the past 40 years. These include different bases of sponsorship, e.g. finance vs. the oil industry, a move toward smaller businesses, and the need to produce managers who can operate in an arena of uncertainty and change. It also identified some of the similarities over time in executive education; those include a general satisfaction level with the programs attended, a desire for rigor, and the benefit of relationships developed with classmates. The strength of the classroom experience, where personal communication is one of the most important benefits noted, was confirmed even by those who had choices of on-line alternatives.

The message that I will carry from this research is that universities need to look at their programs as any profit-making corporation would, as products that require the best resources (up-to-date course selection) and the best managers (professors). Anything less leaves them open to an unforgiving competitive atmosphere.

REFERENCES

American Psychological Association (1994), Publication Manual, Fourth Edition. Washington, D. C. : American Psychological Association

Anderson, C. (1995, May 3). School on the tube. Performance

Andrews, K. (1966). The effectiveness of university management development programs. Boston: Harvard Business School Press.

Banks, H. Aerospace & defense. (1996, January 1). Forbes.

Bannergee, Neela (1993, Sept. 10, p.R9). Battling bias. The Wall Street Journal.

Bardwick, J. (1995). Danger in the Comfort Zone. New York: AMACOM, American Management Association.

Bolt, J. F. (1993, May). Achieving the CEO's agenda: Education for executives. Management Review.

Boone, R. Jr., Christy, J.H., Fluke, C.J., Kehoe, K., Reifman, S, Z., & Sherwood, R.H. (1995, December 4). Private business. Forbes.

Bradford, W. D. (1996), Dean of the University of Washington Graduate School of Business Administration. Remarks in their 1996 EMBA catalog.

Bremner, B. (1996, July 1). Those footsteps you hear are Japan, Inc. Business Week.

Brooks, N.R. Groves, M. (1996, August 23, p.A25). Woman to run the house that Barbie built. The LosAngeles Times.

Brown, T. & Rivas, M. (1993, summer, p.83). Advising multicultural populations for achievement and success. Academic advising.

Boone, R. Jr., Christy, J.H, Fluke, C.J., Kehoe, K., Reifman, S.Z., & Sherwood, R. H. (1995, December 4). Private business. Forbes.

Bradford, W. D., Dean of the University of Washington Graduate School of Business Administration. Remarks in their 1996 EMBA catalog.

Bremner, Brian. (1996, July 1). Those footsteps you hear are Japan, Inc.

> Business Week.

Brooks, N.R. and Groves, M. (1996, August 23). Mattel's new boss, The Los

> Angeles Times, p. A25).

Byrne, J. (1991, October 28). Back to school. Business Week

Byrne, J. A. & Green,C.(1993). The best executive education programs. New York:

> McGraw Hill.

Byrne, J. (1995, October 23, p.64). Virtual B-schools. Business Week.

Byrne, J. & Leonhardt, D. (1996, October 21, p.111). The best B schools. Business

> Week.

Bongiorno, L. & Byrne, J. (1995, September 11. P.6). On the A-list at Harvard B-School.

> Business Week.

California Polytechnic University (1996, March, vol. 6, no.1). Shareholder's report.

Campbell, J. P., Daft R. L., & Hulin, C.L. (1982). What to Study.

> Beverly Hills: Sage Publications.

Capell, K. (1996, November 11, p.134E8). Uncle Sam's Surprise for Grad Students.

> Business Week.

Cheit, E. F.(1985, Spring, vol. XXVII). Business schools and their critics. California

> Management Review.

Comes, F. J. & Power, C. (1994, November 18). 21st century capitalism.

> Business Week

University of Colorado Executive MBA program catalog, 1996.

Deloitte & Touche promotional literature, 1996.

Dillman, D. A. (1978). Mail and Telephone Surveys, New York: John Wiley &

> Sons.

David, Stan and Jim Botkie (1994, September/October). "The Coming of knowledge-based business." Harvard Business Review

De Rouffignac, Ann (1993, September 10). "Teacher, teach thyself : a changing market is forcing business schools to rethink their courses-and their marketing. The Wall Street Journal.

Drew, D. E. (1996). Aptitude Revisited. Baltimore: Johns Hopkins University Press.

Drucker, Peter F. (1988, January/February) The coming of the new organization. Harvard Business Review.

Drucker, P. F. (1992, September/October). The New society of organizations. Harvard Business Review.

Du Jardin, P.E. (1981). Residential general management programs and adult development: An exploratory study. Dissertation Abstracts International, 6369. (University Microfilms No. 8202820).

Eurich, Nel (1985). Corporate classrooms. Princton: The Carnegie Foundation for the Advancement of Teaching, Princeton University Press.

Fertig, Kevin(ed.) (1994). Directory of executive MBA programs. University of Illinois.

Kichen, S. & McCarthy, T.R., ed.(1995, December 4, p.196.) Private business. Forbes.

Flint, J. (1996, January 1, p.110). Consumer durables. Forbes.

Fowler, F. J., Jr. (1984). Survey research methods . Newbury Park, CA : Sage Publications.

Fresina, A. (1988) Executive education in corporate America. Executive

Knowledgeworks.

Goulds Pumps, Inc. 1995 Annual Report.

Graham, Ellen (1993, September 10). Meat and potatoes: Sometimes the most successful courses are the most basic. <u>The Wall Street Journal</u>.

Grant, A. & Schlesinger, L. (1995, September/October). Realize your full profit potential. <u>Harvard Business Review</u>

Greenberg, J. and Baron, R.A. (1993). <u>Behavior in organizations</u>. Needham Heights, MA: Allyn and Bacon.

Glaser, B. G. and Strauss, A. L. (1967), <u>The discovery of grounded theory: strategies for qualitative research</u>. New York: Aldine de Gruyter.

Groves, M.(1996, May 26, p.D1). Women still bumping up against glass ceiling. <u>The Los Angeles Times</u>.

Harvard University (1996). Executive education program recruitment brochure.

Hayes, R. H. & Abernathy, W.J.(1980, July/August). Managing our way to decline. <u>Harvard Business Review</u>.

Hilgert, A. (1992). Personal development aspects of an executive Master of Business Administration degree program, Unpublished dissertation, The Claremont Graduate School, Claremont.

Himelstein,L. (1996, October 28,p.55). Shatterproof glass ceiling. <u>Business Week</u>.

Humble, J. (ed.) (1973). <u>Improving the performance of the experienced manager</u>. England: McGraw-Hill Book Company (UK) Limited.

Johnson, T. R., McLaughlin, S.D., Saari, L.M. & Zimmerle, D.M. (1988). The demand and Supply of University-Based Executive Education. Berkely:GMAC Occasional Papers.

Johnston, William (1991, March/April). Global work force 2000: The new world labor market." <u>Harvard Business Review</u>.

Kuhn, T. R. (1996, May/June). Electric utility deregulation sparks controversy. Harvard Business Review.

Lancaster, H. (1995, November 28,, p.B1). M.B.A. forum can give you a glimpse at schools world-wide. The Wall Street Journal.

Leavitt, H.(1989, Spring). Educating our MBA's: On teaching what we haven't taught. California Management Review.

Leonhardt, D.(1996, September 30, p.104). The way to the top: 'copy shamelessly.' Business Week.

Leonhardt, D. (1996, October 21, p.130). Tenure: an idea whose time has gone. Business Week.

Levenson, E. (1995, August 21). Part-time B-school is a full-time grind. Business Week.

Lopez, J.A. (1993, July 3). Career women are being helped more, and in new ways, when jobs turn sour. The Wall Street Journal.

Lord, M. (1993, March 22). The M.B.A. gets real. U.S. News & World Report.

Lubin, J.S. (1996, September 24, p.B1). Schools boot up to offer on-line M.B.A.'s. Harvard Business Review.

Mann, R. W. & Staudenmer, J. (1991, July). Strategic shifts in executive development. Training and Development.

McKay, Q. G. (1960). The impact of university executive development programs on participating executives. Unpublished doctoral dissertation, Harvard University.

McKay, Q. G. (1996, April 2). Verbal comments regarding his 1960 research findings. Salt Lake City.

Morrissey, C. (1993). Executive MBA directors' perception of issues in management education. Unpublished paper, The Claremont Graduate School.

Moulton, H. W. & Fickel, A.A. (1993). <u>Executive development.</u> New York: Oxford University Press.

Peltz, James F. (1996, March 17,p.D1). A jobless recovery. <u>The Los Angeles Times</u>

Popcorn, F. (1996). <u>Clicking.</u> New York: Harper Collins Publishers, Inc.

Ready, D. A. (1992, December 14, v126n13p39) Executive education: Is it making the grade?" <u>Fortune.</u>

Rheem, H. (1996, July/August, p.12). Equal opportunity for women. <u>Harvard Business Review.</u>

Rudestam, K.E. & Newton, R.R. (1992). <u>Surviving your dissertation,</u> Newbury Park, CA: Sage Publications.

Simon, H.(1976) <u>Administrative Behavior.</u> New York: The Free Press.

University of Utah public relations material, 1996.

U.S. Department of Commerce (1991). The national data book. 111th edition. Washington, D.C.: Bureau of Census

Warwick, D. P. and Lininger, C.A. (1975). <u>The sample survey: Theory and practice.</u> New York: McGraw Hill.

WellPoint Health Networks 1995 Annual Report.

Wentling, R. M. (1996, Fall). A study of the career development and aspirations of women in middle management. <u>Human Resource Development Quarterly.</u> V7n3, 253-270.

White, J.B. & Lublin, J.S. (1996, September 27, p.B1). Some companies try to rebuild loyalty. <u>The Wall Street Journal.</u>

Verlander, E. G. (1986). The use of principles of adult education in six university executive programs. Unpublished doctoral dissertation. Teachers College, Columbia University.

Xerox (1995). Annual report

Xerox (1996). Fact book.

APPENDIX B

Janis Dietz
1352 Darnell Street
Upland, California 91784

January 4, 1996

Ms. Nina Sanders
Director, Executive MBA Program
The University of Washington
322 Lewis Hall
Seattle, WA 98195-3200

Dear Ms. Sanders:

Thank you for your willingness to review the survey I will be using for my dissertation at The Claremont Graduate School. Although the survey has not been finalized yet, I anticipate very few changes. The survey will be printed on Claremont Graduate School stationary.

I will be replicating part of a survey done in 1959 by Kenneth Andrews at Harvard, which included 10,000 graduates of executive management programs from 39 schools, of which the University of Washington was one. The purpose of the original survey was to measure student response to these programs. My purpose is to query today's executive student body for their reaction to the applicability of their coursework, and to see if differences in the student populations (the Harvard sample was entirely white American male) will make a difference.

Please feel free to contact me at 909-985-2103 if you have any questions. I will call you next week to get your reactions to this material.

Thank you again for your agreement to look at the survey.

Sincerely,

Janis Dietz

APPENDIX E.

April 26, 1996

«Title» «FirstName» «LastName»
«Address1»
«City», «State» «PostalCode»

Dear «Title» «LastName»,

Gary Lindblad and The Anderson School have been very kind to work with me in my research on the satisfaction of executive students with their executive education programs. Your experience as one of a select group of alumni from UCLA and three other schools will help answer this question: Are executive programs meeting the needs of today's working executives?

I realize that you are very busy, and hope that you will take just a few minutes to help me. I have designed this instrument to be completed in under 15 minutes.

In 1959, Harvard Professors Kenneth Andrews and Reed Powell began a survey of 10,000 graduates of executive management programs to determine the worth and applicability of their programs. You have been chosen because UCLA was one of the schools used in the 1959 survey and I want to replicate many of the details of the prior work.

The survey is confidential and will be used only for the purposes of the dissertation research. Only statistically aggregated survey data will be reported; no individual respondents will be identified. The number at the bottom of the survey is intended only to keep track of responses, and not for any other purpose. I will also be conducting interviews with those alumni who agree to expand upon the survey. Please note on the first page if you are willing to be interviewed.

Thank you for your valuable time and input. Please return the survey in the enclosed envelope or fax to me at 909-949-2658. If you have any questions, please feel free to call me at 909-981-4387. Your Executive MBA experience is very helpful in determining the worth of today's programs. Again, I would like to express my thanks to the Anderson School for helping me in my dissertation research for the Peter F. Drucker Graduate Management Center.

Sincerely,
Janis Dietz

APPENDIX F

May 10, 1996

«title» «first» «last»
«address1»
«address2»
«address3»
«city», «state» «zip»

Dear «title» «last»,

Two weeks ago, you received a survey that asked your opinion about the executive MBA experience you received at the University of Washington. You were chosen because your school was one of the original schools used in the 1959 Harvard Study of executive education.

If you have already completed the survey, please accept my sincere thanks. Because the sample size is small, it is extremely important that your opinions be included in the research.

If, by some chance, you did not receive the survey, or it was misplaced, please call me at 909-985-2103(or fax to 909-949-2658) and I will send you another copy. If you have questions before you fill out the survey, please don't hesitate to call me so that I can answer them for you.

I really appreciate your help in furthering the effectiveness of executive education programs.

Sincerely,

Janis Dietz

APPENDIX G

May 24, 1996

«title» «firstname» «lastname»
«adress1»
«address2»
«city», «state» «zipcode»

Dear «title» «lastname»,

    About four weeks ago, I wrote to you asking for your opinion about your experience at the University of Utah. This research is being undertaken with the support of Dave Dungan because he is interested in my replication of a 1959 Harvard Study that sought to determine the satisfaction of managers with executive education programs. This is a small study, but we have been very pleased with the response from the University of Utah. I am uncovering some very interesting responses and comments that will be helpful in reporting the results.

    I am writing to you again because of the significance of the response rate for this study. Although the results are confidential, a full response guarantees that the answers will have significance for the schools that have agreed to participate.

    I realize that this is a very busy time of year for you, and hope that you will take a few minutes to return the survey (or fax to 909-949-2658). I have enclosed another copy in case the first one was delayed. If you have any questions, please call me at 909-981-4387.

    I truly appreciate your help.

Sincerely,

Janis Dietz

APPENDIX H

Program Director Interview

1) Do you feel that you are meeting the needs of corporate clients for relevancy in class work?

2) What, specifically, is the University doing to improve the relevancy for corporate executives if the answer to the above is "no?"

3) How has the ethnic/gender make-up of the program changed in the past 10 years? Do you do anything to address these changes in classes or other places in the program?

4) What percentage of your EMBA students have their programs funded? How much?

5) How do you get evaluations of your programs?

6) Do you react to these evaluations in any way when it comes to planning curriculum? If so, how often?

7) Job security has changed greatly in the past ten years. How has that changed your student population and the reasons they come to your school?

8) How many of these people use the Exec MBA as a stepping stone to either change careers or changes employers?

9) Has the support by industry changed in the past 5 years? If so, how?

10) What would you say is the most critical need for your school to face in order to continue to be competitive as we go into the next century?

11) Do you expect enrollment to:

   Continue to climb at x rate?
   Remain steady?
   Decline?

12) How are your marketing plans changing in the light of the above?

13) Do you get any feedback from participants or sponsors regarding the use made of knowledge acquired during the EMBA program?

14) Do you use only full time faculty? If not, what is the % of part-time faculty to full-time.

15) Do faculty from the EMBA program also teach in the regular MBA program?

16) What is the statistical demographic profile of this year's participants?

17) How has your program changed in the past ten years?
    In response to diversity of students?
    In response to diversity and globalization in the business world?

18) How often is the curriculum reviewed?

	Green	Blue	Appendix I Gldrd	Yellow
2 weeks	0.3	0.28	0.3	0.21
3 weeks	0.39	0.34	0.43	0.24
4 weeks	0.52	0.46	0.46	0.34
5 weeks	0.52	0.46	0.48	0.39
6 weeks	0.68	0.55	0.58	0.43
7 weeks	0.82	0.57	0.58	0.49
>7 weeks	0.84	0.57	0.58	0.53

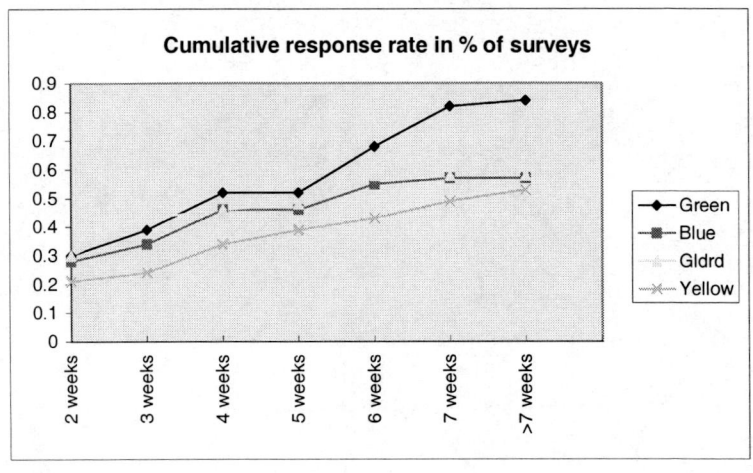

APPENDIX J

(Questions #7 and #8 Position at time of beginning MBA program; Position now)

Table J.1 School Green

Position at the beginning of the program	Position now
Attorney	Partner
Consultant	Marketing Manager
Manager, Budget	Manager, Finance
Analytical lab mgr.	Regional affairs associate
Technical sales representative	Shipping manager
Electrical supervisor	Maintenance supervisor
Graphic artist	Graphic artist
Manager of engineering services	Manager of engineering services
Project engineer	Graduate assistant
Craft supervisor	Craft supervisor
Engineering manager	Director of engineering
Private medical practice	Private medical practice
Newspaper advertising	Vice President, Operations
Systems analyst	Systems analyst
Software engineer	Product engineer
Sales manager	Associate
Manager, materials	Manager, start-up services
Systems programmer	Technical design consultant
Sales agent	Project manager
Engineering team leader	Engineering manager
Computer sales	Real estate sales
Advertising manager	Senior marketing officer
Physician	Senior physician/Medical director
Vice President for a software company	Vice President, Asset liability for a bank
Advanced technical writer	Supervisor, documents
Market researcher	Marketing research manager
General manager	General manager
Senior product analyst	Product manager
Pastor	Pastor of new church
Manager, decision support systems	Retail information technical manager
Contracting officer	Unemployed
Audit supervisor	Audit supervisor
Operations analyst	Operations analyst

Table J.2 School Blue

Position at Beginning of Program	Position Now
General Manager	President
Vice President	Senior V.P.
Manager, public affairs	Director, pubic policy
Transportation analyst	Manager, Corp. Transp.
Operations specialist	Bus.&Regulatory Analyst
Chemist	Supervising chemist
Staff Manager	Mgr, Human Asset/Learning
Manager,construction	General, Div. Mgr.
HR Director, Refining	HR Director, Operations
Marketing Manager	Marketing Manager
Company owner	Unemployed
Mgr. Prog Planning	Dept Mgr. Astronaut
Software Coordinator	Mgr. Acct. Services
Asst. Sec. U. of Colorado	Evaluation Specialist
Teen health advocate	Software Analyst
Project manager	Analyst
Director, Research and Dev.	Dir., Research & Devel.
Product Marketing Manager	Product Marketing Manager
President	President
Acting General Mgr.	Sales & Administration Mgr.
Administrative Analyst	Progress consultant
Mgr, Project Mgmt	Mgr, Project Mgmt
Vice President	Exec.Vice President
Project Manager	Executive Support Mgr.
Director, Remedial Programs	Mgr., Programs
Project Lead Qual. Assurance	Network administrator
Cost accountant	Controller
Engineering Mgt.	Process Eng. Mgr.
Distribution Mgr.	Product Mgr.
President	President
Mgr., Bus. Development	VP, Gen. Mgr.
Financial analyst	Field Specialist, Consultant
Private Law Practice	Special Counsel
Manager, Construction	General Division Manager
Operations support	Contract administrator
Sales manager	Sales manager

Table J.3 School Goldenrod

Position at beginning of program	Present position
Finance manager	Finance manager
Mgr, software engineering	Consultant
Controller-law firm	Controller-software
Asst. Dir/Employee Rel	Mgr/Employee Rel.
National Sales Mgr	President
Mgr, Comm Service	Mgr, Printing&Micro
Engineering Supervisor	Chief engineer
Manager	Self-employed
Mgr of Treasury Services	Mgr., Corp Accting
Management analyst	Director of info systems
Senior asset/liability	Mgr, bank consulting
Program manager	Dir, Mfg operations
Dir, Prof development	Same
Primary care administrator	Marketing administrator
VP, Acct. Supervisor	Senior VP & Acct. Supervisor
Supervisor, Mfg Eng	Manager, Mfg Eng.
Battalion Chief	Battalion Chief
CFO	Vice President, Operations
Director of mfg.	Exec. Dir of operation
Business manager	Business manager
Computing manager	Director, info systems
Manager	Manager
Quality manager	General manager
President	General manager
Dir., Internal audit	VP, Bus. Development
VP finance	VP finance
Sales manager	Marketing manager
Dir utilization	Dir. of operations &finance
President	President
Project officer	Started own company
Licensing assoc.	Director, tech. Trans.
Plant manager	Plant manager

Table J.4 School Yellow

Position before you began the program	Position now
Environmental safety audit manager	Instrument supervisor
Vice President	Vice President
Systems Engineering Manager	Department Business Unit Manager
Assistant Project Manager	Department Manager
Senior Financial Analyst	Case Team Leader
Senior Scientist	Applied Physics Group Manager
National Account Manager	District Sales Manager
Senior Project Engineer	Project Manager
Plant Controller	Mgr, Leasing and Retail
Business Strategy and Planning Manager	Manager, Business Operations
Account Manager	Area Sales Manager
Manager, Product Support	Director, Strategic Planning
Director of Support Services	Director of Support Services
Regional Sales Manager	Area Sales Manager
Attorney	Attorney
Program Manager	Business Analyst
Vice President	Vice President
Manager of Engineering and Quality	Director of Quality and Technology
Director	Senior Director
Surgeon	Surgeon
Senior Financial Analyst	Director, European Logistics
Manager	Manager, Product Engineering
Project Engineer	Engineering Specifications and Project Manager
Director	Director
Finance Manager	Finance Director
Senior Speechwriter	Manager, Executive Communications
Plant Manager	Senior Consultant
Director	Vice President
Director of Engineering	Director of Engineering
Financial Analyst	Financial Consultant
Senior Scientist	Group Manager
Associate Clinical Professor	Tenured Associate Professor
Assistant Chancellor	Senior Associate Dean
Manager	Director
CEO	CEO
Assistant Vice President, Finance	Associate Director, Project Finance
Manager, Systems Integration	Manager, Systems Integration
Regional Manager	Director of Marketing Development
Owner	Owner
Corporate Environmental Manager	Corporate Environmental Manager
Senior Vice President	Executive Vice President
Senior Manager	Senior Manager, Account Director
Plant Manager	Director of Manufacturing
Vice President, Manager	Vice President, Manager